See page 94

AN IRRATIONAL EXPLANATION ...

Aunt Isa has much to answer for, for it was she who regularly wheeled Michael Pearson across the cobblestones and tram lines in his pram to watch the trains at Paisley Canal.

His lifetime interest in railways was further cemented when he emigrated from Scotland to England aboard the luxury Pullman Queen of Scots in 1954. The trauma of leaving his 'hameland' has never left him, but his enthusiasm for trains continued to grow throughout a 1950s childhood spent in the Leicestershire hosiery town of Hinckley.

In 1961 he began commuting to school by train between Burton-on-Trent and Ashby de-la Zouch, at the same time acquiring his first Ian Allan ABC devoted to the locomotives of the Eastern and North Eastern regions; not a great deal of use in Staffordshire, but he was drawn to the Peppercorn A1 Pacific on the cover. Luckily this, subsequently well-thumbed, volume saw full use in his years of incarceration in a Yorkshire boarding school which had the distinction of having a Gresley V2 named after it.

By 1970 he was beginning to display a semblance of interest in girls, pop music and reality, but fortunately this was just a rebellious phase, and he returned to his 'first love' just in time to travel behind *Pinza* from York to Selby in 1980 and miss crossing the channel on the Night Ferry because of a 24 hour seamen's strike.

Very happily married with two children and a massive overdraft, he now divides his time between literary award ceremonies and the end of Platform 12 at Crewe.

Railway Holiday in Scotland

a sequence of journeys by train, stopping off at places of interest and bumping into people of character

Michael Pearson
illustrated by Eric Leslie

WAYZGOOSE

Published by Wayzgoose 2001

Michael Pearson asserts the moral right to
be identified as the author of this work

Wayzgoose
Tatenhill Common
Staffordshire
DE13 9RS
Tel: 01283 713674
www.wayzgoose.org.uk

ISBN 907864 90 2

A CIP catalogue entry for this book is available from the British Library

Printed by Character Graphics of Taunton, Somerset

CONTENTS

To:

My Mother and Father for not using their steamship
tickets to emigrate to Canada before I was born,
Jackie for quarter of a century of love and affection,
Tamar and Eden for making their father so proud of them,
Karen for faith, work and charity,
and Yellowlees for coal and water -
with thanks from the 'implausible frontman'.

First shapes everything: the first goal you score, the first girl you kiss, the first pint you sink.

The first railway book I read was *Four Main Lines* by Hamilton Ellis, the first travel book *The Call of England* by H.V. Morton. Their imprint haunts these pages - although influences should be left fallow to distil into inimitability, and you will meet other heroes in the journeys which follow, equally significant in the genesis of this book.

Older readers, of a railway bent, may recognise the source of this book's title. David & Charles published a Railway Holiday series in the Sixties. It didn't stoop to the parochiality of Scotland,

England or Wales - or even, most regrettably, Ireland - and it petered out with Portugal by D.W. Winkworth in 1968, but it was enough to give me a template, or a mould, if you like, into which to pour my experiences. Telephoning David St John Thomas to clear it with him that, as co-publisher of the original series, he had no objection to me taking up the mantle, I learnt that, in any case, there is no copyright on titles (at which point I considered calling this book *Captain Corelli's Railway Holiday in Scotland with his Mandolin*) and that he thought it was not a bad idea at all. The railways of Scotland, he felt, deserved a literary boost. They were in danger of being taken for granted, and when we take things for granted, they have a knack of disappearing.

With 1,720 route miles to play with, I devised a vaguely clockwise itinerary designed to cover as much of Scotland's rail network as I could. It boiled down to eleven journeys, about the only thing I could thank Beeching for, because if it had still been possible to get to St Andrews or Newton Stewart or Hawick or Forfar by train I would have had to have made choices and sacrifices. I was rarely alone - over sixty million journeys are made annually on ScotRail, making it the fourth most travelled by Train Operating Company. Significantly, I managed to travel over all but 171 miles of the ScotRail network, but only visited 60 of the company's 333 stations; Largs, Weymss Bay, and Oban being notable absences and I apologise profusely to their disgruntled supporters.

While I was writing this book someone I interviewed asked me who it was being written for. I was nonplussed. Creativity and market research should never share a sleeper cabin. Apart from the recurring need to keep my family in the lavish style to which they've become accustomed, my motivation in writing *Railway Holiday in Scotland* is the transparent (and implicitly laudable) desire to encourage people to get out of their cars and on to the trains. And then, having got on the trains, to get off them again and explore this wonderful country; what Ricky Ross of the Scottish rock band Deacon Blue so evocatively called this 'long, narrow land, full of possibility'.

There is nothing like the writing of a book for making new

friends. Votes of thanks go to everyone who appears in these pages and who gave their time and enthusiasm and knowledge so effusively. Others, who didn't get a walk-on part, but remained shadowy (though no less essential) helpers in the background were: Mark Curnock of Character Graphics and everyone else involved in the book's production; Keith Goss for proof-reading, Keith Jones of the Great North of Scotland Railway Association, Angela MacKenzie of GNER for the last bit of the jigsaw, Roy Mitchell of West Lothian Council for information about the Airdrie-Bathgate Cycleway, Ian Rankin for allowing me to go for a walk around Cardenden with John Rebus, Carrie Robb (late of ScotRail) for ticketing logistics, Ricky Ross for letting me quote from *Wages Day*, Doug Small aka Perkin Warbeck and friend and associate of Ricky Ross, Ken Vickers of Cordee, Maria Webb for help with the Spanish at Kingussie, and Richard Wilcox the temporary signalman at Elgin West.

That's it then. I hope you enjoy the journeys, I hope you enjoy the *craic*. It hasn't really been a holiday, it's been hard work; so hard that I'm off for a wee *deoch an doruis*.

Thirst shapes everything.

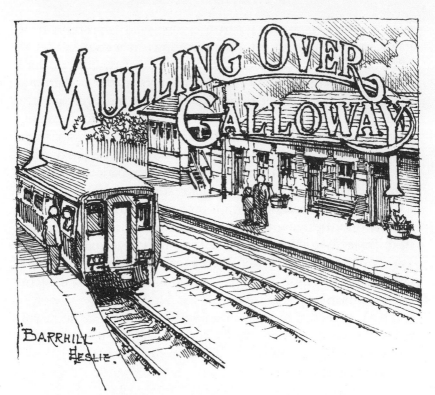

MULLING OVER GALLOWAY

"BARRHILL"
LESLIE.

Crossing the border at Gretna. A lost route across the
Solway Firth. Dumfries and The Thirty-Nine Steps. Robert
Burns in Nithsdale. Sanquhar and the land of coal.
Kilmarnock and the whisky counterfeiters.
The seaside train - Troon to Ayr. Remembering the
Maidens & Dunure Light Railway. Girvan and Ailsa
Craig. Over the moors to Barrhill. Down to the coast
and the port of Stranraer.

Odd, but not entirely inappropriate, to begin a journey of
exploration of Scotland's railways on an English station. It has
always seemed to me that Carlisle should have one of those symbols in *Thomas Cook's European Timetable* that denotes a frontier
station. The kind of station where, at any moment, customs
officials might clump through the train; unctuously requesting
to see your papers, brusquely demanding to know your busi-

ness. But, until the day dawns when the Scottish Parliament becomes the Scottish Government, Carlisle remains free of the petty bureaucracy of nations, and I was able to board the 14.23 to Stranraer without worrying if the cheap Spanish whisky sewn into the lining of my rucksack would be liable to excess duty.

Before setting out I had spoken to Toby Rackliff, Dumfries & Galloway Council's Railway Development Officer, about my intended route. He is enthusiastic about the railways in his area. But then he needs to be, South-West Scotland has suffered proportionately more railway rationalisation than the Highlands. The main line over Beattock holds the unenviable record for the longest distance between stations in Britain. Toby intends to rectify this by re-opening the stations at Beattock (for Moffat) and Symington, but it is not something that can be achieved overnight. Costs have to be identified and allocated. Train operating companies have to be talked into providing a service. Local people encouraged to rediscover rail. On the Nithsdale line Thornhill has been identified as a suitable case for re-opening. On the day of my journey Toby had sent out two thousand questionnaires to local residents to ascertain attitudes towards such a revival. It'll be a long hard slog; there will be 'nimbys' to placate; unforeseeable complications. There is no longer a footbridge between the platforms. If Health & Safety insist on one, with provision for disabled passengers, it could put the project out of reach financially. It seemed to me as I prepared to set off on my exploration of Scotland by train that I was lucky to be making the journey at all.

It was a warm June afternoon, made warmer by the heating arrangements on the Class 156 Sprinter. Hot air was being fired through the ducts at floor level as though they were trying to make a *crème brûlée* of my feet. In my childhood trains used to start sedately, gradually acquiring momentum, like someone taking you out jogging for the first time. Now they just take off in an aeronautical manner, and it won't be long, mark my words, before the Nanny State make seat belts compulsory on trains. Back in that same Fifties childhood, stretching one's legs with a walk along the corridor was one of the joys of rail travel

- one of the joys of life actually. And so Dixon's 19th century textile mill on one side and the Cathedral on the other had been and gone before I could even scribble their names in my notebook, and we were over the glistening Eden in a flash.

The gradual revival of rail freight - another of Toby Rackcliff's missions in life - is well illustrated in Carlisle where, prior to privatisation, it was all but moribund. Direct Rail Services (a subsidiary of British Nuclear Fuels) maintain their fleet in the former Kingmoor depot. Their dark blue coloured locomotives   (of Classes 20, 33 and 37) are predominantly occupied in the carriage of spent nuclear waste to Sellafield, but they have recently won a contract to move container trains for the road haulier Malcolm between Grangemouth and Daventry, and obviously have every intention of broadening their portfolio. Toby told me that he hoped that sidings just north of Carlisle at Longtown might in the future be de-militarised and turned into an inter-modal railhead.

Anyone who's read my book *Coming Up With The Goods* will know I have mixed feelings about Kingmoor Yard, having been marooned there one December night, but I am constantly heartened by its rebirth under the aegis of EWS (English Welsh & Scottish Railway - Britain's biggest operator of freight by rail). The yard held two empty coal trains returning north, some timber traffic and some of the very Hoyer containers that I had travelled with on that occasion, presumably, at this time in the afternoon, making their way back from Workington to Teesside; pitiful, perhaps, in comparison to the road traffic on the neighbouring A74, but at least the patient is responding to treatment.

Both the Eden and the Esk flow into the Solway Firth, either side of Rockcliffe Marsh. From the west side of the train one gets a view of infinity. Now crossing the Esk, I could see Criffell, the most dominant peak on the Dumfriesshire side of the Firth, at this distance a pastel shade of violet against the sky. The tidal Esk was close to high water, but it is an altogether less significant watercourse that has the most impact hereabouts, for at Gretna the little River Sark forms the boundary between

England and Scotland, and at last this book can begin to fulfil the spirit of the Trade Descriptions Act.

Not only do we leave England (and all its shortcomings and shibboleths) behind at Gretna, we also leave the 'main line'. The track singles and the train stops to call at Gretna Green, where one is somehow surprised and disappointed that the station signs do not read: 'Gretna Green - alight here for an instant marriage'. Alternatively, you could be urged here, to alight for Geoffrey Evison, a well known railway enthusiast and activist, campanologist and chum of the author whose alter ego is Hamish McEvison, current incumbent of the stationmaster's post at rail-less Riccarton Junction.

This wasn't always a secondary route, let alone a byway. This was very much the Glasgow & South Western Railway's main line, and their staunch Sassenach allies, the Midland Railway, would conspire with them at Carlisle to out perform the despised Caledonian and London & North Western companies. Rationalisation took its toll in the last quarter of the 20th century, electrification favouring the Beattock route, and sections of singling reducing the Nith Valley line's capacity. A short-sighted saving which has come back to haunt Railtrack now that heavy flows of coal traffic utilise this route down from the Ayrshire coalfield.

There is much Ministry of Defence activity in the vicinity, though not shown on Ordnance Survey mapping in case of threat to security. Our small island outlook defies logic. If the Spanish or the French or the Germans or the Russians had ever really considered invading us, would they have been put off by a lack of maps or signposts or station nameboards? More likely it was the thought of the cooking and the weather that has kept us gloriously intact. Would you march on a country of whom boiled cabbage and rain might be said to be the two most defining characteristics? At Eastriggs (whose station is being considered for re-opening) there's a museum, sweetly called the Devil's Porridge, devoted to the munition workers of the neighbourhood.

Pondering such thoughts and trying unsuccessfully to recall a bar or two of Sir John Blackwood McEwen's somewhat turgid 'Solway' Symphony, I looked across the Firth to the Lake District horizon dominated by Skiddaw. Approaching Annan, I craned my neck to see if I could see any remaining earthworks from the astonishing Solway Junction Railway, a short-lived shortcut between Scotland and England, built to facilitate the carriage of Cumberland ore to Lanarkshire ironworks. Well over a mile long, a single track cast iron viaduct carried the line bravely across the Firth. At least it did until the Arctic winter of 1881 when ice floes brought great sections of it crashing down into the frozen waters. It took three years to repair, but the railway was never really the same again and the line closed completely in 1921, though the viaduct remained intact for another thirteen years, surreptitiously used by locals to effect a foot crossing of the Firth. By all accounts it came into its own on Sundays when, by dint of a brisk walk, Scots could escape their liquor-free Sabbath. In fact a cutting swallowed us up at the wrong moment, but I caught a glimpse of a pipeline which Toby told me follows the course of the railway down from Chapelcross Nuclear Power Station, whose four cooling towers are prominent to the north. Jokingly he told me that it carries waste from the power station out into the Firth and that it glows at night; at least I think he was joking. Annan station - where the line doubles again - is worth a second glance. It dates from 1848 and is built of local sandstone. A canopy protects southbound travellers from the worst of the Solway Firth's frequent rain squalls and there's an imposing timber built signal box of a Glasgow & South Western style I was going to get more and more familiar with as the journey unfolded.

Crossing the Annan, a salmon fishing river of some repute (which has its origins at the Devil's Beeftub by Moffat) the line veers away from the coast and passes two closed stations at Cummertrees and Ruthwell; the later now being notable as the location of a museum devoted to Savings Banks - what will they think of next! A quarter of an hour of pleasant progress through a landscape of isolated farms and conifer plantations ensues. Criffell's 1,866ft summit is much closer now. Close enough for me to see the veining of watercourses on its precipitous eastern flank. A wisp of white cloud clung to its summit like the stray blob of shaving cream I invariably omit to wipe off, much to my wife's irritation. It wasn't the only cloud, merely a scout, big grey reinforcements were being called up. Nearing Dumfries the line skirts the peaty wastes of Lochar Moss. Incredibly, there was another wayside station here, isolated on the edge of the moss except for a few remote cottages, but indicative of the role the railway played in the rural economy.

Not so long ago, Dumfries received the accolade of 'Britain's nicest place to live'. This is not as outrageous as it sounds. My family and I know the place well, and a perfect winter Saturday might consist of a Scottish breakfast (with haggis) in the 'Doonhamer', and an hour or so in James Thin's bookshop and its second-hand neighbour, with the optional extra (as far as my wife and daughter are concerned) of an afternoon at Palmerston Park, watching Queen of the South thwarting football's laws of gravity. Forty years ago I would have been able to add to that appealing list the fascination of Dumfries railway activity. Architecturally the station (aided and abetted by the adjacent Station Hotel) can still hold its own, but in terms of activity and potential for train-watching, the glory days are gone; though it was good to learn that a new traincrew depot was about to open. At the height of my train-spotting powers in the early 1960s this fascinating line might have thrown up half a dozen different types of Pacific, numerous mixed traffic designs and freight locomotives, plus still the odd pre-Grouping class. Sadly I never came here then, and everything had gone before I became a regular in the early 1990s; everything that is but for the occasional BRCW Type 2 shunting timber in the yard behind Safeway. And now even that seems desperately long ago.

In Buchan's famous thriller, *The Thirty-Nine Steps*, Richard Hannay 'woke at Dumfries just in time to bundle out and get into the slow Galloway train'. Three feature films having followed, with varying degrees of accuracy and authenticity in its exciting and inspirational footsteps, it is difficult to accept that the story was first published as long ago as 1915. Our train might be relatively slow, and it will hopefully be heading for Galloway, but the real Galloway line which Buchan used so atmospherically for his novel (as did Dorothy L. Sayers for her *Five Red Herrings* sixteen years later) closed in 1965, one of Beeching's most transparent acts of vandalism. For this direct line, known as the Port Road, between Dumfries and Stranraer - a principal port of embarkation for Ulster - was a whole sixty miles shorter than the route which survives today, and one doesn't necessarily need a post-graduate degree in transport planning to realise that, had it survived the Doctor's flawed and one-dimensional forward planning, it would have had a very useful role to play in the movement of people and freight between the mainland and Northern Ireland in the 21st century. Certainly Dumfries & Galloway Council recognise this and they consider its re-opening (an admittedly massive project) a long term strategic objective.

In the meantime Dumfries station's north-facing bays are infilled and trees now grow where its sizeable engine shed - given the look of a Presbyterian chapel by its tall, round-topped windows - stood, providing motive power for the 'Port Road' and the local branch lines to Lockerbie and Moniaive. Pulling away from the station I saw a rusty single track curve away from the main line, all that's left of the direct line to Stranraer. Toby had every reason to believe that oil trains would begin using it in 2002, whilst a local group of preservationists was also eyeing it with the intention of running steam specials over the remaining three miles of track still in situ. Not such a bad idea, Southwest Scotland could do with such an attraction.

The River Nith is one of Scotland's greatest salmon fishing rivers. Though no angler myself, I have heard several piscatorial friends and acquaintances speak of it in tones more worldy men than us would have reserved for mistresses of the most accommodating and imaginative nature. In some ways, however, the Nith resembles the railway which appropriated its valley, being not quite as good as it was. Climate change or over-fishing might be said to have done for the Nith's fish-stocks what over-rationalisation has done to the trains. Some five miles out from Dumfries, Portrack viaduct carries the railway over the river and, because I knew what to look for, I saw through trees the gabled end of the whitewashed buildings of Ellisland Farm where Scotland's favourite son, Robert Burns, lived between the years of 1788 and 1791. *Auld Lang Syne* was written here, as was *A Man's a Man For A'that*, but Burns was better at poetry than farming, and disillusioned, got himself a steadier career with the excise in Dumfries. It's a great shame Burns did not live into the railway age. His muses, he said, visited him 'short and far between; but I meet them now and then as I jog through the hills of Nithsdale'. I have 'nae doot' he would have been inspired by the building of the railway through his Nith Valley in 1850 and that, unlike Wordsworth, he would have seen the railway as a begetter of opportunity and an improver of man's lot.

I got a glimpse of Closeburn's closed station as the train ran through a very gracious countryside in which the railway, with its red ballast, seems perfectly integrated. A coal train clattered by southwards as, climbing now, at 1 in 200 steepening to 1 in 150, the line reaches Thornhill, where an up loop - with new semaphore signals - has recently been commissioned by Railtrack as a lay-by for southbound freight. The handsome sandstone building has been converted into flats. Standing adjacent is one of those marvellous timber-built circular auction marts which seem to be characteristic of border agriculture. The line's most scenic section follows as it negotiates a passage between the hills. Running through luxuriantly wooded cuttings, I was reminded of the Cornish main line in the vicinity of Bodmin Road and Lostwithiel. Beyond Carronbridge a swarthy cutting leads to Drumlanrig Tunnel (1410yds) which derives its name from the neighbouring 17th century castle, seat of the Buccleuchs. Hopper windows down to provide its passengers with some cool relief, the train made its noisy way through the depths of the tunnel like some avant-garde piece of percussive music. I half expected Evelyn Glennie - a Scot after all - to emerge from the vestibule as daylight returned and take a bow. That daylight revealed a dramatic gorge-like setting, somewhat disappointingly compromised by excessive lineside vegetation;

circumstances which would have been frowned upon by earlier generations of permanent way engineers.

Wheels squealing on the sharp reverse curves, the Class 156 lived up to its sobriquet and 'sprinted' almost too quickly for would-be sightseers. Part of me was gratified that the train so easily overtook cars and lorries on the heavily-trafficked A76, part of me wished it would dawdle a bit so that I could savour the view. We crossed the lofty Enterkin Burn Viaduct, almost organically constructed of the local sandstone. From Mennock, a mile or two further on, the B797 can be seen wriggling eastwards, seeking the pass between the Lowther Hills which will take it to the old lead and silver mining communities of Wanlockhead and Leadhills. But I am beginning to sound like a guidebook, and that's a trap I had promised myself not to fall into. There exists a subtle difference between a travel guide and a travel narrative. It's akin to sitting in a carriage with a well-informed companion, who is forever pointing out objects of interest to be seen through the window, when all you really want to do is gaze in an unfocussed sort of way out of the window and daydream. Daydream, in this instance, of my great-grandmother's roots in the Sanquhar (Sank-her) and Cumnock districts. She was a McAvoy and ended up in Paisley, by way of Helensburgh, we know not how. What was the Sanquhar of the 1880s like? More industrialised for sure. There were brickworks and coal mines. Perhaps my great grandmother was one of the knitters of Sanquhar, renowned for their two-toned patterned gloves. Perhaps she was one of the wee girls in white, captured in a photograph in the Tolbooth Museum, waving a flag the day the Prince of Wales came through in 1871.

Sanquhar station closed in 1965 but opened again in 1994. It beggars belief how a station serving a busy community such as this could ever have been thought of as surplus to requirements. Presumably it was still staffed in 1965, so alright, fair enough, reduce it to an unstaffed halt in status, even if you've no conscience about putting half a dozen folk out of a job, but why close it? Out of sheer spite I expect; the sort of numb negativity that our bureaucrats specialise in. Someone will have worked out figures to prove that it 'didn't pay'. Did the B797 *pay*? And so Sanquhar lost its station for thirty years, just about the same time as it lost its coal mine, and its brickworks and its shovel factory (James Rigg & Sons - medal-winning shovel makers, manufacturers of 'The Drainers Friend'). Bankhead Pit sold its high quality steam coal to the Glasgow & South Western. The brickworks produced a lovely little terracotta number known as 'The Buccleuch', as well as a cheaper composition brick made of clay and pit waste called 'The Sanquhar' which they used to good effect in the miner's houses. Up until the 1950s there was a Sanquhar Dairy as well, producing 26,000 lbs of local cheese *daily* and widely distributing it by *rail*.

'Alight here for the Southern Upland Way' is what the bare (but at least refurbished) platforms offer you now. Yet as long distance footpaths go, the 212 mile walk across the south of Scotland from Portpatrick to Cockburnspath is one of Britain's best and Sanquhar is a useful staging post. They might also bid you to detrain here to see the oldest working post office in the world, the ruins of an 11th century castle, and the pageantry of the 'Riding of the Marches' which climaxes on the closest Sunday to 18th August. But, as usual, there aren't enough hours in my day, and I stayed on the train, as it stood rattling for a moment or two of inactivity, watching rooks fly over the pinnacled tower of the kirk.

A change comes over the countryside. The sylvan flanks recede. Spoil heaps - or 'bings' in the Scots vernacular - infiltrate the landscape like warts. The train rumbled over Crawick Water. Through the open windows came the sick sweet smell of manure. We passed through a rash of black bings just - as if to taunt the abandonment of the local mines - as another long train of perhaps imported coal came past us heading south. Kirkconnel was another mining town, its Faulhead Colliery closed as recently as 1968. The coal here was 450 feet below ground and output over a thousand tons a day when closure was announced. I gleaned these facts from Guthrie Hutton's marvellous book *Mining - Ayrshire's Lost Industry* which triggers ambivalent emotions of pride and despair in equal measure in me, for mining shares with railways an unenviable history of political abuse. Kirkconnel retains another of the lovely GSWR timber signal boxes. In the 1870s, this was the local beat of the surfaceman Alexander Anderson, a self-educated poet, one of whose volumes of verse was called *Songs of the Rail*. With his steady acquisition of knowledge, however, he outgrew the railway and went on to become Chief Librarian of the University of Edinburgh.

Pulling away from Kirkconnel I saw houses of unmistakable Coal Board provenance on the neighbouring hillside and subconsciously acknowledged that uncomfortable juxtaposition of coal and countryside. Beyond the houses, up on the green ridge, a wind farm waved merrily. The railway sways and sashays with the river, as if the two of them are enjoying some Scots country dance. Modest and burn-like now, the Nith encounters the boundary between Dumfries & Galloway and Strathclyde; or formerly, and perhaps more congenially, Dumfriesshire and Ayrshire. This change takes place under the rounded summit of Corsencon Hill (1,554ft). The valley widens out beyond here, becoming slightly, though not disparagingly, featureless. At New Cumnock, Burns's 'Sweet Afton' merges with the Nith and I found its melodic namesake tune entering my head without an invitation as the train pulled up at the station. There's a new loading point for opencast coal here whilst, just west of the station, a branchline runs down across the river, stretching just over a mile to Connel Park and the Knockshinnoch Disposal Point, another coal bunkering centre.

I'd seen the last of the Nith, it disappeared west, curving round to its source above Dalmellington. A trio of lonely lochs marked the line's summit at Polquhan. Under the now cloud solid sky they looked inky black and enigmatic. A rocky cutting led to Cumnock, surprisingly without a station. The railway runs at some height above this sizeable community once known as a centre of snuff box making. A big red, but disused, railway viaduct straddles the town. It carried the Ayr-Cumnock-Muirkirk line. Our own line leapt over Lugar Water on its own lofty viaduct. Down through the trees I glimpsed a quaint outdoor swimming pool which looked as though it might have had Coal Board origins.

If Cumnock, the bigger town, has lost its station, Auchinleck, the smaller neighbour, paradoxically retains its. In the sixty seconds or so that the train stopped I took in a small football ground, an old colliery headstock, and the rooftops of a 'wee toon' as metaphorically grey as its rooftops. A white plume of smoke from a board mill accompanied us out of Auchinleck as myriad plumes of smoke would have filled this landscape in the days of steam. I saw another headstock, belonging to the Barony mine, which closed in 1989, serving as a landmark and a memorial, but, being on the wrong side of the carriage, I didn't see if any earthworks remained from the short spur to Catrine which was once operated by a steam rail-motor known as the Catrine Caur, one of three built in Kilmarnock in 1905. David L. Smith, respected chronicler of the 'Sou Western', tells the story of the day the rail-motor's crew allowed the fire to go out while they were playing dominoes. Embarrassment was averted by the driver's presence of mind, he ran to the fire house where they heated the carriage foot-warmers and purloined its glowing coals, racing back to the rail-motor with them on a shovel.

Ballochmyle Viaduct offers a bird's eye view of the River Ayr, but what you don't see from the train is the 'Listed' bridge's graceful styling; its massive centre arch having a 181 feet span, 163 feet above the water. Obviously it would repay a visit on foot one day, though for photography to be successful, winter's bare trees are said to be best. And it would be a long walk if you come by train, for Mauchline's station is another casualty of 'progress'; though I did hear that it is on SPT's shortlist for re-opening. What does survive at Mauchline, however - and I can only write in a railway sense - is the junction with the direct line to Ayr, nowadays restricted to freight use. Another big signal-box overlooks the pointwork and its signalmen are kept busy by a stream of coal trains working to and from the Ayr line.

I had been travelling for an hour and a half now - not yet half way through the journey - and was glad that Toby had warned me of the lack of catering trolleys on the Glasgow-Carlisle/Stranraer services. I'd bought a bottle of Coke on Carlisle station and it was sustaining me through a patch of tiredness. The railway-side prison on the outskirts of Kilmarnock did nothing to lift my spirits. Neither would the passing trains do much for the inmates, I mused, reminded of A.E. Housman's poem about Shrewsbury Gaol. Past the Burns Memorial and over the River Irvine, the train slowed down for Kilmarnock, a spacious station with north facing bays, elaborate ironwork incorporating the GSWR initials, and stonework the colour of tandoori trout.

Tap, tap, tap, I type Kilmarnock into the memory bank and, whirr, whirr, whirr it comes up with an image of my dad, dropping me off here to catch a Peak-hauled express south circa 1968. But my father has a better Kilmarnock story to tell. Johnny Walker's bottling plant overlooks the station and always prompts the tale of two men coming into my father's print-works and ordering a rather large quantity of whisky bottle labels. Gratified, but suspicious, my father had the common sense to check the order with Johnny Walker's head office and discovered that the men were, in all likelihood, counterfeiters. It gets more exciting here on in, as my father becomes embroiled in a police-commissioned 'sting' to trap them. Climaxing in a cops and robbers sequence and a court case to rival Perry Mason. He has dined out on it for thirty-five years.

Flicking through old copies of *Trains Illustrated* to find references for this chapter, I was delighted to find Kilmarnock featuring as 'Resorts for Railfans - No.17' in the March 1956 issue. From the article - written by G.H. Robin - I learnt that Kilmarnock had been at one end of one of Scotland's earliest railways, a 4ft gauge affair opened in 1812 to carry mostly coal (but sometimes passengers as well) down to the docks at Troon. By 1850 the main line between Glasgow and Carlisle was running through the town and in 1856 the Glasgow & South Western Railway built their locomotive works here. The article analysed Kilmarnock's contemporary train services and made sober reading, listing expresses to London St Pancras, separate sleeper services to St Pancras *and* Euston, through carriages to the West Country, and an intensive service of local trains connecting Kilmarnock with Glasgow St. Enoch, Ayr, Ardrossan, Largs and Darvel.

It speaks volumes of Kilmarnock's railway decline that just two single track routes debouch from the north end of the station now. The right leads by way of Barrhead to Glasgow, the left to Troon and Ayr, and this was the way my train departed, skirting the town's prosperous northern suburbs and clickety-clacking over slow, short-sectioned track across the River Irvine. I still could not shake off my tiredness and was consequently irritated by a noisy child behind me and what I took for his acquiescent granny. Seasoned rail travellers learn to avoid sitting too close to children, but this one had somehow crept up on me. I did my best to ignore the racket, watching the River Irvine lazily meandering alongside. We crossed Shelwalton Moss. The sidings into Hillhouse Quarry were dishearteningly rusty, but the adjacent line into the Caledonian Paper Mill at Irvine was reassuringly shiny and up the line I could see some of the distinctively inward-sloping tank wagons which bring china clay from Cornwall.

The sea came into sight as we curved round to Barassie Junction and I felt my spirits lifting. The sun was breaking through again and I was looking forward to the long scenic run down to Stranraer. A jumbo jet flew out of Prestwick as we entered the land of golf courses. Sandy bays led to Troon. Arran looked glorious and desirable - Goat Fell puncturing what was left of the cloud. Troon's attractive timber station is the work of the well known Scottish architect James Miller. The station's lively styling reflects its end of the19th century development as a resort and residential centre. Possibly some of that status has been eroded, for on the platform signs now read 'No blading or cycling within the station premises'. But in bungalow-land existence remains serene, on and off the links.

The restless boy began clambering over the back of my seat. I carefully considered the pros and cons of elbowing him in the face. The cons won, not on ethical grounds, but because I suspected there would be tears, and consequently even more noise. When I was his age, children were seen and not heard. When I was his age I took off from Prestwick Airport; not on a Trans-Atlantic journey, but for a thirty minute flight over Arran and back. Our pleasures were simple then.

Approaching Ayr, foursomes were silhouetted against the light, putting out on peerless greens. Ailsa Craig is ushered in on the horizon. All is sweetness and, quite literally, 'light', until, suddenly, seaside gives way to sidings, a phalanx of lines filled with coal wagons: René Magritte and/or Edward Hopper would have been inspired. Others sensibilities may be offended, but I am at home here, having visited Falkland Yard (as these sidings are known) to research a chapter of *Coming Up With The Goods*. This seaside marshalling yard is a centre for coal traffic, much of it gathered by opencast techniques in the hills behind Ayr, the balance imported from wherever in the world through Hunterston on the coast above Ardrossan. Marshalled at Falkland, the coal is then carried by EWS to power stations in Yorkshire and the Midlands. I won't bore you with any further technical details, but I must tell you that the two journeys I made from Falkland - one up into the hills to collect coal from Killoch, one to carry it right across Scotland's Central Belt to Longannet Power Station on the Firth of Forth - were close to being the highlights of the twelve journeys I made, courtesy of EWS, for *Coming Up With The Goods*, and I would urge you to get a copy, not simply to boost my royalties, but to enjoy a vicarious pleasure in the wonderful experiences I had. So it was with heavy dollops of nostalgia that I passed the bothy which displays the sign: 'No Idling'; leaving one to pure conjecture whether it refers to the excessive running of locomotive engines or the work ethic of staff.

When I was two and a bit we went on holiday to Ayr for a week; I got knocked over on a gravel drive by a boxer dog and my father played golf with Bill McLaren. Naturally we went by train, overnight from Birmingham, and I can remember crossing the Lune at Lancaster and going through a tunnel but nothing else. A shame that, because Ayr station in 1956 teemed with

activity. Our old friend G.H.Robin wrote another piece for
Trains Illustrated - 'Resorts for Railfans No.32' - albeit five years
later, outlining its history and cataloguing the density of its traffic. By 1961 dieselisation was beginning to bite. Inter-city diesel
units would rush you to St Enoch in three minutes over the
hour, against a fifty minutes best that the Glasgow & South
Western could offer pre-Grouping, a timing matched, but barely bettered, by today's electric trains. Robins was also able to
write in the contemporary tense of the diesel railbus service to
Dalmellington and excursions to Butlins Holiday Camp at the
Heads of Ayr, of Clan Pacifics working between Glasgow and
Stranraer and of sexagenarian ex Caledonian 0-6-0s on local coal
trains; it's often an inescapable fact that wherever you travel,
you travel too late.

It was 16.34 and Ayr's platforms were filled with a teatime
trade of homegoing schoolchildren and shoppers. Its stature
may have diminished but the station retains its dignity, and the
same might be said of the adjoining Station Hotel. With my
spread of maps, timetables and notebooks, I must have looked
more eccentric than I thought, for no one came to sit by me
even though the train was almost full. I was reminded of the tac-
tics one used to keep a compartment to oneself, or at least to
one's family and friends. Casually arranged coats and bags to
hint of occupation was a frequent ruse, though this might
require reinforcement by strategic occupation of the doorway. I
had a school-friend whose father (a shy man who was something big in the rag trade) would habitually fill his compartment
with an array of fully clothed inflatable tailor's dummies to
ensure privacy.

The Ayr-Stranraer main line of the Glasgow & South Western
Railway is notoriously switchback in nature. Even our high-tech
two-car Sprinter had to work hard. We passed a big Safeway
supermarket and then a zone of poor housing, the sort which
always seems to have more washing on the line more often than
is the case in more salubrious suburbs; clearly a metaphor strug-
gling to escape from a packet of Persil. Some three miles out, at
Dalrymple Junction, the shiny rails of what was once the

Dalmellington branch climb and curve away to the coal loading point on the edge of the moors at Chalmerston. The train turned south-west into the sun and crossed the River Doon which snakes through woodland on its way past Burns' birthplace to the sea at Alloway. Wilson MacArthur - a man who wrote books about river journeys in much the same vein as I write books about rail - published an engaging account of the Doon in 1952, enlivened, as was his habit, by black and white photographs in which his pretty dark haired wife was often titillatingly placed.

I hoped fervently that the noisy schoolchildren would evacuate the train at Maybole, and I'm pleased to say my prayers were granted. I wanted peace and quiet to savour the next leg of the journey. We live in pan-European times: a freshly painted seat on Maybole platform bore a 'wet paint' warning in three languages. Unfortunately none of them was Lowland Scots, and a man rose to meet his wife off the train with a red stripe across the back of his white shirt. On we went, into a beguiling landscape of ruined keeps and whitewashed farms. My old map suggested that the monument on Kildoon Hill was something to do with a Vitrified Fort. If this was a guide book I would have to go to the trouble of checking that, but it isn't and I can be as enigmatic as I like. So lovely is the countryside, and so much a part of it is the railway, that I was suddenly reminded forcibly of railway journeys over fairytale branchlines in France that I have made in the past, or in Portugal as I imagine it might be. There are hints of what might have been stations at Kilkerran and Dailly and Killochan, and on my old map the inscription 'mine' at Dalquharran. 'There was once a halt here for workmen's trains', I gleaned from yet another old article in *Trains Illustrated*.

Enjoyable as this part of the journey was proving, I couldn't help feeling that a more intensely scenic route would have lain over the long abandoned and magically named Maidens & Dunure Light Railway, a coastwise line constructed in 1906 to serve the grandiose railway-owned hotel and golf courses at Turnberry. In the M&DLR's heyday the Glasgow & South Western provided passengers with a 'breakfast-car' up to

Glasgow in the morning and a 'tea-car' back in the afternoon - and now we can't even manage a catering trolley on trains going all the way to Stranraer. Perhaps my father travelled on the line, for he knew a fishing family at Dunure with whom he would trawl for herring in the then fish rich waters of the Firth of Clyde. Apparently the railway was also subject to the optical illusion that affects motorists on the Electric Brae at Croy, teasing you that you are travelling up when in fact you're going down; a delusion I have suffered from for much of my career.

The spires of Girvan appeared on the horizon. It has always seemed to me the sort of place one might select if one wished to disappear. I remembered its post-war style station from a journey I made in 1968 by Inter-city diesel multiple unit down to Stranraer. Then it suggested something out of Hornby-Dublo - now it looked like something rather tarnished you might pick up for a bargain at a swap-meet. Judging by the rusty rails, only the up platform appeared to be in use. I sighed and wished it was still 1968, and that the day before I had played a round of pitch and putt at Turnberry with an American air hostess, and that I could wander into Girvan and buy a copy of *Rogue Male* for one and six, and that my O level results wouldn't be so catastrophically bad as they were about to be.

But you will be wishing I would pull myself together and get back to the present day, and I am honour bound to oblige. And I should not be churlish, what with Ailsa Craig doing all the scene-stealing out there in the shimmering, luminescent firth, an upturned soup tureen, darkly opaque in the contre d'jour light. Ailsa Craig (or 'Paddy's Milestone' as some locals were telling an American back-packer further down the train) has magical connotations of childhood for me, not only a topographical landmark but a spiritual one as well. I could have given him some facts as well as folklore: that it is two miles round and over a thousand feet high, that it is the core of an ancient volcano; and that its granite was once quarried for the manufacture of superior curling stones, curling being a sport close to Scottish hearts. Nowadays it's for gannets rather than granite that the rock is known.

Twisting round the slopes of Dow Hill, the line climbs stiffly for three or four miles at 1 in 54/6 out of Girvan. The train had emptied considerably and I was able to swap sides to gain a better view of the sea, which promptly disappeared behind Byne Hill. Pinmore Tunnel is 440 yards long (did platelayers of an athletic bent ever hone their quarter-mileing skills by running through it in pre metric days?) and marks the first of two main summits between Girvan and Stranraer. The summit is a modest 394ft above sea level but the surrounding hills rise to seven, eight or nine hundred feet. Past the site of Pinmore station the line descends at 1 in 69 to cross a curving viaduct of considerable photogenic appeal. Now in the valley of the River Stinchar, the train ran due south between radiant shafts of sunlight slanting through the lineside trees, accompanied by the reassuring percussion of bogies on traditional lengths of track; the rhythmic ancestry of jazz.

Pinwherry is another closed station and abuts the consummation of the Stinchar and Duisk rivers, the former cutting away westwards down to the sea at Ballantrae. In 1919 there was some political suggestion that a light railway might be constructed between Pinwherry and Ballantrae to boost the local economy in much the same way that similar lines were built in rural Ireland. But all those surplus War Department lorries coming back from Flanders and Picardy must have already got a toehold in Carrick transport and no railway ever materialised. It would have been a pretty little line, eight miles long, perfect for preservation. Eight miles of climbing up the Duisk Valley follow. In Glasgow & South Western days it was company policy for locomotivemen to take it easy uphill to conserve coal and to speed downhill to keep to schedule.

We soared over two mellifluously named viaducts - Laggansarroch and Lig Burn, - and the bogies continued to beat out their song: 'We're climbing, we're climbing'. The people left on the train had thoughtful faces. All this beauty must have been getting to them. Suddenly a huge house came into view down in the wooded valley. My map told me it was Kildonan House and I wondered who built it and how they got their fortune. Barrhill is the only station left open between Girvan and

Stranraer. God knows how it escaped the Beeching axe. Perhaps the Laird of Kildonan had some pull in Whitehall, which was often the case. In steam days the locomotives took on water here and it was an important passing place. It still is. A blonde, bronzed signal lady came down from her lair in the tiny signal cabin to swap the token with the driver. We were in such a time warp that the token was carried in a leather pouch attached to a big hoop for ease of handling, particularly at other signal boxes along the line where the train wouldn't necessarily stop. You need a strong arm and a stronger nerve to handle these things and the bronze lady looked as if she had both, plus other attributes besides. Barrhill (along with a number of other Galloway railway stations) featured in *Five Red Herrings* and Dorothy L. Sayers, unlike the majority of novelists who include railway references in their work, was at pains to authenticate the action by careful reference to the timetables of the period.

Beyond Barrhill the line continues climbing. Now we were on the wild, peaty moors themselves with only sheep and cattle for company. At first no longer bare, as my 1955 OS map suggested, but thickly forested, and the railcar rode between the regimented firs like a hiker taking a shortcut through a fire-break. The plantations receded as the train approached the line's summit at Chirmorie, 690 feet above sea level. There was a railwaymen's community here of surfacemen's cottages. On Fridays a train stopped to take their wives down to Stranraer for the weekly shop. You have to acquire some of David L. Smith's out of print essays to get the full flavour of life here in Sou' Western days. In his inimitable fashion he wrote of the great blizzard of December 28th 1908. A Glasgow-Stranraer express was waiting at Girvan for a northbound train to clear the single line. When at last it arrived its driver warned them not to leave, but was over-ruled by control, shades of Emile Zola and *La Bête Humaine*. The Stranraer train got through to Barrhill but stuck in a drift between there and the summit. It stayed there for four days. They got the passengers out on the third.

Now I could understand why I have always held that 1968 trip over the Girvan to Stranraer line so high in my esteem.

Beyond the summit and the watershed the moorlands stretch bare and sensuous towards Kirkudbrightshire and the dominant summit of Merrick. The weather was contriving to set up a golden evening. The view through the carriage window was of Churchill's 'broad sunlit uplands' personified. Glenwhilly's station has gone but its loop survives and we slowed to exchange tokens. In the old days a 'lamb special' was a fast livestock train from Glenwhilly, not something drowned in subaqueous gravy you got from your landlady in a seafront boarding house in Girvan.

By Criagbirnoch Fell the line describes an arc around Lagnabenae Moss, falling at 1 in 58 for three miles. This, in locomotive crew parlance, was the 'Swan's Neck'; not only did you have to battle with the gradient but the sharp curves as well. The Sprinter went rattling downhill, returning to domesticity by the whitewashed chapel at New Luce, sounding its horn like a bugle call to the man on the tractor at Milton of Larg. The map suggested I should swap sides again to see the sea at Luce Bay. The Water of Luce accompanied me. There's a glimpse of Glenluce Abbey in which some 13th century wizard is said to have imprisoned a plague in the vault, presumably it seemed like a good idea at the time.

Luce Sands shone temptingly golden but, according to the map, they are a 'Danger Area' used by the military for target practice. Beyond them the bay stretched out to sea and I thought I could see some land which might just have been the Isle of Man, though more likely the Mull of Galloway. I was too intoxicated by the view to remember to look for the course of the direct line from Dumfries joining from the east at what was Challoch Junction. A mile further on we all but came to a standstill to exchange the token at Dunragit. Dumfries & Galloway Council have earmarked the loop here as a potential site for a station re-opening, to serve as a railhead for The Rhinns, as the twin headland either side of Stranraer is known. It may be just a gleam in Toby Rackliff's eye, but it would be a worthwhile project. At Dunragit in the old days one of the signalmen's wives dispensed teas in her front parlour for passengers changing between the two lines.

Loch Ryan came into view and I could see a ship at berth at Cairnryan where there had been a Military Port with a railway link during the Second World War. Moments later we were entering the outskirts of Stranraer, squealing past the football ground (arch rivals of Queen of the South) and past some rusty sidings littered with containers and road trailers, for no rail freight travels south of Dalrymple Junction anymore, though Dumfries & Galloway are again championing the idea of timber from Barrhill and intermodal activity at Stranraer.

All of a sudden the train emerged from a grassy cutting on to a causeway, with parking facilities for ferry-waiters on one side and the lapping waves of Loch Ryan on the other. The Sprinter shuddered to a halt under a reinforced plastic roof covering the platform and a timber station building of some antiquity. Unexpectedly I noticed that the noisy boy had still been on the train. I had forgotten all about him. Moreover I'd got my facts wrong. It hadn't been his granny at all, just a well-meaning fellow traveller. His parents were a bored young couple further down the carriage. I'd misjudged him and now felt sorry that he should suffer from his parents' indifference. And now on the platform, clutching a small bear, he was excited:

"We're going to Ireland, aren't we mum, we're going to Ireland."

Privately, I said what amounted to a small prayer in the hope that life would take him much, much further than that.

And off he went, along with a little knot of other passengers that had made their way down to Stranraer for the ferry by train. They evaporated and I was left by the buffer stops, staring out over the water horizoned by twin headlines, a sort of Caspar David Friedrich inspired view of eternity. An hour and a quarter away by Stena Seacat lies Belfast, an altogether different part of the United Kingdom, an altogether different country. I could get there before I could get back to Glasgow. Proof, were proof required, that distance is relative. I went into town for some fish & chips and ate them walking through its narrow streets, followed by a flock of seagulls.

Useful Contacts

Ayrshire Tourist Board - Tel: 01292 678100;
www.ayrshire-arran.com

Sanquhar Tolbooth Museum - Tel: 01659 50186

Dumfries & Galloway Tourist Board - Tel: 01387 253862.
www.dumfriesandgalloway.co.uk

Stranraer Tourist Information - Tel: 01776 702595

Stena Line - Tel: 0990 707070

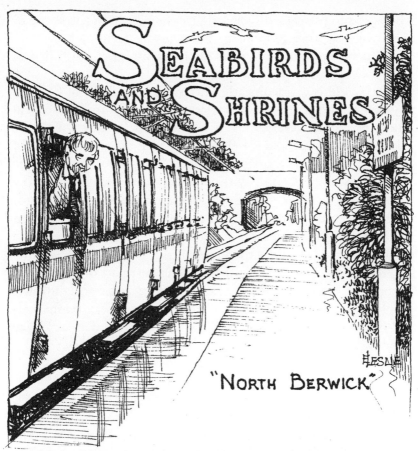

"NORTH BERWICK"

SEABIRDS AND SHRINES

A visit to North Berwick and the Scottish Seabird Centre. Elderly electrics escaped from Essex. The fight for the North Berwick branch. Edinburgh Waverley. Two Presbyterians at the Carfin Grotto. Glasgow to Ardrossan and a mystery island destination.

According to an advertisement in British Railways' 1955 *Holiday Guide to Scotland,* North Berwick is 'phenomenally dry'. So it came as no surprise to me that it was raining when John Yellowlees - ScotRail's erudite and enthusiastic External Relations Manager - and I hastened down from the station into the pretty little seaside town early one morning. Too early, initially, for a cafe to be open, so we perambulated the damp,

33

shop-opening streets, discovering treasure trove in the shape of a pale blue Scottish Region enamel sign, still pointing to the station the best part of forty years after the introduction of British Rail's 'Corporate Image'.

The world is divided neatly into those who think of Gannet, Guillemot and Kittiwake as varieties of seabird and those who know that they were names of Gresley and Peppercorn Pacific locomotives. John and I belong to a well-informed clique of intellectual colossi who straddle both. Thus we could visit the Scottish Seabird Centre with dual interest, recognising how appropriate it had been that 60032 shared its streamlined, aerodynamic outline with a seabird capable of diving from a hundred feet high into the sea for a fish supper at sixty miles an hour. It sort of redefines the concept of a 'carry out', doesn't it?

After a good soaking we still had the best part of an hour to dispose of before the centre opened at ten, so we sought out a salubrious little bistro and ordered coffee, easing our damp bodies on to comfortable sofas as the waitress asked if we'd like scones as well.

"There's cheese, fruit, herb and apricot," she told me.

"That's fine," I said.

"No that's four *different* sorts," she explained sympathetically, as if just noticing, for the first time, that I'd had a lobotomy.

Our host at the Scottish Seabird Centre was Tom Brock, the Director. You mustn't run away with the impression that I am normally shown around places by the top man. Usually it's the nightwatchman. But, in what now seems like a previous existence, Tom and I had collaborated on a book about the canals of Birmingham and the Black Country. It was good to see him again, and to note how well he looked, having swapped the foetid air of South Staffordshire for the bracing sea breezes of East Lothian. And who would not be happy working in such surroundings? If I envied John his giant ScotRail trainset, I could quite equally covet Tom's personal wildlife sanctuary.

By whatever criteria you care to judge it, the Scottish Seabird Centre has been an enormous success. Over espresso in the charming, big-windowed cafe/restaurant Tom outlined its impact. Not in PR mode, for he was amongst friends, but with the ardour of a man who has found a convivial niche in a world where such sinecures are in notoriously short supply. In those far off canal days I hadn't realised that his educational roots were in zoology, and here he was telling us that his graduate thesis had actually been on *gannets*.

Ah yes, the gannets! Through the rain-washed window Tom pointed to one as it began its jet-fighter like dive into the sea. We could have been in no more an appropriate location, for the bird's scientific name is *Morus bassana* and this is derived from its occupation of the Bass Rock. The rock reminded me of Ailsa Craig, and it commands the North Berwick view in the same attention-seeking manner that Ailsa Craig dominates proceedings at Girvan. It looks as impressive, but distances are deceptive, and it is in fact just 350 feet high and a mile in circumference. Forty thousand pairs of North Atlantic Gannets occupy it now, but in the past it has been an austere, windswept home from home to lighthouse-keepers, imprisoned Convenanters and 5th century evangelists.

Until recently the only way to get close to the Bass Rock was to sail round it aboard one of the little cruise ships which ply their tourist trade from North Berwick harbour. They continue to do so, but now a landlubber's alternative is to descend into the bowels of the Seabird Centre and manipulate your very own remote control camera. Unlike some humans, the gannets are not averse to being watched on CCTV - unlike some humans they have nothing to hide. Tom told us to look for the tell-tale signs of a bird leaving the nest, how one or other of a pair will literally 'point' at the sky, as if to say: "I'm awa doon the awf licence, will I be bringing youse back a Guinness?" And that trip down the pub might take one or other of the birds away for a couple of days, no self-respecting gannet thinking twice about popping over to the Norwegian coast for a fresh fish supper.

For those (and OK, I hold my hand up) to whom 'zoom' and 'focus' are alien concepts, helpful members of staff are unobtrusively on hand to offer back-up as and when required. There are three cameras in use: two transmitting pictures from the Bass

Rock; one from the neighbouring island of Fidra, an RSPB reserve occupied by puffins and seals at different times of the year. A new link to the Isle of May, also notable for its seal and puffin colonies, is under construction. The yellow-headed, black-wingtipped gannets don't have exclusive squatters rights on the Bass Rock. Other seabirds nest there; razorbills and fulmars and those railway inspiring guillemots and kittiwakes I mentioned earlier. Which reminded me that we had a train to catch, so we left Tom in paradise and made our way rapidly back to the station. I think I can safely say we'd both had an enjoyable morning. The Seabird Centre and ScotRail have teamed up to market an all-inclusive ticket for both individuals and families from Edinburgh. Tom reported encouraging uptakes of this initiative, good for ScotRail, good for the Centre, good above all for environmentally sustainable transport.

With the 613 feet summit of Berwick Law at our backs, we retraced our early morning steps to the station, making a quick detour to the Tourist Information Centre for a local leaflet - which they were clean out of. No matter, I already owned sundry reference material to the area, whilst John had kindly brought along a copy of Andrew Hajducki's Oakwood book about the North Berwick and Gullane branchlines for railway reference. I'd 'done' the North Berwick branch a year or two previously, on a warm late-summer afternoon, relishing the ride through cuttings thick with wildflowers; window down, emerging past post-harvest fields filled with big circular bales.

Window down? That gives the game away. Then, as now, I was aboard an elderly Class 305/2 suburban electric unit, one of five survivors that had escaped from captivity in Essex when the North Berwick branch was electrified in May 1991. These four-car units were built in Doncaster in 1960 and subsequently worked out of Liverpool Street and Fenchurch Street stations. They must have enjoyed semi-retirement to the familiarity of the seaside, there being little generic difference between the jellied-eel-eaters of Southend and the golfing-links-peregrinators of North Berwick. They may have been someone else's cast-offs, but the 305s endeared themselves to the East Lothian commuters, their 'somewhat antiquated features such as slam-doors and lack of air conditioning were overlooked in favour of such old-fashioned virtues as comfortable seats, opening windows and space for bicycles', as Andrew Hajducki put it. I fully concur, and would add the old-fashioned bell sounded by the guard on departure, and the comfortable clickety-clack of the jointed track beneath our Gresley style bogies.

But all this might well be over by the time you read this. On the very day that John and I were travelling, the first usurping 318 was out on the line, and when enough drivers had been trained on the new stock the 305s would be gone, like the Cravens and Gloucesters before them, and the steam V1s and C16s before them, way back to the horse-drawn Dandy Car which for a time provided the passenger services in 1856. Nothing stays the same, even on a branchline, for long. That horse was called in to effect economies in the early days of the line when the North British Railway found it to be running at a loss. At least a change in motive power showed initiative, even if it resulted in a court case being brought by an Edinburgh solicitor, outraged at the doubling of time taken to travel over the line and the deterioration in passenger comfort. He lost the action. Though, by the time the court had made its ruling, steam had returned with a vengeance.

It's a stiffish climb up to the station, we had hurried and John, I noticed, was a bit out of breath, though, finely honed athlete that I am, I had barely noticed the gradient at all.

"That's (gasp) all that's (deep breath) left of the (total collapse) original station," John told me, pointing to the British Rail symbol perched, somewhat symbolically, on top of one of the former cast iron canopy support pillars. The old, attractively S-shaped platforms and their buildings were demolished in 1985. Photographs in Andrew Hajducki's book reveal elegant symmetry and ill prepare you for current reality, a bare straight platform and buffer stops. Only Ken Denton's kiosk provides humanity now, a dispenser of newsprint, chocolate bars and homespun wisdom; essential antidotes to the vapid minimalism of the basic railway. Back home I poured over archive illustrations: wishing that 67670 would whisk me off in a three cylinder symphony of Walschaerts gear and derived motion; wishing that the Pullman camping coaches were still available for let, so that I could stride down to the beach before breakfast for an exhilarating dip in the Firth of Forth.

That we were catching a train from North Berwick at all is due to the intervention of an unknown lady at the very end of a hearing in 1969 to decide the fate of the line. I telephoned Norman Hall, a key member of the protest committee, to hear the story from the horse's mouth.

"We had appreciated something from the very start of our campaign that similar protesters had failed to grasp," he explained, "and that was that if you didn't win round one, there wouldn't be a round two. We also produced a circular letter which supporters could simply sign and send to the TUCC citing hardship were the line to close. On the day of the hearing there were six hundred people in the hall. We had primed a good number of witnesses, but the last person to get up and speak was a total stranger to us. She told a harrowing story of her cancer-ridden mother in a nursing home beside the station at North Berwick, who she wouldn't be able to visit so frequently if the trains stopped running. There was hardly a dry eye in the place, at least two lady members of the committee were seen to reach for their handkerchiefs."

On 19th September 1969 Richard Marsh, Minister of Transport at the time, formally refused British Rail permission to close the line. By such slender threads have the slings and arrows of railway history's outrageous fortune hung. Many a well meant protest lobby must still be disemboweling themselves that they did not fight longer, harder, dirtier battles against the pernicious railway managements of the Sixties and Seventies, whose perverse doctrine was to close railways rather than operate them. In retrospect it seems bizarre that the essentially local North Berwick line survived, when the much more strategically significant Waverley route closed. Perhaps it simply lacked an angel like the one who winged her way down to that hearing. Walking past the graceful North Berwick frontages on

Quality Street, I'd asked John how he personally viewed Beeching's contribution to railway history, and he'd answered pithily enough: "He trashed the inheritance."

So we owed it to an angel that we were able to board the 12.20 to Edinburgh Waverley: doors slammed, the bell rang, underfloor motors whirred into life and, thumpedy, thumpedy, thump we set off along the bullhead, jointed track to Drem. A whole soundtrack about to be wiped off the tape, as the 318s finally take over, and Railtrack's rolling programme of welded rail is completed. The line climbs south-westwards away from the coast at 1 in 66 into a landscape of largely arable fields, passing the site of a former intermediate station at Dirleton, which closed in 1952. To the north the sea led inscrutably to the horizon. John was flicking through a copy of the *East Lothian Courier*, for "local colour" as he put it. I was enjoying the 'rhythm of the rails' as immortalised in Steve Goodman's song *City of New Orleans*. Judy Collins wide-eyed and soulful, sat on my shoulder and sang about 'the sons of Pullman porters and the sons of engineers...riding their father's magic carpet made of steel'.

Beyond Dirleton the line drops through a rocky cutting towards Drem and the East Coast Main Line. Four and a quarter miles of fun are all too quickly ended, eighteen remain to be gobbled up in a sprint to Edinburgh. Drem station is demurely weatherboarded and photogenic in its red and cream paint, though the down platform waiting room is a replica, built after British Rail set about demolishing the original in 1985 due, as Andrew Hajducki tactfully puts it, to a 'misunderstanding'. We passed a tall obelisk - the Hopetoun Monument - to the south and, nearing Spittal, briefly spied the earthworks of the branchline to Gullane which had lost its passenger trains as long ago as 1932. I bet they wish it was still functioning when 'The Open' is held at Muirfield.

Brakes on by the ruins of Redhouse Castle, the train came to a halt at Longniddry, a garden village with pantiled roofs, adjacent to the Robert Adam designed seat of the Earl of Wemyss at Gosford. Another branchline struck south from here to the old county town of Haddington, a community of considerable antiquity and charm: or as the *Shell Guide to Scotland* used (and the past tense is regrettable) to put it 'one of the finest examples of burghal architecture in Scotland'. Longniddry's rocky shoreline is just a hop, skip and a jump from the station. They used to mine coal here, but it's very much commuter country now. Up until the early Thirties the station marked the point at which the Gullane portion of the Lothian Coast Express - wherein a gentlemen's club atmosphere prevailed - was joined to the Dunbar and North Berwick portions, for a fast morning run to Glasgow Queen Street.

The atmosphere in our 305 was more akin to a dentist's waiting room. John put his paper down and began to take seriously his role as local guide. A GNER whooshed by southbound, we rattled past a half demolished opencast coal bunker, then glimpsed the branchline curving away to Cockenzie Power Station, an industrial intrusion on this romantic, golf-obsessed coast. John's sense of humour rivals mine in its capacity for equivocality and ambiguity. So much so that there are times when it's hard to distinguish who's kidding who. Thus when he told me that the Battle of Prestonpans in 1745 featured the first recorded involvement of a railway in a military action, I attempted the difficult combination of a sage nod with a knowing smile and made a mental note to consult Fitzroy Maclean as soon as I got home. How could I have doubted you Yellowlees? For there, on page 88 of *Bonnie Prince Charlie*, is a map with a waggonway right down the middle of the battleground. Furthermore, my researches threw light on another reference that had always puzzled me, the folk song *Johnny Cope* (as sung by Ewan MacColl) with the line 'gang tae the coals in the morning.' It appeared that the waggonway carried coal and the words were those of Highlanders mocking the beaten Hanoverian general, Sir John Cope.

Next stop Wallyford, opened in 1994 and surrounded by housing estates; all over-cooked concrete and social dysfunction. But custom for the railway, and CCTV controlled, which increases public confidence.

"Railtrack paid for the cabling," explained John: "The Council paid for the cameras and ScotRail pay for the running costs."

It's an effective deterrent to hooliganism. Imagine you're ripping down a fence and a god-like voice booms out from the sky: "Stop that yer wee so and so, yer on camera, and the polis are on their way."

The line crosses the Esk and passes Monktonhall Junction which provides access to Millerhill Yard (an important freight depot and locomotive fuelling point), then skirts Musselburgh, which boasted its own branchline terminus until 1964, but which is now served by a modern station on the main line, the last stop for the North Berwick trains before they sprint into Waverley. While we paused at Musselburgh for a moment, John told me that the esteemed Scots film-maker Bill Douglas had come from nearby Newcraighall, which would soon be a terminus on the Edinburgh Crossrail service, with the firm intention that, in the not too distant future, track will be re-laid over the old Waverley route, at least as far as Galashiels. All very encouraging and commendable, but why was it allowed to close in the first place?

Edinburgh's suburbs embraced us, but the unit was still going at a fair lick. We raced over Portobello Junction and past Craigentinny Maintenance Depot and saw the Powderhall branch, used by refuse trains, veer away to the north. Somewhere around here, I remembered, stood St Margaret's motive power depot, an important engine shed in steam days. *The British Locomotive Shed Directory* of 1947 quotes: 'The shed is on both sides of the line about one and a half miles east of Waverley Station. Tram No.4 operates from Princes Street.' Those were the days; in its place, cranes were erecting the new Scottish Parliament building against the rocky backdrop of Salisbury Crags. Calton Tunnel swallowed us up, and only then did we seem to slow down.

Daylight raises the curtain on Waverley Station and other game of word association. What is Waverley to you: the eponymous Captain of Sir Walter Scott's novels, the last sea-going paddle steamer in the world, a minor character in the New

Zealand soap opera *Shortland Street,* or this wonderful railway station, in its chasm like setting between the Old Town and the New Town? Your response defines you, and the fact that you are reading a book with 'railway' in the title suggests you'll have plumped for the last answer. The station you see today dates back to the turn of the 19th and 20th centuries, a replacement born out of crises of congestion. It stands on the site of a loch, drained to make way for the city's expansion northwards into the New Town. The *Shell Guide* haughtily refrains from even mentioning it, so I sought out the more dependable Hamilton Ellis in *Four Main Lines.* There I found an earlier reference, by a Professor Foxwell, to the abundant chaos of Waverley's predecessor: 'Trains of caravan length come in portentously late from Perth, so that each is mistaken for its successor; these have to be broken up and remade on insufficient sidings, while bewildered crowds of tourists sway up and down amongst equally bewildered porters; the higher officials stand lost in subtle thought, returning to repeated inquiries some masterpiece of reply couched in the cautious conditional.' Having arrived three hours late on the Caledonian Sleeper that very morning, and thereafter watched a further hour elapse before the three portions were separated, allocated the correct locomotive and allowed to proceed respectively to Inverness, Aberdeen and Fort William; and having watched numerous members of the mystified public engage officials in Pinteresque question and answer routines, I had every reason to suspect that nothing had changed.

Waiting, that morning, for Yellowlees to arrive from Haymarket, I had explored the station precincts, suddenly reminded how, in boyhood, I had admired it, not because of its imposing architecture, but because, in common with London Waterloo, it boasted a staggering total of twenty-one platforms. It does to this day, though some are trackless gaps now, missing in old age like fondly remembered teeth. As with dogs, it's often the case that railway stations physically resemble their owners. Thus, Waverley is spacious, cultured and more couth than its Glaswegian counterparts. Here the staff call you 'Sir' instead of 'Jimmy', and if your accent is unaccountably anglicised you won't necessarily have to spell your destination out to them phonetically. Indeed, tannoy announcements are nowadays in the soothingly angelic tones of a Morningside nanny, as if to say:

"The Dundee train is about to depart, but don't break into a run darlings or you'll crease your clothes."

Even Waverley's pigeons seem politer, patiently waiting at a distance for you to brush off your crumbs, unlike their counterparts at Aberdeen or Inverness who fly straight into your lap and rip the bacon out of your BLT, leaving a tip behind in the form of a sticky stain on your suit.

John and I had a few minutes to spare before our next leg of the journey. We went and paid homage to a new plaque commemorating the birth of Sir Nigel Gresley in Edinburgh. Being familiar with his scandalously unkempt grave in the South Derbyshire village of Netherseal, I expressed surprise that this most famous of locomotive engineers should have been born in Edinburgh.

"His parents didn't live here," John explained, "they were on a visit to Edinburgh and he arrived a bit early."

Obviously a 'streamlined' birth, I thought, but kept the comment to myself, sometimes you can have just too much wit in one day.

Then we proceeded to the ScotRail Booking Office, a rather less grand affair than GNER's, tucked apologetically away behind W.H.Smith. The reason for our visit was to check how sales of *Iron Road to the Isles* were going. The booking clerk, an affable man I feel sure I would have got on with in other circumstances, shrugged his ample shoulders and admitted that they had yet to sell a single copy. An author's nightmare, akin to a politician mounting the platform after a by-election, and being told they've received no votes at all.

"Dinna worry," smiled the clerk, "nae doubt wull sell sum when the two-fur-one offer's on."

Finally we snatched a picnic from Peckham's and boarded the 13.22 to Glasgow Central via Shotts.

My plan was to travel across the Central Belt from coast to coast, heading for a mysteriously romantic island destination.

First, though, I talked John into a sojourn at Carfin to visit the Lourdes Grotto. We had a carmine & cream 156, refurbished - as John knowledgeably pointed out - with 'teal breeze' upholstery. He shared my respect for this type of Sprinter unit, admiring, from the professional railwayman's point of view, their reliability as much as any aesthetic consideration. We pulled out of Platform 13, vanished into the Mound Tunnel (straddled by those twin bastions of Scottish art: the Royal Scottish Academy and the National Gallery of Scotland) and emerged into the oft-photographed cutting overlooked by Edinburgh Castle and bisecting Princes Street Gardens. Hamilton Ellis confessed to leaning so long on the parapet above the tunnel, 'that a stately policeman ranged up with a fatherly look in his eye, apparently ready to point out that things were not quite as bad as that'.

We paused at Haymarket before cutting away on to the Midcalder line, encountering the Caledonian Brewery and Tynecastle, home of Heart of Midlothian Football Club. Come Slateford Junction we were in the territory of the Caledonian Railway whose services would, traditionally, have run in and out of Edinburgh's fondly remembered Princes Street terminus, until rationalisation brought about its closure in 1965. Beyond Slateford station - the second of eighteen stops this train would make on its forty-seven mile, hour and a half long journey to Glasgow - we crossed a lengthy viaduct spanning the Water of Leith in close proximity to an equally imposing aqueduct carrying the Union Canal over the same defile; a new juxtaposition of viaduct and aqueduct for me to add to mental images of Chirk and Marple.

It would be tedious to list each station we called at, too prone to guidebook authorship. It pays to be selective, knowing what to leave out being just as important as knowing what to put in. But I couldn't ignore Wester Hailes, whose high rise horrors have steadily been replaced by more human, or perhaps that should be more humane, housing.

"There was a film shot here," said John, "about two boys who held up tour coaches on a motorbike."

"I know it," I laughed, *"Restless Natives,"* chuckling at the memory of a gentle comedy that occupies a privileged position in our video collection at home.

We crossed the Edinburgh by-pass, passed close to the campus of the Heriot-Watt University, and escaped into a semblance of open countryside. Conversation lapsed as we munched our lunch. I had a particularly tasty broccoli and blue cheese wrap and I wanted to concentrate on each flavour-exploding morsel. John interjected to bring attention to what had been the Balerno branch, a loop off the Shotts line which John Thomas described as 'a lovely rural line' and 'a favourite with picnickers'. Losing its passenger service during the Second World War (an opportunity the LMS took to rid itself of a lot of unremunerative railways and canals while people's backs were turned) the trackbed is now a sylvan public footpath.

It was time to swap Ordnance Survey sheets, from 66 to 65. At Midcalder Junction the main line swerved south-westwards to Carstairs, abandoning us to inter-urban introspection. No one would expect the Shotts line to hold over much appeal for tourists, but I was beginning to respond to its gently understated mixture of countryside and suburbia, a potentially antagonistic interface, melded here - by accident or design I would not care to say - into a cohesive whole. Out of the right hand window at West Calder I saw a little mountain range of pink coloured 'bings', glowing in a sudden burst of sunshine like miniature Alps.

"They're the Five Sisters," explained John, reading my thoughts in a Holmesian manner. "They're listed now, they belonged to the shale oil mines."

Wary of being impaled on the prongs of Yellowlees's spiky humour, I nodded knowingly but took care to read up about what one historian has termed Scotland's Shale Oil Bonanza before going into print myself. Now I modestly consider myself an expert on the subject, able to enliven many a dull dinner party with a homily devoted to its rise and fall. I give you the edited version here, because the train continues to climb slowly towards the summit at Fauldhouse, and we do not want to be left behind. But in essence the shale oil industry flourished hereabouts between the middle of the nineteenth century and the middle of the twentieth. It owed its existence to James Paraffin Young - his middle name, it's safe to assume, being acquired by repute and not bestowed at birth. He discovered that various oils could be extracted from the plentiful beds of shale in West Lothian. Petrol, paraffin, paint - numerous uses were found for shale oil; it was even used to make mothballs. Young built a big refinery at Addiewell, the next station along the line from West Calder. The foundation stone was laid by David Livingstone, a friend of Young's from student days, whose missionary work in the Dark Continent Young was only too happy to finance from his shale mining, oil making fortunes. The industry might well have continued into the present day were it not for post war competition from the Persian Gulf. Britain might be good at inventing things, but we're rubbish at keeping them going. When it comes to competition - be it in shipbuilding, coal mining, textiles, car making - God help us even football - there is only ever one winner - Johnny Foreigner.

The remains of an old mine were apparent at Breich, backed now by big forestry plantations on what had once been melancholy waves of open moorland. Breich station is spurned by most trains and has latterly been something of a crusade for its sole regular passenger. We were being shadowed by an old North British line. Its trackbed passed under us as the Shotts line essayed a suddenly twisting course through Fauldhouse, crossing into North Lanarkshire and coming under the control of Motherwell signal box. The line's summit was passed as well, and now the train was bowling down to Shotts, mere mention of which invariably invokes a Pavlovian dog-like response in me on account of Bells pies.

Two late forty-somethings of vaguely Presbyterian persuasion, one in a suit, one wearing jeans, detrained at Carfin, once merely another Lanarkshire coal mining village, now a celebrated Catholic centre of pilgrimage. Carfin Grotto dates from 1922. It was the inspiration of one Father Taylor who wished to alleviate the misery of unemployed miners, disenfranchised by the Depression. Though he was in no position to help them financially, he could lend them something perhaps more valuable, dignity. A series of shrines and statues were erected on land adjoining the railway, land, it was later discovered, already hallowed by an order of monks centuries before. The majority of the local workforce were displaced Irish, Polish, Lithuanian and Ukrainian refugees, naturally Catholic in their upbringing. The grotto rapidly became a place of pilgrimage. When the London Midland & Scottish Railway opened a halt here in 1927, sixty-seven thousand pilgrims had passed through its narrow platforms within six months. Its two latest pilgrims proceeded hesitantly from shrine to shrine, cautiously encountering each statue, untutored in our response. In time we came to Calvary, most potent of all symbols. A light rain fell. I explained to John that although my father was staunchly Presbyterian, I had, by virtue of my mother's influence, spent the first five years of my education in a convent school being taught by nuns. I think he appreciated the paradox. We went for a coffee, stealing inconspicuously into the Pilgrimage Centre like undercover agents in a foreign land, keeping up morale with Tunnock's Caramel Wafers, eavesdropping on parishional gossip of pilgrimages, visions, miracles and rumoured manifestations of stigmata.

Back on the next train, we found ourselves calling, appropriately enough, at Holytown, and we had moved from the country of Old King Coal into an area still contaminated by the closure of Ravenscraig Steel Works. The press was full of plans for redevelopment of the site - 'an £800m initiative to regenerate a vast area of derelict land by creating a state-of-the-art community and leisure destination'. It was being suggested that 12,000 jobs would be created, 3,500 new homes built, £1bn of private sector investment attracted, 1,125 acres transformed. They are as enamoured with numbers as trainspotters, these developers, and a good deal less concerned to be accurate.

I was retracing the steps of the previous chapter: skirting Mossend, crossing the Clyde at Uddingston (where we reminisced over the cement trains from Kent, reaching mutual agreement that the 'Southern' diesels had come off at Skelton Yard, to the north of York) thrumming through Newton on the fast line;

and reaching Rutherglen, and the land of tenements, in no time at all. We followed the main line into Glasgow Central, past Polmadie, in engine shed terms, the West Coast equivalent of Edinburgh's Haymarket, former lair of Stanier Pacifics, Royal Scots and Jubilees and now a maintenance depot for Virgin Trains.

John was jumping ship, he needed to check that his desk in Caledonian Chambers was still there. We met John Boyle, his immediate superior, on the staircase. I said something flippant about Yellowlees deserving a day out now and again. Mr Boyle fixed me with a look that has terrorised many an RPC meeting and said:

"Day out! Don't you believe it, this guy's *never* in the office."

I left them to their office politics and stole down onto the concourse for a Coca Cola and a bar of chocolate. Four-thirty in the afternoon and, as usual, I was flagging. They play the popular 'what platform will your train leave from' game at Central as well as Queen Street. I'm sketching out a proposal for Waddingtons as I write. Oh yes, and the Patent's in the post, so don't go getting any ideas. I had a par for the course three minutes to get from the concourse to Platform 12 for the 16.50 to Ardrossan Harbour. No wonder the 318 electric unit was surprisingly empty for a teatime commuter run, most of the prospective, deep-fried-Mars-bar eating passengers were probably still wheezing their way past Franco's. We ran fast to Paisley Gilmour Street along the old Glasgow & Paisley Joint, racing the cars on the M8 through Cardonald and leaving the law-abiders for dead. It used to be the only quadruple main line in Scotland, but the slow lines were lifted in 1967. The six-car 318 was comfortable, if a tad reminiscent of the abysmal diesel 150s for my liking; though John Yellowlees (proudly towing the company line) had told me that the whole class of twenty-one, mid-Eighties, York built 3 car units are currently being refurbished to a high standard. At Hillingdon an eastbound train of coal hoppers went by behind an EWS Class 66. A few minutes later we crossed the White Cart Water, with Paisley's imposing Abbey on my left, and came to a halt in the Ayrshire platforms at Gilmour Street.

The train became busier here, filling with life stories. The travel writer extrapolates, creating scenarios from the flimsiest evidence. I am no less guilty, and at each successive stop people got off, unaware that I had neatly, and very likely inaccurately, pigeon-holed their existences for them. We were racing along the metals of the old Glasgow & South Western Railway; blue skies now, reflecting in a sequence of lochs. There'd been a parallel line to the north. I traced its dismantled outline on the map, straining my eyes to catch a glimpse of its earthworks beyond the water. It seemed an unnecessary duplication even given the excesses of the era. Over-enthusiasm always gives way to embarrassment. Between Barr Loch and Kilbirnie Loch the line ran alongside marshland with bog grass and I wondered why this line, and its ghostly neighbour, had not enjoyed more photographic coverage by enthusiasts over the years.

Whisky bonds accompanied us into Glengarnock, once the site of a sizeable steelworks. A bearded man, who'd been reading a book about riveting tools, got off. South flowing off the apparently unnamed high ground between Largs and Paisley, the River Garnock kept convivial company with the railway as far as the outskirts of Kilwinning. The weather was improving as the evening wore on. On the approach to Dalry it was satisfying to see use being made of the railway to carry freight into a pharmaceutical works, though a big ruined textile mill bore witness to the ephemerality of industry. The purple flowers of rosebay willowherb stood intensified by the evening sunshine. A bare embankment carried the trackbed of the old GSWR line to Kilmarnock away to the south-east. I was entering that trance-like state that precedes sleep.

A sudden lurch to the right at Kilwinning rudely returned me to wakefulness. It's one of those 'V' shaped stations which are never less than interesting. The sun was sending catenary shadows on to my notepad as Arran's craggy outline came into view. You knew all along, didn't you, that Arran was my aim? Did you play those 'Merrymaker' Mystery Trip games as well, back in the Seventies, when the railways still had enough surplus rolling stock to compete with coaches for the excursion trade? Cheap, and by definition, cheerful trips to the coast, which always - in my experience - ended up in Rhyl or Llandudno. In Scotland it was probably this Ayrshire coast to which the 'Merrymakers' were invariably destined. Now it was upon me - sand dunes at Stevenston, caravans at Saltcoats - and I sensed an involuntary excitement, a surge of ozone induced frenzy, a strong desire to feel lugworm casts under my bare feet and vanilla ice cream on the tip of my tongue.

At Ardrossan South Beach, the train, and the line, split in two, just three cars proceeding to the harbour, the line to Largs continuing past wastegrounds, which must once have been sidings, I supposed. In the planning stage, I'd toyed with the idea of carrying on to Largs and sampling ScotRail's open top bus tie-in tour of Cumbrae, but it was too late in the day for that now. My carriage had emptied, save for a girl curled up on the seat opposite, long dark hair framing a pale face, barely perceptible eyebrows, reading a novel by Jonathan Coe. We were what Philip Larkin has called a 'frail travelling coincidence', a modern day, visual equivalent of Leopold Augustus Egg's painting *The Travelling Companions*, differing only in age and gender. And I realised how strange it is, that had the train been as empty when one or other of us got on, we wouldn't have dreamt of sitting so intimately together. But we had been left this way, by the deserting crowd, and it would have been too embarrassing for either of us to move.

The girl and I, and our own personal train, took the slow curve on jointed track, under a ruined tower and a tall obelisk to Ardrossan Town. We stood there for barely thirty seconds. I listened to the level crossing warning siren and the girl turning a page. Then the driver blew the horn and we rumbled round to the harbour station, which shared a strange symmetry with North Berwick in its electric status, absence of pointwork, and a similarly foreshortened, all but bare platform. Long ago, both the Glasgow & South Western and the Caledonian railways had separate and busy pier stations at Ardrossan Harbour. Now the railway presence is minimal, and it falls to Caledonian MacBrayne to provide succour for travellers. In their modern terminal building, I asked for a return ticket to Brodick . The young woman behind the counter wanted to know when I was coming back. When I answered "immediately", she gave me that uncomprehending, patronising look familiar to anyone who travels for travel's sake. Why should she have been so amazed, I am only a throw-back to previous generations of Clydesiders who liked nothing better than an excursion 'doon the watter'.

Caledonian Isles was launched by the Princess Royal at Lowestoft in 1993. She felt like a small liner. I understand she is to all intents and purposes the largest Clyde 'steamer.' ever. With a restaurant and cafe and bars and shops on board, plus several decks to get lost on, I began to feel as if I was about to embark upon a voyage across the Bay of Biscay and not the Firth of Clyde. The last cars were quickly driven on through the bow, Captain McRindle introduced himself over the public address with the panache of an airline pilot, and we reversed out of the berth. I took up my favoured position on the stern deck, having, since boyhood, been both captivated and mesmerised by the foaming wake of a sea-going vessel. Occasionally, on the just short of an hour long journey, I wandered round to the starboard side to see Goat Fell - Arran's dominant peak, 2,868ft high - grow ever larger. It stood out against the orange-tinted western sky like a three-dimensional theatre set. I was in the stalls and ready to be entertained. Then my mobile went and it was Tamar, my daughter, wanting to know where I was.

"Sailing over to Arran," I said, shouting over the engine noise.

"Did you say *heaven*?" she asked, and I laughed, knowing that it could well be the case.

Useful Contacts

Scottish Seabird Centre - Tel: 01620 890202. www.seabird.org

North Berwick Tourist Information - Tel: 01620 892197

Carfin Pilgrimage Centre - Tel: 01698 268941

Caledonian MacBrayne - Tel: 01294 463470

Brodick Tourist Information - Tel: 01770 302401

THE DAY RANGER & TINTO.

MAXWELL PARK
LESLIE.

Early morning at Garelochhead. The north bank of the Clyde.
Glasgow Queen Street and George Square. Springburn and
Cumbernauld. A quick walk around Motherwell. Hamilton
and the Cathcart Circle. A pilgrimage to Paisley. Port
Glasgow and Gourock. A rough crossing to Helensburgh.
Kelvin Hall and the Museum of Transport. Following the
tracks of The Tinto to Carstairs.

The American songwriter Paul Simon is most famously known
in railway circles for writing *Homeward Bound* on Widnes station where there's a plaque - stolen from time to time by over
zealous souvenir hunters - to prove it. But he also wrote a song
called *Train in the Distance,* and this was the one I was humming
at Garelochhead one June morning as the Caledonian Sleeper
growled throatily away up the 1 in 61 to Whistlefield, still three
hours short of its destination on the banks of Loch Linnhe.

My complimentary copy of the morning's *Herald* had pre-
dicted 'rain all day' and its pragmatic pessimism was proving
only too accurate. A cold wind from the east was sending low
cloud scudding over the sleeping warships and submarines of

Faslane; the metaphorical cold wind from the East, that our political masters had brought them so expensively into being for, never having materialised. The Vulcan Foundry strains of 37426's exhaust became blurred with a loquacious breeze in the lineside trees. Garelochhead is a pristine example of West Highland architecture. Pristine, but unstaffed and unoccupied. A waiting room would have been welcome, and some *craic* with a resident railwayman, but I made do with the station's solitary bench until the empty stock of the 07.32 to Queen Street trundled in, just after seven.

Garelochhead is the north-western extremity of Strathclyde Passenger Transport territory which boasts 334 route miles, 180 stations and 42 million passengers per annum. My plan was to explore as much of Britain's second largest suburban network as I uncomfortably could in a day. By half past the ScotRail coloured, two coach Class 156 Sprinter unit (whose purple lines chimed so harmoniously with clumps of railside rhododendron) began to fill with fellow travellers. They arrived at the last minute with the nonchalance of season ticket holders, though I would like to think that in true *Titfield Thunderbolt* tradition the crew would have delayed departure for any stragglers. Most of them were smartly blazered schoolchildren with whom I could empathise, having been conveyed to and from school by train myself more years ago than I care to remember. Of course we were much better behaved in those days, though not averse to hurling lightbulbs out of compartment windows, opening carriage doors in tunnels, holding massed snowball battles from platform to platform, keeping close surveillance on passengers we suspected of being smugglers and using the station yard as a football pitch.

Bang on time we started away, rhythmically clattering along the unwelded track on tight curves past the high security fencing of Faslane, which the railway had been instrumental in the construction of as Military Port No.1 in the early 1940s. You can still see the trackbed of the connecting branch sloping down through the woods to the waterside, the ghost of a line which would never have existed but for man's inhumanity to man. It was too early on this weekday morning to buy an SPT 'ranger' ticket, or 'Daytripper' as it is snappily known - 9am being the watershed Monday to Friday - so I purchased a single to Glasgow from the guard; noticing, with regret, that the point of departure was printed out as 'Helensburgh Stations'; not quite so collectable in years to come as 'Garelochhead'.

A naval tug punched its way down channel to the Clyde as we echoed through rocky cuttings to Helensburgh Upper where more commuters and schoolchildren awaited the ritual of our arrival. Ritual for them, novelty for me; eavesdropping on class-room gossip and outrageous teacher slander. And then, describing an arc around the pebble-dashed periphery of Helensburgh, we came to the Clyde at Craigendoran, where two derelict timber groynes jut disconsolately out into the estuary, remnants of the North British Railway's once extensive steamer network.

Virtually all the way from Craigendoran to Kilpatrick, the line hugs the Clyde and I very much doubt if it is possible to tire of the view. There is a classic Terence Cuneo poster of the railway at Bowling with one of the electric Blue Trains gliding past some tugs, and my only sorrow is that whilst the Blue Trains survive (albeit less glamorously) the shipping doesn't. Endlessly fascinating as the day's itinerary was going to prove, I was to be left with a degree of muted grief that most of Clydeside's great commercial successes - its shipbuilding and mercantile trade, its locomotive construction, its engineering - were enterprises now spoken of only in the past tense.

Pewits were ducking and diving over the little grey bays leading to Cardross. Lumps of dark coloured rock lined the trackside to protect it from the incursion of spring tides. It was high water and shelduck and cormorants were foraging at the tideline. This stretch of line was opened in 1858 by the Glasgow, Dumbarton & Helensburgh Railway; though, within seven years, it had become part of the mighty North British empire who operated a dense network of suburban lines on the north bank of the Clyde. Such facts I gleaned from the *Illustrated History of Glasgow's Railways* written by W.A.C. Smith and Paul Anderson and published by the Irwell Press in 1993 which I would commend to all followers in my footsteps, even those who would normally disdain such material, for it is enjoyably written and nostalgically illustrated.

Initially restrained, the growing numbers of schoolchildren, swollen with each stop, were becoming more raucous; winding themselves up, perhaps, for a full day's confrontation with authority. At Dalreoch we temporarily left the Clyde, veered inland through a short twin bore tunnel, passed the junction for the line to Balloch (which, though of undoubted interest, I wouldn't have time to explore) and crossed the River Leven into Dumbarton, whose handsome Central station I had encountered when researching *Iron Road to the Isles,* my 'ridiculously cheap' - as one enthusiastic reviewer somewhat ambivalently put it - travellers guide to the West Highland Lines. Here was the journey's first clear encounter with the sort of typical 19th century Scottish tenement housing which would characterise my Clydeside travels. They solved the area's burgeoning population explosion but fell foul of the post war period's misplaced enlightenment, being replaced in the Fifties and Sixties by hideous high rise blocks which only served to exacerbate social problems. Now some of the better maintained survivors are considered highly desirable residences, whilst even the less well preserved exude at least an exterior dignity. For me they seem palpably in touch with the past, as though their sandstone had absorbed the atmosphere of previous generations, retaining it almost photographically - a necromantic alchemy of zinc and albumen - so that you could feel yourself once more in the presence of the steam trains and trams that had rattled by their windows in years gone by.

The railway travellers' view of Dumbarton's famous volanic crag is compromised by an ASDA supermarket, an enclave of modern housing and a gasholder. Bloated now with Dumbarton commuters, the diesel unit regained its grandstand view of the Clyde, and I was given a glimpse of the trackbed of the original GD&H route, somewhat confusingly abandoned in favour of the rival Lanarkshire & Dumbartonshire line between Dumbarton and Bowling. You certainly have to swot up on railway history to be in the know on Clydeside. Simpler, and more rational perhaps, to concentrate on the fast approaching focus of the Erksine Bridge of 1971, forming a symmetric backdrop to Bowling Harbour; though here again, the ghost of an old railway manifests itself, as the self same L&D is carried over us by way of a hefty skewed girder bridge. The Lanark & Dumbartonshire was a Caledonian Railway route, a bitterly resented incursion into rival North British territory - the equivalent, should you want to gauge its impact, of a Rangers gift shop opening in Parkhead.

The clock on Kilpatrick church read five past eight. ScotRail's Media Relations Manager, Eddie Toal, had told me to look out for Phil Benson's sycamore-sculpted eagle on the westbound platform, but we were going too rapidly to see anything more than a blur of branches and boles. Sandstone tenements introduced Dalmuir, junction for the more direct route through Clydebank to Glasgow Queen Street Low Level. Several electric multiple units were bustling about, contributing to the rush hour. Mostly they still wore SPT's old, predominantly orange colour scheme, that had seemed bright enough in its time, and a welcome antidote to British Rail's drab blue, but which now pales in comparison to the present carmine and cream livery, appearing as obsolete and so very 'Eighties' as Afghan Hounds or Abba LPs. We didn't deign to stop at Dalmuir, but called instead at Singer (named after the world famous sewing machine manufacturer who had a massive factory here, and such a large workforce that they had their own, separate six platformed terminus) where the schoolchildren detrained and bundled into the shelter - whether to wait for a connecting train or for a furtive pre-school smoke I could only speculate.

Electric trains swished by at frequent intervals, several of them belonging to Class 303, the original Blue Train design which revolutionised travel on north Clydeside forty years ago. Delays in the introduction of new stock have extended their life - a familiar scenario on Britain's railway system, but a welcome one for those railway nostalgics among us who hold on to the 'old ways' as nodal points of stability in an unstable world; in much the same way that we re-read Sherlock Holmes, try and sit in the front seat of the top deck of a double-decker bus, save the tickets and still drink Vimto. Notwithstanding the fact that they were withdrawn *en masse* with a generic electrical fault for the best part of a year (just months after being introduced to an appreciative travelling public), they have served both sides of the Clyde wonderfully well, burying themselves almost as deep in the Glaswegian psyche as the city's trams. Refurbishment in the 1980s regrettably subtracted some of the chic out of their original design. The driver's stylish wrap-round windows (an attractive trait they shared with Trans-Pennine and Clacton stock) were in-filled, and additional bulkheads prevented passengers from enjoying a view over the driver's shoulder along the track ahead. And, of course, that gorgeous (though initially inappropriate in former rival North British territory) Caledonian blue livery got lost in the process as well, leaving one to hope (though probably fruitlessly) that at least one unit might be saved from the breaker's yard, restored to its original condition, and allowed to trundle around the network on high-days and holidays, as a sort of railway equivalent of the PS *Waverley*.

Dalmuir, Drumry, Drumchapel: the alliterative qualities of Glasgow's suburbs have poetic potential it occurred to me as we crossed the administrative boundary between East Dunbartonshire and the City of Glasgow. Prodigious amounts of excess water were flowing over the lockgates on the newly restored Forth & Clyde Canal at Westerton where you are urged to alight for Canniesburn Hospital. A mischievous image of heavily bandaged, walking wounded outpatients descending from the train to a waiting committee of paramedics passed wickedly through my mind.

Beyond Westerton the 07.32 from Garelochhead became one of the comparatively few passenger services each day (other than West Highland trains) to pass over the unelectrified section of line to Maryhill, beyond which there is a frequent inner-suburban diesel service to and from Queen Street High Level. This was launched, with several new well-sited stations, in 1993, and there are proposals for the revival of the spur between Maryhill and Anniesland, along with a new station at Dawsholm, to further enhance the network. But such schemes are prone to gather dust on drawing boards, to be becalmed in stagnant pools of political intrigue, and to get caught in interminable queues for the sourcing of funding.

Summerston station is cold-shouldered by high rise housing of disheartening decrepitude. A sad little playground with a solitary swing encapsulates the hopelessness of life reared in such surroundings. We passed under the Forth & Clyde Canal and my eye was caught by the gaunt tower of the old fever hospital at Ruchill, before the train curved slowly round to Cowlairs. In the holding sidings at Eastfield (all that's left of a once massive motive power depot) a steam locomotive, Peppercorn K1 2-6-0, 62005, was waiting with its support coach to make the journey up to Fort William for a summer season of steam hauled services to Mallaig. It stood wistfully in the rainy siding like a lost link with a prehistoric era.

Cowlairs is a hundred and fifty feet higher than Queen Street. Such was the discrepancy in height, and the resultant intensity of grade, that when the line opened in 1842, the Edinburgh & Glasgow Railway's engineers were of the opinion that a gradient of 1 in 41 was just too steep for the steam locomotives of that time to cope with. Instead they left their engines at the top of the bank and provided specially designed four-wheel brake wagons to control each train's descent into the terminus. In the opposite direction trains were hauled to the top by a five inch thick hemp rope - later made somewhat more tensile by the adoption of wire. This unique method of expediting the arrival and departure from a major city terminus amazingly stayed in use for sixty-six years.

In August 1909 the first trains used Queen Street under locomotive power. But even then, and indeed until the end of steam in the early Sixties, much use was made of banking engines which suffocated the approach tunnel, and the high-roofed station itself, with an almost permanent blanket of all-enveloping and pungent smoke. Perhaps it felt like a slow descent into an active volcano. Nowadays there's just a rush for the door, a necessary ritual since the designers of modern rolling stock reckoned the provision of access points to each bay of seats on suburban routes an unnecessary luxury. And were they not in such a hurry, these commuters might be more receptive to James Carswell's magnificent segmentally arched trainshed, 78 feet high and 250 feet in span, revelling in the smokeless atmosphere of the modern age. In *A Postillion Struck by Lightning*, Dirk Bogarde called it 'an enormous inverted iron colander', and certainly it's the sort of place in which you might well feel all the juices running out of you.

Too much the gentleman, I was last off the train, but in no particular hurry, having half an hour to purchase my day ranger ticket before setting off on the next leg of the itinerary. Not in a rush, but not concentrating either, picking up a *Roundabout* Glasgow leaflet and too quickly purchasing the equivalent ticket, only to realise, on closer inspection, that it would restrict me to an inner city zone bounded by Paisley, Dumbarton and Motherwell, when what I actually needed was a *Daytripper* ticket which offers unlimited travel throughout the whole of the SPT empire, including the Underground, the majority of bus services and even some ferries. Tail between my legs, I had to rejoin the burgeoning queue and sheepishly explain my error to the good humoured booking clerk, who happily gave me a refund and the ticket I really required for the very reasonable price of £7.50; for which, additionally, I could have taken two children with me on my travels, always assuming I was temporarily unhinged enough to engage in such an undertaking. Had I entirely lost grip with reality, I could have enjoyed the jaunt with my wife (or, equally, someone else's) and up to four of the little blighters for just £13.00. Confirmation, were any required, of the boundless altruism and largesse of the Strathclyde Passenger Transport Authority.

To regain some measure of self-control, I left the station and strolled around George Square, passing the time of day with the statuesque soldier, poet and inventor occupants of the square. By five to nine I was back in the station and in the queue for a cappuccino before boarding the 09.06 for Falkirk. Momentarily I was visited by ghosts: my two year old self catching the Queen of Scots as we emigrated to England in 1954; and a twenty-two year old version of the same guy, sharing a coffee, and subsequently a fitful sort of sleep, on the night train to King's Cross with a raven haired West Highland beauty on her way to a fresher's Michaelmas Term at Cambridge.

Perhaps out of sheer devilment, they are inclined to keep you on the hop at Queen Street. Not until four minutes past nine did the departure boards reveal what platform the 09.06 would leave from, and even then it wasn't there. A small knot of prospective passengers, swimming against the morning's incoming tide, watched patiently as an approaching Sprinter's headlight burnished the trackwork, emerging from the saturnine depths of the tunnel portal like a miner rising from the cage at the end of his shift. Clutching my cappuccino, there was no problem in finding a seat towards the front of the carmine & cream coloured Class 156 unit, and we were away within seconds, ascending effortlessly through the tunnel and veering right onto the Cowlairs chord to Springburn.

For this next leg of the journey I had elected to go to Cumbernauld, on a route which lay through Springburn, a Glasgow suburb traditionally associated with the manufacture of locomotives for railways all over the world. Epicentre of this activity was the North British Locomotive Company, a 1903 amalgamation of the famous 19th century manufacturers Dubs, Neilson and Sharp Stewart. It is highly unlikely that you could visit any railway museum in the world (with the possible exception of North America) and not find examples of their prodigious output. In their heyday NBL were employing eight thousand workers and outputing five hundred locomotives a year. The K1 I had seen earlier in the morning was built here, as were many locomotives under contract to the Big Four - Royal Scots for the LMS; King Arthurs for the Southern, pannier tanks for the Great Western and even twenty Gresley Pacifics for the LNER. They were not quite so good at building diesel locomotives. Terrible in fact, and the huge company went into liquidation in 1962. The company's offices remain intact, however, not inappropriately in use as an engineering college. The Scottish based video company, Panamint, has released two enjoyable films about the works, *North British* and *The Other Man's Job* as part of a series of 'Treasures' from the Scottish Screen Archive. Watching the men at work on their lathes, you wonder where all their children and grandchildren have found gainful employment, saddened when you realise the answer is probably call centres and retail parks.

Wastegrounds colonised by sturdy saplings and littered with burnt out cars mock at all the lost activity. From Springburn the electrified City of Glasgow Union line circumnavigates the city's east end, running through Queen Street Low Level and out to Milngavie, which Glaswegians pronounce 'Millguy'. Our train climbed and curved over the CGU to meet what had once been the Caledonian Railway's main line to the north from its notoriously dingy Buchanan Street terminus. I went there in 1965, attracted like many others by Gresley's streamlined A4 Pacific's last fling on the Aberdeen 'Three Hour' expresses. My trainspotting alter ego 'needed' *Golden Plover* for the set, but it eluded me. Sensing disappointment, my ever supportive father drove me out into the badlands of St Rollox to see if it was 'on shed'. But, having unwisely left Ian Allan's invaluable *Shed Directory* at home, we came unstuck in the backstreets of Balornock and had to beat a retreat, fearful of becoming embroiled in the fierce ice cream war being waged at that time.

The train crossed the M80 and called at Stepps before passing the unmistakably horrifying towers of an asylum at Gartloch, retracing the route that the sleeper had carried me over, still comatose, some four hours previously. At Gartcosh we crossed the M73 and turned north-eastwards (past the site of a not so long ago sizeable steelworks) to Glenboig. For two or three succeeding miles the train ran almost bucolically through pastureland, albeit compromised by electricity pylons and pockets of scrubland typical of the latent, post-industrial melancholy of the Central Belt. I had two contrasting Ordnance Survey maps in my haversack: a 1957 one inch Sheet 61 and a pretty much up to date Landranger Sheet 64 issued forty years later. The more elderly map showed Cumbernauld station out in the wilds, a country mile south west of the eponymous village it cheekily claimed to represent. Present day Cumbernauld sprawls gratuitously between the two, nightmarishly utopian in its unkept promise of a better life. I hesitated before alighting. In the station forecourt lines of taxis and minibuses waited menacingly to whisk me off for interrogation and torture by the Collector of Taxes. How odd, I mused, that one of the British film industry's gentlest, most benignly humorous of modern comedies, Bill Forsyth's *Gregory's Girl,* could have been inspired by this nebulous prospect of arterial roads and underpasses. Back on the platform I came upon a throwback, a genuine Caledonian Railway quarter milepost, sadly rubbing shoulders with a plastic replacement, indicating that I was a hundred and one and a quarter miles from Carlisle, if not a million miles from reality.

The 09.59 to Motherwell saved me. It was provided by another 156, indisputably the most human and ergonomic of the Sprinter derivatives. Why, the seats even correspond to the windows and are high enough for you to see out of, as if some reactionary designer with a grudge had been inadvertently allowed to tinker with the blueprints and got clean away with it. One or two transparently anorak types were sharing the journey with me, strategically positioned on the right hand side of the carriage to get the best view possible of the railway installations at Coatbridge, Mossend and Motherwell. We do our best to disguise our obsession, but it is the intensity of our gaze that gives us away. Where other travellers stare blankly into the middle distance, we focus intently on the minutest railway detail, like men possessed, which of course in a way we are. Freightliner's Coatbridge container depot was disappointingly bereft of locomotives, though reassuringly busy with containers and their corresponding flats. In a misguided country where only 6% of freight travels by rail one needs all the reassurance one can get.

I can't help thinking of Coatbridge and Whifflet as Gary Lennon country, Gary being an entertainingly precocious and well informed, Celtic-mad adolescent whose copious train sightings enliven many a dull evening on the internet. I would have enjoyed his company as a local guide, but thought him better off at school; even though I knew his gaze would be drifting from the blackboard to identify each passing train.

"Lennon!" shouts the maths master. "Suppose you give us the benefit of your attention and tell us what you make if you add 66 to 92 ?"

"A 158 sir !"

EWS's yard at Mossend provided more motive power action than Coatbridge and we lost souls scribbled furiously in our notebooks. On the left the sidings were filled with containers and cars, on the right timber and coal. In the stabling sidings *D.H.Lawrence* was having a deep and meaningful literary discussion concerning syntax with *Kipling*. A green Freightliner Canadian built General Motors Class 66 diesel locomotive contrasted vividly with a red EWS example. The variety in types of locomotive contracts almost in proportion to the bewildering growth of colour schemes.

A cats cradle of interconnecting lines lies to the south of Mossend, and then there's a brief almost pastoral interlude, as what was once the Caledonian main line to the north is carried loftily, by Braidwood Viaduct, across the South Calder Water (which rises by Shotts where Bells make wonderful pies) on its way down to meet the Clyde. Obligingly a red signal held us tantalisingly by Motherwell's traction depot where we could see only too well what effect standardisation of the EWS fleet was having, for rows of discarded locomotives stood achingly exposed to the elements. Three of the already almost extinct Class 33 locomotives; a 56 and a 47, and several bonnet-nosed 37s lay disused, their life support systems shut terminally down, in sidings behind the ancient sandstone engine shed. Their disreputable appearance contrasted tellingly with more modern examples of Classes 60, 66 and 67 and electric Class 325 Royal Mail units undergoing routine maintenance.

I had half an hour to kill in Motherwell. It refused to die without a fight. The station architecture appeared to take its cue from KwikSave. I ventured briefly into town and found it patrolled by a bewildering array of buses. Call me old fashioned, but I was immune to the 'tropical delight' of the Aquatec leisure centre. Back at the station a poster was advertising a book called *Life Strategies* by Dr Philip C. McGraw. 'Over one million copies sold - as seen on *Oprah*. Do what works, do what matters!' I didn't think there was anything he could teach me about life, but about selling books ...

'Airbles - alight here for Motherwell Football Ground'. Fir Park to the cognoscenti. I took my father and my son there for a cup game against Ayr United a year or two back and we were treated to a seven goal thriller; three penalties and a sending off. The meat pies weren't half bad either. But how sad that a pygmy team like Motherwell can only eke out a twilight existence in the giant shadows cast by the Old Firm, never having the financial clout to compete and always having to sell their best players just to keep the bank off their backs. Such were my thoughts as the first former Blue Train of my journey carried me across Camps Viaduct high above the Clyde. At Haughhead Junction, where the line spanned the M74, another railway used to head off southwards into a delta of lines serving the Lanarkshire coalfield. What an education it would have been to rattle down to Brocketsbrae (where my Grandpa once lived), or to Strathaven, or to Lesmahagow (where in my memory bank I have a much valued image of a Fairburn tank crossing the viaduct with a couple of non corridor suburban carriages) and on across the bare 'broon' moorlands to Coalburn. There are proposals that the line should be relaid as far as Larkhall as an add-on to the Strathclyde suburban network. But each time the paperwork reaches the top of the tray, someone raises bushy eyebrows at the cost and it goes back to the bottom again.

For a forty-something, the 303 rode surprisingly well on its pre-war bogies, negotiating the single track section through Barncluith Tunnel and bursting out into daylight above the deep wooded gorge of Avon Water. In the stillness of our stop at Hamilton Central I listened to two women opposite, or rather one woman talking incessantly while her companion read the newspaper with male-like concentration punctuated by a succession of sighs. Through Hamilton West and Blantyre ('for the David Livingstone Memorial') we ran, keeping close, but largely invisible, company with the meandering Clyde, coming upon another watercourse, libellously known as the Rotten Calder, before reaching Newton, a pair of rain swept platforms at the intersection of the Hamilton, Kirkhill and West Coast lines. Once there had been a steelworks and a colliery here, but only the latter's bing remained. I regarded it with due solemnity, hunched up to keep dry (for there is a marked absence of canopies at this lonely interchange) whilst waiting for another 303 to exit the turnback siding and carry me deeper into Glasgow by way of the Cathcart Circle.

It was 303019, looking second best only to its original kingfisher blue in SPT's carmine & cream. The Kirkhill line was a comparative latecomer, opening early in the twentieth century, primarily for coal trains to run from Lanarkshire to the Clyde, but between the wars finding fresh impetus as Glasgow's suburbs burgeoned southwards. Generally the housing seemed much better appointed than that of the east end; neat villas rising up to the Cathkin Braes. Island platforms in various guises came and went. Beyond King's Park a triangular junction sent us on to the Cathcart Circle proper. The Saltire fluttered damply from the tower of an old stone kirk overlooking Cathcart station itself, perched on girders above the White Cart Water. But we by-passed its platform, negotiating the West Junction and travelling clockwise along the Outer Circle to Langside.

I had read in advance of the architectural merits of the Cathcart Circle's stations, though unsure just as to which had survived alteration or demolition. My plan was to travel round the circle until I found a well preserved example to alight at. Langside, Pollokshaws East and Shawlands served me up with disappointing bus shelters, but Maxwell Park was original and intact, so I jumped off the train to take some photographs for Eric to use as reference material for his illustrations. This inner suburban 'horseshoe' route, a five and a half mile loop out of Central Station, was completed in the 1890s under the nominally independent control of the Cathcart District Railway. At its zenith it operated an astonishing forty-five trains daily on each of its inner (anti-clockwise) and outer (clockwise) circuits, and is said to have proved an effective marriage-broker for generations of commuters, its fourpenny tickets being an economic alternative to the florin cost of a cinema seat, whilst the privacy of its compartment stock was of even greater supine potential.

Even in the rain Maxwell Park was gorgeous. Sometimes one shudders at the thought of 'regeneration', but here Railtrack Scotland have waved a sympathetic wand over the wooden structure, and my only regret was the unrequited 'To Let' notice on the old booking hall. Surely Railtrack should relinquish the rental on such properties and be happy just to have them occupied as insurance against decay and vandalism. A nice little tea room would be just the job at the edge of the adjoining park, filled with the mellifluous gossip of the discreetly charming bourgeois who occupy all the neighbouring sandstone tenements.

It was a pleasant enclave on which to wait three quarters of an hour for an anti-clockwise inner circle connection into Glasgow Central. Blackbirds sang from the sycamores beside the park. A demure crescent of flats looked serenely over the station, making me think of all the trains their occupants had seen and heard down the years. Picturing Edwardian worthies and their wives taking the train to the fleshpots of Sauchiehall Street and the West End. As if to crystallize these thoughts, an elderly lady came down the steps and asked me from which side trains ran to Glasgow. I sensed that I would only confuse her if I told the truth, so I kept it simple and suggested she board the imminent 11.59 outer circle service.

My inner circle train left at 12.12, another 303. It was not exactly a chore to retrace my steps to Cathcart. At Shawlands (where the station-master's house stood directly beneath the tracks) I got a glimpse of the Barrhead and East Kilbride line heading southwestwards out of the city. Between Pollokshaws East and Langside I saw more clearly how closely the White

Cart Water parallels the railway, wending its way through man made channels between high tenements. Curving into Cathcart I was on fresh ground, an increasingly fascinating nineteenth century urban landscape, largely unspoilt by the twentieth century's usual clod-hopping progress. Framed by high stone retaining walls, Crosshill station (where once you could get off to go and watch Third Lanark) remains in its original state, similarly Queen's Park (where you can *still* get off and go and watch Scotland's first football club), but Pollokshields East had been given the bus shelter treatment; though the adjacent theatre, housed in a former tram depot, provides consolation.

There is something symbolic about crossing the Clyde into Glasgow Central, recently revealed by Railtrack Scotland's regeneration programme for what it is - one of the great railway stations in the world. Though is it just me who believes it somehow diminished by the disappearance of its old sparring partner St Enoch? Recently, I met a perfectly charming old gentleman who told me, quite casually in passing and with a certain amount of professional pride, that he had overseen the closure of Buchanan Street *and* St Enoch. I responded by enquiring how he ever slept at night. Of course, financially and operationally, no adequate case could have been made - even by romantics such as me - for their survival, but *emotionally?* Moreover, St Enoch was so architecturally outstanding that it should have been retained for another use, in much the same way that Manchester Central became G-Mex. As for Central, I can't pretend to do its engineering and its architecture justice here; both are simply riveting (as well as riveted), all glass and girders supported by big stone walls the colour of that fudge the Scots call tablet. Take an extended stroll along Platform 11 and you can stand above the Clyde itself and look back towards the station's all embracing magnificence. And Central is pure theatre as well: sudden bursts of people off incoming trains, some of whom look as though they know where they're going, some who look as though they don't and never will. And in the opposite direction knots of potential travellers wait on the concourse; long distance people with swagger or anxiety in their mien, commuters who just look dazed. What I love most - in common with all truly great termini - is the way the public gather on its concourse, gazing upwards in rapt attention at the arrival and departure boards, as if waiting for Moses to come down from the mountain, as though waiting for a shooting star to wish upon, as if trying to second guess what platform their train would leave from despite Railtrack's panic-inducing habit of leaving it to the last minute.

I caught the train to Paisley Canal from Platform 12, a ScotRail liveried Sprinter 156493. Thirty-six years earlier I had boarded a train hauled by a Standard Class 4 2-6-0 (operating tender first) from the adjacent Platform 13 (the main station's westernmost) to Paisley Gilmour Street. I would be heading there soon enough, but first I wanted to make something of a pilgrimage to Paisley Canal, the station where - according to family folklore - I had first become infected with the irrational railway virus. My Aunt Isa was apparently to blame, being in the habit of wheeling my pram from Espedair Street, down Causeyside to Canal where I would gurgle with delight at the passing trains. You will all have similar stories to tell, similar case histories for filing under I for insanity or O for obsession. By all accounts it was the 'crashers' which thrilled me most, the buffering crescendo of a slowly starting goods train.

Back across the Clyde we went, with a glimpse of the Broomielaw, and out across labyrinthine pointwork to Shields Junction and the old Glasgow & South Western line, formerly umbilically linked to St Enoch. Shields Electric Traction Depot revealed brand new Class 334 'Junipers' poignantly sharing siding space with soon to be redundant 303s; rolling stock continues perhaps not so much to evolve in the strictest scientific sense, but to find new variations to an old theme. Beyond Dumbreck our route lay past the legendary Glasgow motive power depot of Corkerhill, a provider of maintenance for multiple units now, but once a Glasgow & South Western Railway stronghold, a community within a community distinguished by a model village of high quality employee housing.

West of Corkerhill the Canal line is effectively a single track siding. During the seven mile journey from Glasgow the route weaves uncharacteristically for a railway. The truth lies in the title of its present terminus, for this was indeed once a canal, the Glasgow, Paisley & Johnstone, opened in 1811 in an ultimately futile attempt to by-pass the shallow Clyde. It had been intended that the canal should reach Ardrossan but the company ran out of capital and the Government were deaf to pleas for subsidy; an all too familiar scenario to this day. Before the railways came in the middle of the 19th century the canal was an economic success and even operated a passenger service of packet boats which could get you from Paisley to Glasgow in one hour and eleven minutes. Impressive stuff, but not good enough to beat the railways, let alone the trams, and in 1881 the canal was abandoned and the railway built on its bed. Ironically the railway itself closed in 1983 amidst considerable controversy, only to re-open seven years later at much expense.

The journey proved a case study in urban and social disparity. On the Cathcart Circle side of Pollok Park the houses exuded wealth. A mile across town in Mosspark and Crookston poverty is endemic. On a previous journey along the line in a Metropolitan Cammell Class 101 diesel multiple unit - a 1950s design now extinct in Scotland - I remember being pelted with stones by a gang of boys standing on the roofs of a row of lockup garages near Hawkhead. On this occasion they were mercifully absent, probably at school, but then again probably not; disenfranchisement begins early in such squalid surroundings.

The gloomy ruins of a roofless and derelict hospital stood beyond the White Cart Water. Behind some lineside flats, and their strange coruscation of telephone wires, an imposing textile mill came into view. Paisley, of course, being known world wide for its threads and its shawls; though perhaps not quite so much for its custard and marmalade. Through deceptively bosky glades the single line track winds to its abrupt single platform terminus, a premature halt on the opposite side of Causeyside Street to the original station of my babyhood. Beyond here the Glasgow & South Western continued through Elderslie and Kilmacolm to Greenock Princes Pier, a stirring journey over high ground deemed too replicative of the Caledonian's Gilmour Street to Gourock line to survive.

Briefly I paid my respects to 31 Espedair Street before hurrying down Causeyside where a man was helping the 'polis' with their enquiries. Paisley's reputation as the crime capital of Scotland must embarrass my father. He is justly proud of the Paisley of his boyhood and the Paisley he came back to after the Second World War with a Tyneside girl for a wife, setting up home first in Cochran Street and then on Espedair with a mongrel collie called Eager who had a predilection for travelling about on the trams on his own. By the time I came along my father was making his mark in the print trade, and so it is not perhaps entirely coincidental that I should have come to rely on that industry for the propagation of my thoughts.

It took me twenty minutes to walk down to Gilmour Street station. You could do it in half the time but I joined a lengthy lunchtime queue in a baker's shop for a warm Scotch pie. Gilmour Street is an extraordinarily handsome station whose frontage somehow reminds me of Shrewsbury; all those Tudor overtones I suppose. It is the junction of the Caledonian line to Gourock and Glasgow & South Western route to the Ayrshire coast. Eastwards to Glasgow the two companies shared running rights over the Glasgow & Paisley Joint. I am old enough to remember the intensive steam worked services through Gilmour Street, predominantly operated in my time by Standard Class 4 2-6-4 tank locomotives hauling lengthy trains of maroon suburban stock. Perhaps now the services are even more frequent, though am I only being subjective if I say that they lack the soul of their predecessors?

The slow train to Gourock was a 314, a somewhat utilitarian design of electric multiple unit of late 1970s vintage built by British Rail at York. What I'd really hoped for was the chance to sample one of the new 'Juniper' sets, so I decided to alight at Port Glasgow and see if one was on the following service, a 'fast'. Out of Paisley the line headed in a north-westerly direction past Glasgow Airport and parallel to the M8 before coming within sight of the Clyde opposite Dumbarton. In the six hours or so that had elapsed since I last saw it the tide had ebbed, exposing large expanses of bruise coloured mud.

Port Glasgow may sound grandiose, but it's a well past its sell-by date dockyard town barely capable of sustaining close scrutiny. Even the gulls, wheeling and screeching over the wet platforms and neighbouring rooftops, seemed to be lamenting this once proud shipbuilding community's obvious decline. Like tidal rivers, commerce can ebb and flow, but it is difficult to see the Clyde ever re-establishing itself as an artery of trade and engineering.

I was in luck! The fast train was indeed an all singing, all dancing Class 334 - No.019. Comfortable and well-appointed, after the rather antiseptic twenty-first century manner, the 'Juniper' accelerated smoothly away to the accompaniment of pre-recorded announcements by a pleasantly accented Scots lass regarding approaching stations. A tad unnecessary, I thought, on routes where the bulk of passengers would know their stops like Catholics know the stations of the cross. But, as the saying goes, if you have the technology, flaunt it. Both of Greenock's remaining stations, Central and West, looked as though the guts had been ripped out of them, only some residual high, pink coloured walls remaining as a distant echo of former grandeur. At least they are still served by trains, unlike the Glasgow & South Western station at Princes Pier, the terminus of many a priority given boat train in the days of intense competition with 'The Caley'.

Scotland's longest railway tunnel separates Greenock West from Fort Matilda. Then the train skirts Gourock Bay on the last lap down to the end of the line, where the curving platforms and canopies of Gourock station reach out in an all embracing hug of welcome for arriving trains. One glance at the firth was enough to make me wonder at the wisdom of my itinerary, for here I planned to temporarily leave the train behind and travel across to Helensburgh on a ferry. Waves were whipping playfully in like boisterous porpoises. *Saturn*, the Caledonian MacBrayne ferry from Dunoon, rolled at the gale-swept quay with the 'stocious' gait of a Jamaica Street drunk. Ludicrously toylike in comparison, the Kilcreggan and Helensburgh ferry approached the pier as if it were a new boy sent with a message to the prefect's study. I anticipated forty minutes of purgatory, but in truth the plucky little ship rode the swell like an accomplished surfer while, along with four other passengers, I sat in the upper cabin quite impervious to *mal de mer.* Its name was *Kenilworth*, formerly *Hotspur II,* and it had been built by Rowhedge Ironworks in Colchester, of all places, three years before the outbreak of the Second World War.

Presently we bumped politely into the barnacle-encrusted jetty at Kilcreggan, then set off again, with just me, and a young blood going to visit his girlfriend in Helensburgh, left of the fee-paying complement. We skirted Roseneath Point. Naturally the firth was almost bereft of shipping, save for a yacht under engine power and some sort of Naval supply vessel anchored midstream. I took a turn around the deck, doing my best to evade the spray. Helensburgh hove into view on the port side, and I assumed what I fondly imagined might be the attitude of Ulysses returning to Troy. On the hillside behind the town a West Highland train slowed down to pay its respects to Helensburgh Upper. The Gare Loch stretched away to a horizon of cloud covered summits. Astern, the Renfrewshire shore had all but disappeared within the inscrutable face of a heavy squall. Partly to regain my land legs, partly because it's difficult to resist, a detour along the promenade to McLaren's second-hand bookshop recommended itself. It cost me five pounds, the asking price of P.B.Whitehouse's *Railway Anthology,* published by Ian Allan in 1965, the sort of amiably discursive railway book nobody seems to bother publishing anymore - well not until now anyway. McLaren's is also excellent if you are into maritime literature, and the fact that HM Naval Base Clyde is just up the road is obviously not coincidental.

Helensburgh Central is a pleasant little terminus with a short but beautiful curved trainshed over its buffer stops. I wish I could have known it when Gresley V1 2-6-2 tanks were the mainstay, or even the original Blue Trains. The BREL built, Class 320 electric unit, which whisked me on the next leg of my journey to Partick, proved an uncharismatic replacement, though I admired the bulkhead illustrations of Clydeside landmarks. The generic fault with all BREL designs of the 1980s lay in the fact that the juxtaposition of windows with seats appeared to have become a lost art. Just as well, then, that beyond Craigendoran I was lapping myself as far as Dalmuir. Indeed, the duration of my travelling day was emphasised by the appearance on the train of homecoming schoolchildren. Whilst the seabirds I had seen breakfasting at the tideline were now saying to each other:

"You'll have had your tea."

By Dumbarton I was beginning to feel I was in a remake of *Groundhog Day*, only there was no compensating sign of Andi MacDowell. At Dalmuir the spell was broken, for the train took the Yoker line, ducking down to pass beneath the Singer route my morning train had taken, and tunnelling under the Forth & Clyde Canal. Being an Airdrie bound semi-fast it sped haughtily through Clydebank, Yoker, Garscadden (which crept into the title of the A.L.Kennedy short story *Night Geometry and the Garscadden Trains*), Scotstounhill and Jordanhill; bequeathing me a blur of dockyard cranes, an electric train servicing depot and an athletics stadium. We did however stop at Hyndland which once had its own impressive terminus at the end of a spur that curved away towards the Great Western Road; why, you could even catch a through carriage to London King's Cross from here!

It was to pay homage to just this kind of Glasgow's railway past that I alighted at Partick and scurried along Dumbarton Road for a whistlestop tour of the Museum of Transport at Kelvin Hall. Preserved in aspic they may be - and you could argue they'd be better served by trundling along one or other of Scotland's private railways in steam - there is nevertheless a latent dignity to the Highland Railway's 'Jones Goods', the Great North of Scotland Railway's *Gordon Highlander* (nicknamed 'The Sodjer'), and the famous racing Caledonian No.123 that it is impossible not to find poignant. Lesser exhibits have equal appeal: from King George VI's wartime saloon carriage to the Aberdeen breakfast barrow used by royalty on their way to Ballater. I paid particular attention to a model of the Glasgow & South Western Railway's St Enoch station, the only one of the four main Glasgow termini that I never had the chance to visit. It was closed to passengers in 1966 and demolished a few years later. With more time at my disposal I might have taken equal notice of the museum's other exhibits: trams, motor cars, a room full of model ships representing some of Clydeside's maritime magnificence, and a reconstruction of a typical Glasgow Street as it might have appeared in 1938. But it was time to get back to Partick for the final train of this narrative.

We live in an era of 'clockface' timetabling and standardised starting points and destinations, so I am always much taken with one-offs; trains which run just once a day, throwbacks, perhaps, to some traditional service whose origins are buried deep in the ancestral subconscious of the timetable planners. That is why I was standing on Partick station, an impostor amongst homegoing commuters, anxious lest some hungover employee had failed to materialise for the 17.20 to Carstairs and caused its cancellation. By my reckoning this quirk of timetabling science has its roots in The Tinto, the Caledonian Railway's businessmen's express for the well-heeled autocrats of Lanarkshire's 'Upper Ward'. The train drew its inspiring name from Tinto Hill, a glowering 2,320ft summit above the Clyde seven miles due south of Carstairs. Originally it ran as far as Moffat, leaving Glasgow at 5pm and arriving in that pleasant Dumfriesshire spa town (after reversing at Beattock) at 6.54pm, just in time for a malt before dinner. At one time The Tinto even boasted a Pullman buffet car, but this disappeared, along with other frivolities, on the outbreak of the First World War.

No Pullman now. Just an egalitarian 303 whilst, judging by their attire, my fellow travellers no longer represented the cream of Glasgow's business community. I coped with that disappointment, acquiring solace, as so often, from the view beyond the carriage window. It was dominated by the new Glasgow Tower, the 'Armadillo' auditorium, and the giant bulk of the

Finnieston Crane, a potent reminder of Glasgow's lost river trade and the thousands of locomotives which this massive, Meccano like machine had lifted on to ships for export around the world. Then the train was swallowed up by a series of tunnels leading to Glasgow Central Low Level. This subterranean traverse of the city centre was completed in 1895 at enormous cost. The link might have been achieved less expensively had a scheme for an overhead railway like Liverpool's not been rejected on aesthetic grounds. When the trains did start running the atmosphere in the underground stations must have closely resembled Sunday School illustrations of hell. Doubtless many Glaswegians felt at home, and looked upon the experience as good training for the after life. Many of them carried brown paper bags to put over their hands to protect them from the soot on the window straps, John Yellowlees had told me. The line closed in 1964 and lay in sepulchral limbo for fifteen years before being reinvented as the electrified Argyle Line.

Daylight returned completely at Dalmarnock. The Clyde was crossed at Rutherglen, where we joined the West Coast Main Line. The old, but still skittish, electric unit picked up its skirts (or rather its Gresley bogies) and began to impart a sense of hurry to its time-honoured itinerary. After Cambuslang we crossed the Clyde again into Uddingston (celebrated for cement and caramel wafers), called at Bellshill (birthplace of Sheena Easton), and returned (full circle as far as I was concerned) to the signal that had stopped me that morning outside Motherwell's engine shed. But it wasn't a signal stop at all, we'd pulled up obligingly for an EWS driver to jump down from the driver's cab and nip across the tracks at the start of his shift.

No names, no pack drill. We had our own crew change at Motherwell, beyond which the emptying train (and I wish I could tell you, like Betjeman's Cornish train at Egloskerry, that there was 'wind in the ventilators') ran in suitably sombre frame of mind past the scorched earth zone of Ravenscraig ('Save Gartcosh, Save Ravenscraig, Save Scottish Steel' implored a painted slogan on a crumbling wall) to Shieldmuir, where the impressive Royal Mail rail terminal spoke more optimistically of a railway future. It's difficult now to pass through Wishaw without thinking about the e-coli outbreak, but I have a fonder memory of a disconcertingly lovely and dark haired schoolgirl who always seemed to alight here whenever I could contrive to be aboard a Lanark bound train at tea time.

At Law Junction 303089 rejoined the main line, emerging into a potentially pretty landscape of farms and conifer plantations. A sunnier evening would have gilded the bountiful hawthorn. But this day, which had started so drearily, was determined to stay 'dreich' to the end. By Carluke, the penultimate stop, our diminishing complement of passengers was beginning to resemble the sort of detective story in which everyone keeps disappearing in mysterious circumstances. It was a shame to have to snub Lanark at the end of its two mile single track branch. With more time at my disposal I might have taken up ScotRail's special offer to go by train to Robert Owen's preserved cotton mills in the Clyde gorge at New Lanark. We ran past the Ravenstruther (pronounced 'Rastrie') coal terminal and into Carstairs. I was one of just five passengers left to alight, and it felt as if we were the sole survivors of some cataclysmic disaster upon whom the future of mankind depended. Luckily that was just my imagination working overtime, for we were all male.

Three other generations of the Pearson clan have shared the Carstairs experience with me. In 1965 I descended the steps to the island platform with my father and my grandfather as *William Whitelaw* shuffled in with the southbound Postal. It was a busy place then, filled with railway staff who vastly outnumbered prospective passengers. Not that there can ever have been many of them (save perhaps for those bound for incarceration in the neighbouring high security psychiatric establishment) in this comparatively remote location on the north bank of a bend in the Clyde: a river so uncertain of its direction in life that it literally boxes the compass hereabouts in its search for the sea. An archetypal country junction, then, a place of railway operating expediency, where the Edinburgh and Glasgow portions of expresses were divided or joined amidst a soft cacophony of shunting sounds. Only the Caledonian Sleeper goes through this ritual now, few of the Virgin and none of the GNER expresses deigning even to call here anymore. In 1995 another trio of Pearsons stood on Carstairs' platform watching them swish haughtily by. My then four year old son regarded these with glee and his excitement was infectious, but how I wished he could have heard No.4 steam away southwards under the saffron-anointed shoulders of Tinto, its American chime whistle enhanced by the Clyde's auricular proximity into a haunting coda to the end of steam.

Useful Contacts

Strathclyde Passenger Transport Tel: 0141 332 7133

Gourock-Kilcreggan-Helensburgh Ferry - Tel: 01475 721281

McLaren's Bookshop - Tel: 01436 676453

Greater Glasgow & Clyde Valley Tourist Board -
Tel: 0141 204 4400

Museum of Transport - Tel: 0141 287 2720

"ABERDOUR STATION

LESLIE.

*Perth's sprawling station. The little known line to Ladybank.
Falling for Kirkcaldy. The beautiful Fife Coast. Aberdour:
the castle, the beach and the station gardens. North
Queensferry and the Forth Bridge. A spontaneous visit to
Dunfermline. Exploring Cardenden with Inspector Rebus.
Kirkcaldy again. The Tay Bridge and Dundee.*

Perth railway station is so rambling and sprawling and
Gothically dysfunctional that I understand the SAS requisition
it from time to time for survival seminars. People have been
known to go insane just finding their way from Platform 2 to
Platform 7. It's the sort of place you half expect to bump into
one of the lost tribes of Africa: and the goats tied sacrificially to
Sir William Tite's elegant cast iron columns lend credence to
this impression. Come to think of it, one or two of the railway

staff look as if they might have been missionaries in previous existences. I asked one of them why the 08.49 to Edinburgh was late and he told me it was God's will; though perhaps that was just a euphemism for Railtrack.

Divine intervention notwithstanding, it was a relief to sink into the comfortable Business Class cushions of 170410 when it eventually found its way in from that outpost of civilisation otherwise known as Inverness. I had already come to terms with missing my first connection at Kirkcaldy, these days ScotRail's services are so intensive in Fife that one acquires a Central European sense of fatalism, and feels the better for it. Acres of weedgrown sidings testify to Perth's lost importance as a railway centre. Modern diesels negate its former frontier status. Long gone the days when the Caledonian gave way to the Highland here. But Moncrieff Tunnel swallows up such melancholy thoughts, and adrenalin pumped at the commencement of a 'figure of eight' itinerary designed to take in all the remaining railways of the Ancient Kingdom of Fife.

Emerging from the 1,210 yards long tunnel, my train veered sharply left at Hilton Junction onto the old North British line to Ladybank. The width of the ballast base suggested that the track had once been double. Few Scottish lines have received less publicity than this, yet it has an interesting story to tell of near abandonment then revitalisation. It opened as early as 1845, but lost out to a more direct route between Edinburgh and Perth via Kinross. Its passenger services were withdrawn in 1955, but reintroduced twenty years later. Rarely discussed in the railway press, I was little prepared for its scenic attractions which, right from the outset, manifested themselves as the line crossed the River Earn, arcing away through fields of cabbage and corn on jointed track. The M90 crosses the line at Bridge of Earn, having cuckolded the course of the direct railway between Perth and Edinburgh via Kinross and Cowdenbeath. I was soaking up the scenery and enjoying a complimentary cup of coffee.

"Are you first class sir?" the catering trolley attendant had enquired. And I had to bite my lip not to reply:

"How perceptive of you."

The Turbostar slowed to negotiate a temporary speed limit. Old track panels were strewn beside the line, and by the sudden silence it was evident that new welded track was being put in. I had time to savour the view of a harvested field with jackdaws and black headed gulls feeding off the stooks before the train gathered speed again. At Newburgh, an ancient royal town, I thought I saw a ruined timber station building, but my gaze was more focused on the elevated view the railway offered of the widening Tay. Obviously I was travelling over one of Scotland's most unsung and undersold scenic railways.

Bearing inland, so to speak, the train ran through cuttings clothed in wild flowers, past a ruined keep and a small village, which my map informed me, goes by the charming name of Den of Lindores. As we ran into a cutting I saw earthworks which marked the egress of a line which ran to St Fort. Throughout the journey I was to be reminded of the former density of Fife's railway system. Lindores Loch lay beautifully still. Half a dozen anglers, fly-fishing from rowing boats, lent it the air of an Impressionist painting. Then the line shimmied and climbed to make its way through a narrow pass between rounded hills. The church at Collessie has an English look about it. James V of Scotland was apparently in the habit of wandering around these parts disguised as a beggar so that he could talk with commoners on an equal footing. I masquerade as a travel writer for similar motives. A neighbourhood of gravel workings ensued as the landscape bottomed out, and there were views over the Howe of Fife towards the twin peaks of the Lomond Hills; the East being clear of cloud, the West smudged by it.

The car park at Ladybank Golf Club was already busy with the vehicles of golfers wanting to get out on the fairways early. The train didn't stop at Ladybank, but it joined the main line from Edinburgh to Dundee; or from London to Aberdeen if you want to be all-encompassing about it. We crossed the River Eden and began a stiff, curving climb at 1 in 90 to the summit at Lochmuir. This was the line, I remembered, that Sir Nigel Gresley had designed half a dozen monster Mikado 2-8-2 locomotives for. Machines bestowed with stirring Scots names like

Cock o' the North, Thane of Fife and *Mons Meg* which his jealous successor, Edward Thompson, pettily converted into Pacifics, and unsuccessful ones at that, during the Second World War.

A high embankment took us past the potato fields of Freuchie, and then a procession of rocky cuttings led to the summit. I sensed that even the high-tech Turbostar felt the climb, and it showed its relief by proceeding to hurtle downhill, past a curiously isolated lineside cemetery, into Markinch. I was now on the home patch of two of my heroes: the late railway photographer W.J.V. Anderson; and the singer/songwriter Jackie Leven. Bill Anderson was a paper maker and Jackie Leven has sung of those very mills. Anderson's heyday was the late Fifties, when he recorded in a sequence of beautifully crafted black & white photographs, the last days of steam on Scotland's railways. Apparently he used a cumbersome plate camera for most of his work, and took with him a changing bag and portable developing tank so that he could develop each plate by the lineside, so as to ascertain the quality of each shot, long before the days of digital cameras. I mean no denigration when I write that his work was not of the most creative kind. He owed more to Eric Treacy than Colin Gifford, and the trains are almost always neatly caught by the lens in a 'three-quarter' view. But the clarity is unparalleled, and I guess I just envy him his period and his locality. What I admire most in Jackie Leven - apart from the number of bars he seems familiar with - is an altogether different clarity of vision, his ability to write and sing about male angst without descending into bathos. But what I respect even more is his capacity for turning out album after album to critical acclaim and public indifference in equal proportions.

A high viaduct - echoed and duplicated by an abandoned neighbour across which the daily goods used to rumble down to the paper mills at Leslie - carried us over Jackie Leven's fluvial namesake and into the heart of Fife's former coal mining region. Now, though, instead of mineral sidings set against horizons of colliery headstocks there were fields of lavender beside the line, and the rusty track of a disused branch leading to the coast at Leven. This was once part of the lovely East Fife line, an enchanting railway perambulation of the coast serving St Andrews and a series of poetically named stations such as Largo, Kilconquhar, Elie, St Monance, Pittenweem, Anstruther and Crail. Lucky the collector who has any of these resonant, pale blue 'totem' nameplates on their living room wall. I can think of few lost lines I would liked to have travelled on more, preferably aboard the Fife Coast Express, which used carriages displaced from the crack pre-war streamliner, Silver Jubilee. It left Queen Street just after four and got you into St Andrews before seven, just in time for dinner. I have mentally traced the journey on many occasions, though undecided in my preference for a 'Director' or a 'Shire' up front. We live in an era where rapprochement is deemed preferable to the bearing of grudges and the pursuit of vengeance, but this is one closure I can never forgive Beeching and his compliant politicians for.

The Turbostar swayed through the junction at Thornton, and was I imagining the smell of methane? We came upon a bing and then the surprise of a deepish hole where yellow earthmovers seemed to be working by opencast methods for coal. By Dysart I was enjoying my first view of the sea, millpond calm and sprinkled with ships at anchor. On the horizon Bass Rock and Berwick Law stood clearly outlined, inland, five industrial tank engines stood rusting in Muir's scrapyard, waggishly known as the Scottish Barry, but I was distracted by the outskirts of Kirkcaldy and the need to gather my belongings and leave the train.

Kirkcaldy's modern station was hooching with prospective passengers. The sun was out and there seemed a festive mood to the proceedings, which made me wonder if it was a holiday week. I had missed my assignation with one of the Fife Circle's clockwise, coastal stopping trains, so I went into the station building to check the time of the next one. Simple, but effective in its modern styling, a plaque informed me that it dates from 1991, whilst the provision of linoleum floor covering reminded me of the 'Lang Toun's' stock in trade. A charming plaque on the wall quotes in full *The Boy in the Train*, a poem by Mary Campbell Smith which finishes with the immortal lines:

'I ken mysel' by the queer-like smell

That the next stop's Kirkcaddy'.

I wandered out into the road and found myself beside an imposing art gallery and museum. I hadn't originally intended to spend any time in Kirkcaldy, but I felt swayed, and began to think about re-jigging my itinerary to allow me time to visit the museum in the afternoon.

The platform was still packed when I got back. It became apparent that the next train was for London. Over the tannoy came the announcement:

"May we remind members of the public *not* travelling, *not* to board this train for their own *safety*."

I have never been much enamoured with London myself, but I have never perceived it as *such* a threat to life and limb.

Undeterred, most of the public were swallowed up by the GNER express; cool, calm and collected in its dark blue with a red stripe livery. A brusque whistle from one of the station staff, a wave from the guard, and power cars 43109 and 115 whined into life, puffed burnt diesel from their roofs, and purred purposefully away to the south, leaving the less ambitious travellers like me to await the stopping train. The sun was warm on our backs and gulls wheeled overhead. I leant against a lamp-post between flower-filled tubs eavesdropping on unintelligible Fife accents. An EWS 66 came through on a coal train, whipping up the hems of summer dresses. My abiding image of Kirkcaldy is an array of knobbly knees.

John Yellowlees had insisted that I visit the floral station gardens at Aberdour. But first I had a quarter of an hour run along the coast to savour. Most of the Fife Circle services are provided by Class 150 Sprinters, the most basic version of the genre; my train was an exception, a much more comfortable 158. The train ran within shooting distance of Raith Rovers football ground. Out at sea I counted five ships at anchor. In Guthrie Hutton's *Fife - The Mining Kingdom* (Stenlake Publishing 1999) a double page spread illustrates Seafield, a massively modern coal mine at which production began in 1960. It was envisaged that it would deliver 5,000 tonnes a day for sixty years and then, after the sinking of new shafts, be good for another one hundred and fifty. It closed in 1988 - after the miner's strike of 1984, the heart went out of British coal mining. New housing covers the site of Seafield pit; though, with the irony of history, a medieval tower survives nearby.

The tide was turning on a rocky foreshore. Two or three miles offshore, Inchkeith island basked like a sea monster in the sunshine. Caravans heralded Kinghorn, and I looked down on pantiled rooftops, small boats in the harbour and a curious looking church with an exposed bell tower, which looked as though it might have been stolen by enterprising Scots pirates from some little town on the Low Countries coast in the Middle Ages. The station building is constructed of timber and stone. I looked it up when I got home and discovered that it dates from 1847, and that the street frontage, obscured from me, is in Tudor style. Nowadays, under the care of Linda Mullen, it enjoys a burnished reputation for the loveliness of its loos. I could find no reference to the fish & chip cabin adjoining the up platform, dated 1936 and melancholically boarded up, its last fish supper served a long time ago.

A 260 yard long tunnel ushered the train under a headland that Alexander III, Scotland's last Celtic king, accidentally fell from on a windy March night in 1285. Then, across the broad sandy sweep of Pettycur Bay, I was rewarded with panoramic views southwards to the skyline of Scotland's capital city and a backdrop of the Pentland Hills. Burntisland is traditionally associated with fairs - there's an Edwardian Fair Museum in the town - and a modern day successor was taking place as I passed. But this was no time to have my fortune told, the next stop was my goal, and we pulled out over a curving cast iron viaduct, past a dock busy with tugs, barges and cranes. Two seals were bobbing in the water close inshore at Silversands Bay, bringing home to me how beautiful this line is, beating the North Wales Coast run and the South Devon main line in my opinion.

I wasn't prepared for Aberdour. I don't mean that I wasn't by the door - I'm the sort of traveller that never prepares to get off less than five minutes before we're due to arrive - but that, in stepping from the train, I felt as if I stepped back forty years or more, to a time when almost every village station boasted a well cared for garden. This sort of thing survives on preserved lines, but on the profit-pinned, multi-owned, technology-led railway of the 21st century there's little room for decoration. I resolved to interview the man responsible, but first I wanted to see the neighbourhood, and if his conversation was as good as his horticulture, I'd be in for a long delay.

Aberdour Castle overlooks the railway and you can reach it in two minutes from the station. The man in the shop sold me my ticket and told me I'd have the company of fifteen female artists: "Though I wouldn't like to say what their average age is," he added wryly, just in case I was beginning to get excited. This is no place to go all guide-booky on you. Let me just advise you to follow in my footsteps as fast as you can. You never know, they may still be there, imprinted on the dewy grass that I crossed to reach the dovecot. I have had a thing about dovecots ever since I came upon one in the heat of an August day in the village of Wadenhoe on the banks of the River Nene in Northamptonshire. Aberdour's did not disappoint. Inside its dusky, beehive-shaped interior six hundred stone nesting boxes bore witness to the fact that they already knew all about convenience shopping in the 16th century. A gap in a wall invited me into the neighbouring churchyard of St Fillans, snoozing in the mid-morning's burgeoning warmth. It dates from the 12th century, but the most peculiar thing is that it lay disused and near derelict from 1796 until 1925. I opened the door and entered its cool nave, signed the visitor's book and left it as I found it, a haunt of ancient peace. Back outside I stood in the graveyard, watching a tanker move out of the Firth. Once it had disappeared behind the headland, I indulged in a bit of grave-spotting; discovering the stone of Robert Thomson, a ship master who'd died aged 84 on January 1st 1815, perhaps having over-indulged himself on Hogmanay. At the other extreme of lifespan I found one stone commemorating Charles H. Rowden and Isabella Salmond, who'd died aged two and four respectively, though I couldn't fathom why they had different surnames, let alone why their father was called James Cumming! Another feature of the castle grounds is the walled garden. I would have liked to have sat there, watching the shadow move slowly over the sundial, but all this dilly-dallying was getting me nowhere fast, and I wanted to go down to the beach before returning to the station.

I bought a Scots pie in Lonie's bakery. The stationmaster was in the queue but still I didn't talk to him. The lady who served me said "it's warum now," but I didn't know if she meant the weather or the pie. I consumed it walking down Shore Road, beginning to think I'd died and gone to heaven. I felt like a child again, excitement mounting as I walked down to the sea. Aberdour was dozing, you could hear a pin drop. The local noise-abatement officer popped up from behind his privet hedge and remonstrated with me for the sound my jeans were making, rubbing against my thighs. Gracious houses, some sprouting envy-provoking balconies, overlooked a small, but perfectly formed, crescent-shaped bay. What is the secret of making so much money you can afford to live in a paradise like this?

The waves were barely whispering, a line of yachts lay unmoving at anchor, I had to take a firm grip on myself not to strip down to my boxer shorts and join the children paddling in the sea. A love of ice cream and saltwater, perhaps the only two things we retain from childhood into senility. Instead, I spread out the map and set about identifying various landmarks, as a herring gull fished for its elevenses. A mile offshore lay Inchcolm, the 'Iona of the East', which can be reached by boat from South Queensferry. From this distance it looked the sort of place where miracles might occur. Behind it lay the Lothian shoreline: Cramond Island, Leith, Edinburgh - pinpointed by Arthur's Seat and Salisbury Crags - and, away to the south-east, the chimneys of Cockenzie power station.

With great reluctance I went back to the station, having lingered in Aberdour twice as long as I'd meant to. But I paid the price. Trevor Francis, the stationmaster, wasn't there. The station dog was, but he was too busy drooling over some boys eating sandwiches, to pay any attention to a mere journalist. His name is Buster and he's six years old. I learnt that from Trevor when I telephoned him a day or two later. Trevor had been various things before he'd become a stationmaster - a psychiatric nurse, a social-worker and an undertaker. British Rail took some convincing that he was the man for the job.

"They asked me what retail experience I'd had," he explained to me, "and I told them I'd 'sold' nurses and coffins."

They must have been impressed, he got the job eight years ago and has never looked back.

"There was a tradition of gardening at Aberdour, I just kept it going."

He works a twenty-four hour week, plus four hours a week officially on the gardens, though of course no gardener is ever a clock-watcher. He's meant to finish in the booking-office each morning at ten, but he likes, as he put it, "to see the 10.42 away." The village is jealous of its well-kept station and gives Trevor both moral and financial support to keep it that way.

"I recently got some money from the Resident's Association to buy some heavier hanging baskets to go under the canopy. The ones we had before used to swing in the slipstream of the merry-go-round coal trains. The Floral Society gave me some support for the garden on Platform 2, but to do it properly we need three thousand pounds, and I'm hopeful there might be a three-way partnership between ScotRail, Railtrack and the Fife Council. It all comes down to money as usual!"

Sadly, doesn't everything? I could only admire his determination and hope that the decision-makers would not be as green as Trevor's fingers. Aberdour station is a gem, as vital to the community as the bank or the bakery. But in a perfect world there would be nothing special about it, all wayside stations would be just so.

A pair of 150 Sprinters whisked me away from Aberdour. At first grassy cuttings obscured the coast, so I looked inland, where rolling pastures were being grazed by cattle of variegated hues. The carriages ran along the line making that hollow, whooshing sound characteristic of their kind - a sighing, moaning sort of train altogether. At Dalgety Bay (a new station opened in 1998 to serve housing and industrial developments) the guard, rotund with a chipper manner, emerged from the driver's cab and called down the platform: "Edinburgh train, all aboard please," as though he'd learnt the trade by watching Spencer Tracey films. At Inverkeithing, where the Fife Circle bifurcates, he reprised his act, muttering to the driver about a couple too busy kissing each other goodbye to stand clear of the doors. The paper this book is printed on came from Caldwells Mill at Inverkeithing.

From Inverkeithing a rusty branch, travelled only by the occasional mystery train, leads under the main line to the dockyard at Rosyth. My train climbed past the harbour, with its scrapyard and huddle of cranes like Airfix used to make, and through a tunnel to North Queensferry, a little timber station perched on the jutting jaw of a headland from which no railway could conceivably proceed without some feat of civil engineering. That feat was what I had come to see.

I walked downhill, under a pigeon-haunted railway bridge and past a plashing well, restored in 1897 'by lovers of the ferry for the solace of wayfarers'. Jackie Leven, I felt, would approve the sentiments. Being drawn to the well delayed the dramatic moment when Sir John Fowler's world famous Forth Bridge was all but overpoweringly exposed to view through telephone wires and over chimney pots in front of me. So well known a sight, yet so stupendously remarkable when seen up close. Hackneyed, I know, but it took my breath away.

As if to demonstrate scientifically its method of operation, right on cue a Sprinter emerged from the station on to the approach viaduct. It looked like an N gauge model. Facts? Oh go away, when you look at a beautiful woman do you want to know the dimensions of her bone structure? You surprise me! Alright then, just for you. The Forth Bridge consists of three giant double cantilevers. The top of each tower is 361 feet high, the bridge is 1 mile 1,005 yards long, 51,000 tons of steel were used in its construction, it was opened on 4th March 1890 by the Prince of Wales (later Edward VII, who obviously had a moment to spare between romantic assignations) and 56 men perished during its construction. Satisfied?

From the old ferry pier, the bridge soared above me like an oxide-coloured, triple-backed dinosaur; massive though far from malignant. In common with many cathedrals it was covered in maintenance scaffolding. Looking up at it this close induced vertigo. To recover some semblance of balance, I glanced down into the water and found myself eyeball to eyeball with an evil looking, purple-headed jellyfish. I returned to the safety of dry land as if returning from a sea voyage. On summer Sundays a ferry plies from North Queensferry to Inchcolm and I would commend the experience to you, only sorry that the regular car ferry was rendered obsolete by the adjacent Forth Road Bridge in 1964. By all means replace ferries with road bridges if you're in such a tearing hurry, but at least have the decency to pay the ferryman to remain at his post, should any traveller perchance appear, desirous to cross the water in the old way. The Greeks were never crass enough to bridge the Styx, were they!

I had no intention of leaving the Kingdom of Fife, not on this occasion anyway. So I caught a clockwise Fife Circle train from the station and retraced my route to Inverkeithing (where a small coaster was now entering the harbour) and turned west through Rosyth towards Dunfermline. I wasn't sure where to get off next. Cowdenbeath had caught my eye. But when a low curving viaduct had brought the train into Dunfermline Town, I was drawn spontaneously to alight by a poster depicting the inviting nave of the abbey.

Always be wary of town's surrounded by ring-roads, more often than not they'll have sold their soul. The first building I encountered endorsed these suspicions, a once gracious classical stone pile with elegant balconies mocked by defenestrated windows. Furthermore the streets were unaccountably empty, as though Dunfermline observed the Mediterranean habit of siesta. Unnervingly there were no signposts to the abbey. But no self-respecting guide book compiler is ever cowed into submission by municipal inscrutability. I forged uphill, knowing that monks favoured heights, and was rewarded at the next bend in the road by Monastery Street.

For the second time in the day I was dumb-struck by what confronted me. I had not been prepared for such imposing ecclesiastic splendour. My ignorance was embarrassing. I did not know, for example, anything of Dunfermline's royal or religious status, that it had once been the capital of Scotland, that the remains of Robert the Bruce are entombed in the abbey and that King Charles I was born in the palace in 1600. The abbey is in two parts, a new 19th century church having been added to the east end of what remains of the original medieval buildings. They sit together harmoniously enough, as substantial as many a better known English cathedral. I was impressed by the town centre too, especially the astonishingly ornate Town Hall, which wouldn't look out of place in a Belgian square. I walked up High Street, ducking right into Guildhall Street before becoming disillusioned by branches of Vodafone, the Halifax Building Society and McDonalds. I had made the right choice, for not many towns can boast such a fair prospect of fine countryside beyond one of their main thoroughfares. I was drawn to the salmon pink walls of the Abbot House, now a Heritage Centre celebrating, amongst many other facets of local history, Dunfermline's connections with Andrew Carnegie, the American steelmaster, who in the early years of the 20th century was the richest man in the world. But I felt it was time to shake the dust of Dunfermline from my feet and move on to another destination.

East of Dunfermline the sole remaining railway, of what was once a dense network of lines built to serve the Central Fife coalfield, traverses a landscape transformed by a conjuror's trick of regeneration. They used to pull rabbits out of a hat, now they pull retail parks. On an old map I counted sixteen pits in the vicinity of Cowdenbeath. Needless to say there are none now, the only coal in Cowdenbeath these days travels through by train on its way to Longannet power station, having been mined by opencast means in Ayrshire or imported through Hunterston. And with the mines have gone the railways; all the lost junctions: Touch South, Townhill (and its wagon works), Lumphinnans, Kelty South, and Box; whole litanies of them, mingling in purgatory with the forgotten pits: Minto, Jenny Gray, Dora, Fordell, Benarty and Blairenbathie. And now I gazed through the window at reclaimed pasturelands, plantations and housing developments, knowing which era I would rather inhabit. I got a glimpse of Cowdenbeath's main street. It reminded me of Auchinleck. The same spiritual vacuum. On to Lochgelly, the train beating out a sombre, funereal rhythm. Yet there was beauty in the scars: youths fishing in a lochan fringed by reeds; black cattle swishing flies away with their tails in the heat; emerald glades of bracken for lovemaking. Three teenage girls were waiting on Lochgelly station, miners' daughters perhaps, or more likely *gran*daughters now. Away in the distance, the headframe of Mary pit at Lochore has been retained in a country park, as a reminder of an old industry as ancient as an Aztec tin mine. Lochgelly, I am given to understand, was once known for the manufacture of tawses, but that's a painful subject.

Rebus was waiting for me on the platform at Cardenden. DI John Rebus of Lothian & Borders police. He was going to guide me round Bowhill in advance of the tourist trails that will inevitably materialise in the wake of Ian Rankin's stunningly successful (and now televised) fictional detective.

"It's good to see you," he said, but lacked conviction, and led the way down a cinder path on to Station Road.

"Thanks for sparing the time, I replied, "I'm a big fan, I found you in a Dumfries bookshop before you were famous."

It's not easy speaking with celebrities. You don't want worship to turn into overkill. The trick is to speak to them as if they were an intellectual equal; no different from you at all, except that they are rich and famous and successful with women, and you have no hope of acquiring any of those labels.

"Fancy a drink in the Railway Tavern?" Rebus asked. But I knew his reputation, and I only had an hour between trains. For a while he looked crestfallen, but cheered up when I took him into Mathieson's bakery and treated him to a chocolate coated Battenburg. Having crossed the River Ore, we were in Bowhill.

"There was a railway bridge across the road here," he said, "linking the different shafts. Bowhill was famous for its high carbon content coal, the Navy bought it in large quantities for the ships at Rosyth. The Goth was along here."

I'd read about the Goth in *Dead Souls*, his dad had drunk there and it was the first place Rebus had ever bought a round. But what the book didn't tell you was that the Goth got its name from Gothenburg and the Swedish concept of providing miners with co-operative drinking dens, profits being channeled into community coffers. It was a subtle scheme, if your conscience told you you were drinking too much, you turned round and told it that you were only drinking heavily to help pay for a new village hall, or a day out in Pittenweem.

"They've taken the bing away too," he sighed. In his youth it had had a volcano like propensity to smoulder. Post-industrial landscaping had taken the mystery out of the landscape. Now the only mystery was why people bothered to live here any longer, one case Rebus couldn't be expected to solve.

We didn't get as far as the cemetery where John Thomson, the Celtic goalie is buried. As a youth he'd worked at Bowhill Colliery, but was seen by a scout and signed for Celtic at 18. On September 5th 1931 he was playing in an Old Firm clash at Ibrox when he took a kick on the head. Jeered off the pitch on a stretcher, he died of a compressed fracture in Glasgow's Victoria hospital the same night. Thirty thousand people attended his funeral procession through Cardenden.

A car went by, windows down, blaring *House of the Rising Sun* out from its audio. That gave us our cue to walk back to the station deep in a discussion about rock music - we ran the gamut, Del Amitri to the Blue Nile. Passing the Railway Tavern we noticed an advert for karaoke on Fridays and Saturdays - Top Prize £25.

"Janice Playfair, John?", I said, "What was it she sang?"

"*Baker Street*," he said, almost in a whisper.

Poor symbolic Janice Playfair, a metaphor for all the Janices and Gillians and Sandras and Susans we never got hitched to. Two of them were sitting on the clockwise platform back at the station. One thin and passably pretty, the other plump and plain; a not unusual mix. The former happy to be unchallenged by the latter's homeliness, the latter taking a vicarious pleasure in the former's looks.

Without enthusiasm Rebus said: "We must keep in touch," and drove off back to his altogether different sort of station. The only seat occupied, I sat on the gravel, back against the station nameboard, feeling like Paul Simon must have felt on Widnes station, waiting for a song to come along. Or failing that, a train! I must have dozed off. I dreamt I was in the Railway Tavern, belting out *Thunder Road* for all I was worth. But it was the rails singing, not me, as my sixth train of the day came to scoop me up.

Sixth train? It seemed like sixty, four o'clock in the afternoon and as you well know by now, my sugar levels were shin high. A mile or two along the line, having crossed the River Ore, we came to Thornton Yard. Silver birch masked lines of hoppers. A pair of Class 66s stood purposefully at the head of two east-facing trains, coal empties waiting to return to Ayr. Thornton dates from 1956, part of British Railways' much vaunted Modernisation Plan. It was high-tech for its time, the first to use radar and closed circuit television as aids to wagon control. It was sited to accommodate central Fife's burgeoning coal output. After a press visit, Geoffrey Freeman Allen wrote in *Trains Illustrated*: 'To see Thornton is to have a heartening reassurance that the railways are more than just in the fight to hold their rightful share of the country's freight traffic - with equipment like this and not the least the enthusiasm it arouses in the men who use it, they are going to win.' Win? Why yes, if you think six out of a hundred constitutes a win.

Reference to Table 242 in the *National Rail Timetable* suggests to the uninitiated that Glenrothes With Thornton is a terminal station served by two separate lines from Inverkeithing, one via Dunfermline, one via Kirkcaldy. In fact it's a through station and, like Glasgow's Cathcart Circle, the trains run clockwise and anti-clockwise from Edinburgh. Furthermore the length of the journey is virtually the same whichever way you go, rendering Glenrothes unique on Britain's railway network. Nine minutes after leaving it I was back in Kirkcaldy, looking forward to seeing the Museum & Art Gallery, but more than anything, to having a pot of tea.

In the Cafe Wemyss - an integral part of the Museum named after the local pottery - I caused something of a sensation by being the first customer of the afternoon, three quarters of an hour before they were due to close. There was a certain plaintiveness about the way the woman behind the counter asked if I'd like anything else with my tea which made me regret the Battenburg I'd had with Rebus in Bowhill. Probably it was best not to encourage her, I thought, picturing a plate piled high with all the afternoon's uneaten cakes. Invigorated by the scalding tea I toured the upstairs gallery first, discovering a Lowry and some charming landscapes by the 'Glasgow Boys'. The museum was equally fascinating, a sequence of displays illustrating each facet of Kirkcaldy's social and industrial past in turn. It was the sort of small town museum which easily gets overlooked as we rush about from visitor centre to visitor centre, which is a shame because sometimes these simple collections in their glass cabinets seem so much more eloquently in touch with the past than any number of all-singing, all-dancing, hands-on, interpretive fire-crackers.

My next train, the 16.43 Turbostar to Dundee, took me back along the route I'd journeyed along that morning from Ladybank. It was not an irksome reprise. I saw things I'd missed in the morning, and remembered to look and see if there was any sign of Thornton Junction station, former epicentre of Fife's railway activity. All there is now is a golf course, and one has to rely on archive photographs from the likes of Bill Anderson's collection to see what it might have looked like with a 'Scot' or 'Glen' 4-4-0 waiting in the bay with a local for Dunfermline Upper. Furthermore I was recognised by the guard, who'd just bought a copy of *Iron Road to the Isles* on a trip up the West

Highland Line, and by the time we'd finished chatting we were almost in Ladybank. His name was Roger Booth and he felt Fife's lines could do with the guide book treatment, if only to help him answer tourists' questions. I gave him the details of my bank account and told him I'd see what I could do!

There followed a pleasant run along the Eden Valley past fields of potatoes and sundry other vegetables; enough to give children the collywobbles. A lineside laundry heralded Cupar, once the county town of Fife, and a man was fast asleep on a station seat in such an unlikely pose as to look as though he'd been hit by a poisoned blow pipe dart. I was sitting on the wrong side to take much notice of the Italianate station building. I made a mental note of the sort which used to litter my school reports: 'must try harder next term'.

With the Eden living up to its imagery, sweet rolling countryside led to Leuchars, the Turbostar eating up the miles. Leuchars' wide platforms once included bays for the connecting services to St Andrews and Tayport. Now it's a matter of finding a bus or a taxi to get to the home of golf; not quite the same thing. The five mile line to St Andrews closed in 1969, a ludicrous abandonment given the status of this ancient seat of learning, its historic importance to the game of golf, and its capacity for attracting holidaymakers and tourists. Leuchars' other branchline described an arc through Tayport and Newport-on-Tay to rejoin the main line at Wormit Junction, at the south end of the Tay Bridge. Together these lines would have offered modern day Dundee a lively suburban network. Far too often the railway administrators of even the post Beeching era gave no thought to the future. But Leuchars remains a useful railhead, not least because of the RAF airfield on its doorstep.

The main line curves inland under the watchful eye of Lucklaw Hill. We passed a rail-served oil depot and some not rail-served sand pits. What can I tell you about the Tay Bridge that you don't already know? I could recommend John Prebble's *The High Girders*, a classic 1957 account of the debacle of 28th December 1879 when winds of hurricane like intensity blew a train off the central span of the bridge, drowning all seventy-five people on board. The bridge's collapse - blamed on cheeseparing engineering and shoddy workmanship as well as nature's worst - destroyed the life and reputation of its designer, Sir Thomas Bouch who was at the height of his career. Within a year he had died, insane and a broken man. A replacement bridge, built to the design of W.H. Barlow and his son Crawford, was opened in 1887. It is fifty yards over two miles long and, in the words of Hamilton Ellis: 'Since then it has stood fast'.

I looked out of the window opposite me as we crossed the Firth of Tay, and it felt no different than being in an aeroplane. Ricky Ross of Deacon Blue wrote a song called *Back Here in Beanoland* which incorporates the lyrics: 'Everyday they cross that great bridge, I watch those trains pull in and out.' Beanoland, of course, pays reference to one of Dundee's staple industries, the comic publishing activities of D.C.Thomson. Three days after I'd passed through the city new statues were unveiled celebrating Dennis the Menace and Minnie the Minx. I could have done with some light relief. I'd tried to get into Discovery Point, a new museum built around Captain Scott's ship *Discovery* and his ill-fated exploration of Antarctica in 1901. OK, I know that strictly speaking I marched up to the entrance counter after five o'clock, but they give visitors an hour to clear the exhibits, and I promised to be out by six. Polite but firm, the attendant seemed incapable of discriminating, of making a human decision. Over-trained no doubt, all initiative removed as a matter of policy. I wondered what Scott would have done if he'd arrived late only to be told by some officious penguin that Antarctica was already closed for the day.

Dundee I summed up as a seagull-haunted city of blue & cream buses. Like Discovery Point it was closing down for the day. Its bars filling up as fast as its offices emptied. I had one eye on finding a place to eat, but they all looked smoky and noisey and cliquey. I admired some imposing architecture, discovered a little oasis called The Howff, and bumped into a statue of Burns, a guy who seemed to get about a bit, long before ScotRail offered such attractively priced Travelpasses. You never know, the railway might have inspired him, something along the lines of: 'Wee, sleekit, cowrin, tim'rous Sprinter', or 'Fair fa' your honest, sonsie face, Great Chieftain o' the Turbo race!'

Disgruntled, but not despondent, I returned to Dundee's only remaining station. Once there were four of them, this one was known as Tay Bridge and belonged to the North British Railway, as did the former ticket station at Esplanade. No one has ever worked out why Tay Bridge station was built in a rather dank cutting below sea level, lending it the atmosphere of a partially subterranean station on the London Undergound's District Line. It features one long island platform, sharply curved at the east end, with two long bays at the west end where my wife, Jackie, and I once memorably arrived after a laryngitic run up from Edinburgh behind a Class 27. Dundee West station was a Caledonian Railway terminus which stood adjacent to Tay Bridge on the city side. Old photographs depict an impressive trainshed straddling four platform roads from which trains ran to Perth and Glasgow Buchanan Street. East station was more modest, though still boasted an overall roof. It belonged jointly to the North British and Caledonian and sent its trains up the golfing coast to Carnoustie and Arbroath, and over the Sidlaw Hills to Forfar.

So much railway history, so little left I reflected, easing my weary body down onto a sunlit bench while sparrows fluttered to and fro amidst the cast iron canopies. I'd reconciled myself to dining when I got back, full circle of eight, to Perth. I was looking forward to the last lap, a twenty minute sprint across the Corse of Gowrie, that fertile plain of fruit farms between the north bank of the Tay and the Braes of the Carse. To take me there I had the original ScotRail Turbostar, 170401. Smooth-riding, well-soundproofed, I was beginning to be a fan of these units. It was one of those perfect evenings which supplement a perfect day. All was temporarily right with the world as we raced past the glistening mud of Dog Bank. As the Tay narrowed, so did my mental horizon, all I wanted now was a cold lager and a hot meal. All, that is, and that this racing train would somehow contrive to run on into the golden evening for eternity.

Useful Contacts

Perth Tourist Information - Tel: 01738 450600

Kirkcaldy Museum & Art Gallery - Tel: 01592 412860

Kirkcaldy Tourist Information - Tel: 01592 267775

Aberdour Castle - Tel: 01383 860519

Maid of the Forth Cruises - Tel: 0131 331 4857

Dunfermline Tourist Information - Tel: 01383 720999

Dunfermline Abbey - Tel: 01383 739026

Discovery Point, Dundee - Tel: 01382 201245.
www.rrsdiscovery.com

Dundee Tourist Information - Tel: 01382 527527.
www.angusanddundee.co.uk

Boarding the sleeper at Euston. Supper in the Lounge Car.
Things which go bump in the night. Dawn over Loch Lomond.
Superman at Rannoch. Cab-riding a Thirty-Seven.
Footplating 'The Jacobite' from Fort William to Mallaig.
Fish & chips in the harbour.

Clearly it marks the apotheosis of civilisation when you can stroll into a railway terminus from London's Euston Road, board a small cabin with a bed in it, snuggle under the sheets, then wake to the sound of a discreet knock on your door, as dawn and the upcoming sun's rays are applying rouge to the cheeks of the hills above Loch Lomond. Made human again by an injection of caffeine, you can spend the next couple of hours in the lounge car, flipping through *The Herald* over scrambled eggs and smoked salmon, but focussed on some of Scotland's - if not Western Europe's - most savagely sublime scenery. How is this miracle achieved, who are the people who make it possible, what can you do when you get to the end of the line, where does the Sound of Sleat come into the title? All will be revealed.

"Platform 1 for the Caledonian Sleeper to Fort William, Inverness and Aberdeen," came the voice over the public address at Euston. It would be difficult to not feel excitement on hearing such an announcement. Do less ambitious passengers shake their heads and make into the night for Hatch End and Hemel Hempstead with a sigh? In time honoured fashion I walked the length of the huge sixteen coach train to see what was at the 'country' end and found 90030, a powerful Bo-Bo electric locomotive dating from the late Eighties, not very imaginatively named *Crewe Locomotive Works*, though looking puissant enough in English Welsh & Scottish Railway red and yellow livery. Getting this ScotRail operated sleeper train over the border is a team event, with EWS and Virgin staff also involved, not to mention Railtrack and, if you want to be pedantic about it, several rail engineering contractors.

It was only the beginning of August and not yet quite nine, but from the end of the platform the sky already looked dark. I'd been allocated berth 3 in coach G, which just happened to be at the front of the train. Marjorie, my stewardess, was tactfully explaining to an alcohol-reeking latecomer called Mr Lloyd that she had no spare berths available. He did not take the bad news gracefully. As he went back down the platform muttering, she showed me to my cabin, asked when I required my morning call and whether I preferred tea or coffee with my breakfast tray. Formalities completed, I walked through several coaches to the Lounge Car, procuring one of the last available seats, for the train was more or less full, and regulars know that it pays to stake an early claim.

According to my watch we pulled out two minutes early, perhaps Mr Lloyd had become irascible and the train crew had elected to make a quick getaway, leaving him jumping up and down at the barrier, enraged. Effortlessly 90030 launched its heavy train at Camden bank. Fifty years ago a Stanier Duchess, charged with the same task, would have sent starbursts of burning cinders into the Mornington Terrace sky. The bank was breasted by Chalk Farm, and Primrose Hill Tunnel negotiated. At speed we overtook Underground trains incandescent as glow-worms; gobbling up and spitting out a litany of inner city stations: South Hampstead, Kilburn High Road, Queens Park and Kensal Green. We may have been destined for the north, but to get out of London we went west to begin with. Willesden and Wembley brought acres of railway sidings; depots for EWS and the Royal Mail. Under baleful floodlights, lines of locomotives stood in shadowy repose. 66s and 92s for the most part, but also a 37 called *City of Worcester*, a cousin of the kind of locomotive that I would regain consciousness with, growling through Glasgow's suburbs in the morning.

I ordered a McEwan's Export and a Swiss cheese and ham roll for supper and took stock of my travelling companions. I was sharing a table with a man in late middle age who looked vaguely familiar, he was drinking a half bottle of red. Across the aisle sat a man and wife and young daughter, the man savouring a Traquair Ale. Behind me another group, all male whom, I couldn't see, but I could hear discussing climbs about Arrochar. Opposite them a young Scots couple, he of shaven head, she at too much of an angle to describe, but talking about finding work in the finance sector. In all of them I sensed suppressed excitement, a recognition of the special nature of the journey they were making. Of course they could fly to Los Angeles or Jakarta in the twelve hours it will take them to get to Fort William or Inverness or Aberdeen, but we are blasé about air travel in this day and age; sleeper trains are still an awfully big adventure.

Watford Junction, Berkhamsted, Tring: behind me someone said, "We're on the slow line," engineering activity seemingly everywhere; the West Coast Main Line upgrade. People began to wander off to bed in varying permutations. Like a hotel guest, ensconced in the lounge behind a magazine, I mathematically calculated relationships. The man opposite me had gone to join another table further up the carriage and I was left to the dregs of my beer and the unsolved clues of the *Railway Magazine* crossword, it being the names of Halls and Jubilees that always stump me. We came to a stop outside a large town which, after a few minutes delay, revealed itself as

Northampton, a place I knew well from boat trips on the Nene. Well enough, at any rate, to recognize without needing to read the station signs. I paid for my supper and went back to my cabin, the long walk an evening constitutional before bed. Marjorie wished me a good night and reminded me to lock my door.

"There's nothing valuable in there," I replied, "Except, that is, for me."

Between the sheets is like being at sea. You have to learn to roll with the punches. People tell me they have to get their land legs again when they get off the train in the morning. Me, I'm pleasantly relaxed by the womb-like rattle and hum. Unless, that is, I've had a beer, in which case there's an inevitable trudge to the loo in the wee small hours. Luckily I was only two doors along from the WC, less distance than I have to walk at home. Returning to my cabin, I glanced out of the window. It was what the comedians call 'a braw bricht moonlit nicht' and I immediately recognized my whereabouts. It was Beattock, and we were passing the park where Eden and I go to play football and watch trains. In many respects, I was sad to be only travelling over this route in the middle of the night, for there is an austere beauty about the famous climb to Beattock summit, and the subsequent traverse of the Upper Clyde Valley, which repays a daylight run.

Something goes bump in the night, something called Waverley, where the train trifurcates and the shunting tends, shall I say, towards the spirited; nothing, however, that you haven't already felt a thousand times when your spouse knees you in the groin whilst turning over in the marital bed. A diesel adds two day coaches to the Fort William sleeping cars and you head off through Princes Street Gardens and Haymarket, searching for sleep again, as the train makes its way through the Central Belt.

Willie Black of ScotRail had kindly furnished me with some interesting facts and figures relating to the sleeper operation. Sixty-nine on board staff are employed to look after the likes of you and me. On a typical night each portion would be staffed by a Team Leader and three hosts, the former looking after the Lounge Car while the latter take care of the sleeping quarters. There are sleeper depots at London, Aberdeen, Inverness, Fort William, Glasgow and Edinburgh. If all the 800 berths are occupied, 3,372 items of laundry are removed and replaced each day, whilst 864 bottles of water are provided for the cabins. ScotRail use the services of four laundries, the northernmost being in Elgin, the southernmost in London. Oh, and the southbound Inverness sleeper carries fresh shell fish for the smart restaurants of London town.

I woke to the rallentando rhythm of wheels on jointed track and timber wagons being loaded at Arrochar & Tarbet. The climbers got off as I reached for my complimentary toilet bag. Far from applying colour to her cheeks, dawn appeared to be lathering her face in shaving cream. The pointed summit of Ben Lomond was clear of cloud, but only just. Perhaps dawn wasn't Dawn at all, but Donald. The sleeper's in no apparent hurry. The wheels beat out a loping rhythm suitable for something by Travis perhaps, or in an earlier era, The Eagles. Nae bother, all the more time to soak up the scenery; even under a dull sky Loch Lomond can be 'in your face' gorgeous.

Marjorie knocked on my door with the breakfast tray and newspaper, but I was washed and dressed and decided to take it to the Lounge Car. A woman was hovering by the serving hatch, wondering if she could have toast for her children. "We haven't done toast for fifteen years," said Colin Parkington, the steward, who came on with the Fort William car at Edinburgh. He was making smoked salmon and scrambled egg for a man and boy at the table opposite me. I made a mental note to emulate them next time I breakfasted on the sleeper. There wasn't much in *The Herald*, it was still the summer recess and the country was getting on very nicely without politicians. Celtic had beaten Manchester United in Ryan Gigg's testimonial, but he was happy, he'd made a cool, tax free million. In any case the view through the window is the real winner round here.

"I've known us serve twenty-five breakfasts," Colin said, as he took my neighbours' empty dishes away, and mournfully looked round the almost empty carriage. We were climbing up to Crianlarich past hillsides where the waterfalls stood out like varicose veins. The man, whose name was Mr. Duke, and whose voice reminded me, in a rather silly, giggly way of Peter Cook's E.L.Wisty, told the boy, who wasn't his son, to look out for the locomotive.

"It's a thirty-seven-four," he told him, "Which means its got electric heating."

"Is Trev a trainspotter?" the boy asked.

"A bit of one," the man replied, guardedly.

"I used to be able to do his accent, we've got him on camcorder doing his funny walk."

"There's quite a nice Youth Hostel at Crianlarich," said Mr. Duke, adroit master of the *non sequitur.*

There were more timber wagons at Crianlarich and a welcoming glow from Mr. & Mrs. Cull's popular tea room. The railway to Oban curves away to the west here and I felt a pang of guilt for not including it in my portfolio of lines explored, anticipating the receipt of a vituperative letter of complaint from Michael Magnay, the notoriously Obanocentric engine driver. But you can read of its charms in *Iron Road to the Isles*, and I thoroughly recommend its sinuous, strath-busting, lochloping progress to the coast. The luxury Royal Scotsman travels the line regularly, not quite reaching Oban, but overnighting at Taynuilt to sample some locally caught and cured fish. Most of the regular service Sprinters - Class 156 on this line - split at Crianlarich into Oban and Fort William or Mallaig portions, so you have to be careful to be in the right carriage.

We pulled away and crossed the River Fillan.

"That's Ben More," said Mr Duke who, I was beginning to suspect, wrote guide books for a living. It was a disconcerting thought, made particularly galling by the fact that his head was only inches beneath a poster in the window of the bulkhead advertising that copies of my guide book to the West Highland Lines were obtainable from the buffet counter at the ('ridiculously cheap', you'll remember) price of £4.99. If you have a copy of it, it will tell you that: 'Climbing out of Tyndrum, the

West Highland Railway reaches County March Summit, entering a landscape with an increased sense of wildness about it, as emphasised by snow posts on the adjoining A82'. Looking through the window, six months after having written that, it seemed a pretty accurate description. The road was busy with lorries. Since publication of my guide two freight flows had disappointingly defected from the railway.

"That's the A82," said Mr Duke, "It goes all the way to Skye."

Ah, got you, I thought, knowing full well that the A82 swerves north-east at Fort William and goes off to Inverness.

Bog Cotton - not to be confused with Billy - was blowing in the wind on Rannoch Moor. The last time I crossed the moor it was waist-deep in snow. Under an azure sky it had glistened like silver. I had walked gingerly across its frozen surface thinking of lemon meringues, crunchy on top but treacherously soft underneath. It was February, but it was a lot warmer than this second day in August was looking like being. The seasons are becoming as unpredictable as a Connex South Central timetable.

Mr Duke and the boy had gone back to their cabins to pack. I got talking to Colin, who'd known who I was all along.

"John Yellowlees told me you were coming up and to keep an eye out for you."

The machiavellian Mr Y again, dogging my steps. What was it John Boyle had said to me once? Something about Yellowlees's knack of getting you to do things, yet making you think you had thought of it yourself.

Colin hails from Bury and is a sixth generation railway worker. He'd been a Senior Conductor working out of Preston on the sleeper trains when he met his wife, Kate, already a stewardess on the Fort William sleeper.

"At two or three in the morning there wasn't much else we could do but get to know each other," he told me with a chuckle.

"Eddie Toal at ScotRail did a piece about us called 'Sleeping Partners'."

Now Colin and Kate and their family live in Fort William but rarely work on the same shift, so that I pictured them always passing at the garden gate like the couple in *Brassed Off.*

On Rannoch station I looked for a telephone kiosk to change in. Like Clark Kent I was about to become a Superman - well, a railway engine driver's mate, which to my way of thinking is tantamount to the same thing. Luckily there was no box handy, because I had doubts concerning the sartorial protocol of wearing underpants over shorts. ScotRail, Fort William driver John Hynd was waiting, both for me, and a cup of tea from Colin. He had come down with the 07.35 from The Fort (06.10 off Mallaig) and exchanged cabs with the Glasgow driver who had driven the sleeper from Dalmuir. John and I had worked together on *Iron Road to the Isles,* so there was no need for introductions or small talk as we walked up the platform to where 37421 stood pawing the tracks.

I bundled my bag under the secondman's seat and tried politely to shut the door. Too politely, John had to give it a hefty kick to close it properly, par for the course on a 35 year old diesel locomotive with six thousand plus engine hours under its belt since its last overhaul. Built at English Electric's Vulcan Foundry at Newton-le-Willows in 1965, and originally numbered D6967, 37421 is one of nine of its class retained by EWS, by virtue of its capacity to provide heat and light to the carriages it pulls, for sub-letting to ScotRail to haul the Fort William portion of the sleeper. I know that I run the risk of general readers going all glazed on me here, but I think it's important to point out how charismatically, in certain railway circles, these engines are perceived. Enthusiasts travel the length and breadth of the country to ride behind them, and the sleeper to The Fort is undoubtedly going to be their last regular duty. So how can I convey my excitement? To other men it might equate to being given a lift in a Maserati. To women it might equate to being given a lift in a Maserati by George Clooney.

John Hynd is, as far as I am in a position to judge, no George Clooney (except, perhaps, in the eyes of Mrs Hynd) but he's a mine of railway lore, past and present; another professional railwayman from a family of railwaymen, and another whose interest in them goes far beyond the confines of his job. He is one of four ScotRail drivers based in Fort William. They cover three duties between Crianlarich and Mallaig. Mostly their work is on Class 156 Sprinters, the sleeper being the exception. Being August, and the peak holiday season, the four drivers frequently find themselves covering for their colleagues. John had just come back from a week at Alton Towers with his family. My daughter, Tamar, goes to school within earshot of this epicentre of British fun and frolics. It seemed paradoxical that Highlanders should find that a source of amusement when all I wanted to do on holiday was escape to Scotland.

Ensconced in the secondman's seat on the right hand side of the cab, I peered over the locomotive's long bonnet. Raindrops bejeweled the windscreen as we rumbled over Rannoch Viaduct, climbing towards the even lonelier summit at Corrour. I asked John how '421 compared with the other members of its dwindling sub-class, suddenly remembering that the last time I'd ridden behind it was right at the end of its stay on the North Wales Coast, at the finish of a snowbound day when Karen, Eden, Robyn and I had boarded its train at Bangor for a poignant run back to Crewe.

"It's one of the worst," John grimaced, "Reliable enough, but not strong. '418's a strong one. They're talking about giving five or six of them a good overhaul."

I knew that ScotRail had put tenders out for the provision of all three diesel locomotives required for the six days a week haulage of the Fort William, Inverness and Aberdeen portions of the Caledonian Sleeper north of Edinburgh, but even on the normally loquacious railway grapevine, nothing was being heard about imminent replacements for the classes 37, 47 and 67 leased respectively for those duties from EWS now. How often do they change the Fort William engine I wondered.

"They go sixty hours between exams. This one goes to Millerhill, in Edinburgh every other night for refuelling. They average about four return trips before another engine takes their place."

I had travelled over the West Highland in the cab of a

Sprinter before, but that experience, fascinating as it had been, paled in comparison to this 'heavy metal' thrash over the route. It was good to be on a *proper* train with a *proper* locomotive hauling *proper* carriages; an occurrence of increasing rarity value in Britain. Soon after leaving Rannoch we rumbled through Cruach Snowshed, erected to protect the line from the worst of the moor's snowdrifts.

"I see you, man," laughed John as we slowed to a halt at what was, for the sleeper train, the request stop of Corrour. The man in question had been holding up his hand like a policeman on point duty, as if physically attempting to stop the train by sheer force of will-power. I was remembering an idyllic evening spent in the Station House Restaurant, nursing a Caledonian Brewery bottled beer or two before the Glasgow train arrived to pluck me out of the winter night. Now I was sorry to hear that my amiable hosts, Rick and Angela Brown, had left Corrour and that the restaurant and adjoining bunkhouse were, for the moment at least, shut down. Corrour is known in cinematic circles for its use as the country station in *Trainspotting*. All I can tell you is that the sense of wilderness engendered is no exaggeration.

The last time we'd come along this line together, John had told me, that on good days, you get a glimpse of Ben Nevis, to the north-west, soon after leaving Corrour. Mutually, we agreed that this would not qualify as a good day either.

"When I was just starting," John continued, "There was an old driver I worked with who said to me one October: 'See those sheep, huddling together? That means we're in for a bad winter!' He said the same thing to me in November, December and January. When at last it snowed in February he said: 'There, I told you so!'"

Beyond the summit, John shut off power, and we coasted, with occasional brake applications, downhill on a narrow ledge above Loch Treig. I trust, that when you follow in my footsteps, the weather will be more kindly disposed towards you, for the scenery really is scintillating hereabouts. The variegated peaks of the Grey Corries bare their heads beyond the loch on sunny days. This is not only hill-walking country, but a skier's paradise too. A curving viaduct carries the railway over the River Spean, and the line makes an almost right-angled turn to the west. Tulloch station has been converted into a friendly and comfortable bunkhouse where I fondly remember the quality of Belinda's breakfasts.

With the river now a close companion, the line proceeds through Glen Spean, curving with the river's contours as if learning a new dance routine, which climaxes to spontaneous applause in the Monessie Gorge. 'Proud, turbulent and untamable' is how a Victorian guide-book writer described the Spean's spectacular passage through the awesome gorge, words my wife has often used of her husband, much to the envy of women friends. Unfortunately, hydro-electric installations have tamed the Spean since the 19th century, whilst middle age has had a similar enervating effect upon your author.

At Roy Bridge, a young man and woman, dressed up as human sponges, seemed hysterically grateful for the train's appearance. For a moment I thought they were going to try and get in the cab and embrace us, but John and I were too engrossed in football talk to pay anything but scant attention to this desperately unBritish show of feeling. On Thursday evenings, duties permitting, John plays with a team made up of Lochaber based railway professionals, 'bhoys' from ScotRail, EWS, Railtrack and First Engineering.

"We go over and play in Europe every year," John added modestly, but leaving me with the impression that they'd give Real Madrid a run for their money.

"Twenty-one of us went over this year. We went to Budapest and took two pipers."

'Piper', I would add here for the non-expert, being an indigenous Scots musician, and not a kind of footballer like 'sweeper' or 'striker'.

"We didn't do very well this time," John ruefully admitted, then added, as if the reason had suddenly become resolved in his mind, "Possibly our performance may have been affected by excess alcohol, and the fact that some of our players didn't sleep in their beds, but turned up for the eight o'clock morning coach at five to eight, straight from various bars in the town."

I was impressed by John's shrewd assessment of how his team's form had suffered, realising that ScotRail's gain was the Scottish national team's loss.

Before leaving Roy Bridge, John radioed through to Banavie signal box to get permission to proceed. The whole of the West Highland network is radio-controlled from Banavie (on the outskirts of Fort William) but even in the age of the micro-chip the train still requires a 'token' to pass from one single track section to the next. You will recall how I saw the token being handed over in a leather pouch on the way down to Stranraer? Well the same procedure applies on the West Highland, and indeed the lines to Kyle and the Far North, but on these three routes the token in question is a 'virtual' one, computer controlled in its giving and receiving.

Rain beating down on the bonnet, we continued to the penultimate stop at Spean Bridge. On the level track of the valley floor, John opened up the throttle, and blew the horn for good measure, a sonorous bugle call echoing through the deluged woods.

"Normally the wheels would spin on the wet rail if I did that," he explained, "But this one isn't powerful enough for that to happen," he added with an ironic shrug. At Spean Bridge I lowered the window and drank in the sound of the engine growling behind us. The cooling fan cut in to add to the cacophony and John recalled an incident where one of the fans had worked loose and mangled the roof mesh in the engine room.

"I think it was trying to get out of the roof," laughed John. "I had a chap in with me once wearing a deerstalker. It was a hot summer's day and I opened the engine room door to let the fan suck the midges out, but it sucked his hat off his head and cut it into a thousand pieces."

The second stage of my journey to the Sound of Sleat was coming to an end. We rumbled over the gleaming pointwork into Fort William station as John was telling me that he'd given a ride over the Mallaig Extension to a film producer on the lookout for suitable locations for the second Harry Potter film. The upshot being that John's thirteen year old daughter, Fiona, had been offered a part in the film. 'Dash', I thought, another missed opportunity, if I'd been around I might have got a cameo scene as a disorientated travel writer. Lochaber is that sort of district, anything can happen.

What was going to happen to me was that I was going to swap a diesel locomotive footplate for a steam one. For this I had James Shuttleworth, General Manager of the West Coast Railway Company to thank. WCRC operate The Jacobite, a steam-hauled tourist train which runs through the summer months between Fort William and Mallaig. Footplate passes are fiendishly difficult to come by, but James and I had collaborated over *Iron Road to the Isles* and, with the additional approval of the steam locomotive's owners, the Thompson B1 Locomotive Trust, the last leg of my journey from London was done and dusted.

A young piper was playing a lament on the platform. Large amounts of people were milling about before taking their seats on the train. Vapours were swirling about the maroon, steam-heated carriages in a way that reminded me of a scene from *I Know Where I'm Going*, which of course I did. Prospective passengers were trying to procure last minute tickets - on The Jacobite it pays to book in advance. Naturally, the most charismatic figure in this steamy crowd scene was the locomotive: Class B1, 4-6-0 No.61264 built to the design of Edward Thompson and completed by the North British Locomotive Company in Glasgow at the end of 1947, just twenty-six days before the railways were nationalised. The B1s were Thompson's most successful engines - cruel observers might say *only* successful engine. Over four hundred of them were built for mixed traffic work. Only two examples are preserved. I knew them well when I was at school in York, though 61264 is not amongst those underlined in my 1962 Ian Allan ABC. However, I am pretty certain I saw it heating carriages in a siding outside Rotherham Masboro round about 1967. It was rescued from Barry scrapyard in 1974 and restored at

Loughborough in 1997. Locomotives, you will begin to appreciate, have life stories the same as people do.

James had advised me to liase with a Bill Andrew. I was told he would be wearing a beret. After eliminating a French onion salesman and a Frank Spencer strip-o-gram from my enquiries, I came upon him, down by the buffet car, a big grin on his face. Bill is from Bacup and retains his soft, East Lancashire vowels. In railway circles you don't waste time with the weather.

"I started as a cleaner at Rose Grove in 1950," Bill told me. "I did my National Service on Salisbury Plain, then went to Crewe North in 1956 as a fireman. I passed out as a driver in 1963. It was a dream come true. Then the diesels and leckys came along."

Story book stuff. He had fired and driven Duchesses to Perth, taken ammunition to Sudbury, collected peat from Ellesmere and coffee from Tutbury, worked the Pines Express to Wolverhampton, grappled with the first electrics. In short, a hero; but modest with it.

"I went with Transrail in '94, then EWS, but found myself increasingly pushing paper. So I took early retirement. That lasted two months then DRS phoned and I found myself driving again, nuclear flasks from Bridgwater and Willesden. I did a stint writing drivers' manuals at First North Western for the new 175s, then David Smith of Carnforth called me. It was manna from heaven, it turned the clock back."

"What," I asked him, "was your favourite engine?"

"The Duchess class. I thought it was a crime when they cut up *Sir William Stanier*."

But it had come full circle. A week or two before, Bill had been the inspector when *Duchess of Sutherland* had run her first main line trial since being restored, not bad for a former Butlin's 'red coat' - the engine that is, not Bill.

It was a one way conversation. Bill had been there, done it, got the beret. All I had done was spot *Princess Helena Victoria* on Crewe North shed.

It was nearing ten-twenty and time to be off. We pushed through the throng, figures of stature, and made for the end of the platform where 61264 was soaking up both the rain and the adulation. Short of *Blue Peter* or *Green Arrow*, I couldn't think of a locomotive I'd rather ride on. Bill introduced me to the driver, Frank 'The Legend' Santrian, and the fireman, John 'Fingers' Fletcher. Frank drives full time for the West Coast Railway Company, but originally he was a Stoke-on-Trent man and nowadays he lives in Biddulph with a PMT Leyland Leopard (with a Marshall body) he's restored. John started at Lostock Hall - judging by his youthful looks, at the age of eight - and now lives in Grosmont and works for the North Yorks Moors Railway. All three men are consummate professionals, but the atmosphere on the footplate was like something out of a Marx Brothers movie.

The guard, Florence MacLean, blew the whistle and waved her green flag. Frank opened up the red painted regulator, and smoothly we pulled out of the platform at the beginning of a two hour journey to Mallaig. The B1 was running tender first. A turntable has been installed at Fort William at some expense, but until a corresponding structure can be provided at Mallaig, and until some political manoeuvring achieves compromise over charges to use them, the steam locomotives which work The Jacobite have, by definition, to run with their tenders first in one direction, mostly to the chagrin of lineside photographers, who like things neat and as they used to be.

I had been ushered into the fireman's seat on the left hand side. Running backwards, so to speak, the fireman has the responsibility for not only keeping the pressure up and attending to water intake, but sighting signals and other lineside boards as well; by no means an easy task, given that the locomotive is designed for running forwards, and that the view along the tender is less than ideal. For his part, Frank had to have the agility of a contortionist to operate the regulator with his arm behind his back, and he needed eyes in the back of his head to keep a look out on the various gauges pertaining to steam pressure levels and vacuum brake supplies.

Both scenically, and in railway operating terms, the route out of Fort William gives little hint of what is to come. In the yard between the Glasgow and Mallaig lines this season's other loco-motive for The Jacobite, the Peppercorn K1, 2-6-0 No. 62005, stood out of steam, waiting its next share of the duty. In October, both engines were going to be in steam on a special 'plandampf' day, when they would work *all* the services between Fort William and Mallaig, a concept of preserved steam opera-tion devised in Germany, hence the name. Curving round to cross the River Lochy, the engine takes it easy, like a middle dis-tance runner at the start of a race. I looked back along the train and saw a scowling Ben Nevis, half concealed by cloud, as we slowed for a token change at Banavie and a regulatory five miles an hour across the Caledonian Canal swingbridge. A cabin cruiser was tied to a pontoon, waiting for us to cross before climbing Neptune's Staircase of locks. We waved to June, the signal lady on duty, her dulcet tones would be heard over the radio all the way to Mallaig.

Picking up speed, the B1 emitted its high pitched whistle. We saluted to 'Lackey' at Annat Crossing, where a branch runs off to serve the paper mill, one of those recent freight casualties in respect of outbound finished goods, though china clay is still railed in from Cornwall in tanker wagons. Frank worked the engine hard up to forty miles an hour before applying the brake for the platform at Loch Eil Outward Bound. The sea loch was wide and still and inscrutable, herons and oystercatchers seemed impervious to our passing. Some canoeists were gathered on the shore, waiting to launch themselves into the water. It was necessary for the radio token to be exchanged. John spoke care-fully into the microphone, clearly enunciating each word to make himself heard over the general clatter of the footplate. Reception by the lochside was, however, relatively good. Up in the mountains, they told me, it was sometimes necessary to climb on to the top of the tender and wave the aerial about to make contact with Banavie.

Frank was looking back along the engine's gun barrel like boiler, waiting for a wave from Florence. When it came he eased the regulator open and we barked away along the edge of the loch, making good speed before we hit the hills. How can I describe the sensation of riding on the footplate without being trite? Imagine a massive Aga range on wheels, imagine a particularly fierce sauna, imagine a kennel-full of howling dogs, imagine you're riding bareback on a fire-eating dragon with a mind of its own. Small wonder generations of steam engine drivers and firemen have forcefully maintained that their locomotives have living, breathing personalities.

At the end of the loch the track curved to the right and began climbing towards Glenfinnan. John was shovelling coal like a whirling dervish, Frank maintained a steady grip on the regulator, ready at a moment's notice to throttle back if the engine began to slip. From time to time Bill offered me a running commentary, but it would have needed Murray Walker to be heard above such din. I write what I heard. If it's wrong, I apologise.

"We'll be alright when we get over 'the knob'," he shouted. "We're shaving the flanges on the tight curves."

Suddenly, as if frightened by the noise, a stag ran out of the woods and across the rails right in front of us.

"That was close," called Frank.

We slowed down to cross Glenfinnan's famous and photogenic viaduct, a curving symphony in concrete, if that doesn't sound too implausible. On the way back, apparently, The Jacobite takes it even more slowly over the viaduct, so as to make the most of the view down Loch Shiel of Bonnie Prince Charlie fame.

"We can't afford to take it too slowly in this direction," Frank explained, "because we'd not get up the 1 in 50 to the station."

The Jacobite has a twenty minute rest at Glenfinnan on the outward run, just time for passengers to have a quick look round John Barnes's Station Museum. John also operates a sales counter in the guard's van, offering souvenirs and railwayana not necessarily obtainable from other sources in the area. With another hat on he runs a static restaurant car and camping coach in the old goods yard, a busy man who also finds time to be Vice President of the Friends of the West Highland Lines.

The piper had started up again, the platform was a mêlée of

leg-stretching excursionists, John was attending to the fire, I had been subcontracted to operate the lever draining the cylinder cocks, Bill and Frank were enthusiastically reprising for my benefit their starring roles in the first Harry Potter film.

"We had *Olton Hall* masquerading as *Hogwart's Castle* down at King's Cross on two successive Sundays, twelve hours filming each. We were told to make some smoke, Frank was firing, I was driving," said Bill. "Frank built up the fire and we'd just got some good thick smoke out of the chimney when the director came running down the platform shouting: 'Switch it off, switch it off!' As we pulled out of the station I had to blow the whistle as a signal for all the children to get their heads back through the windows. That's where I got my new nickname 'Action, Bill'!"

We got all the passengers back on the train - well most of them anyway, some of them had found in Glenfinnan a sort of personal Damascus, and were queuing for the phone box to tell their bosses they'd quit. It's a stiff climb out of Glenfinnan. Bill, who had taken over the driver's role, had the engine on 45% cut off, second valve and full regulator. Fleetingly satisfied with the state of the fire, John was hosing down the floor to clean it of coal dust. At frequent intervals he would look out of the gap between the tender and the locomotive to check the road ahead, then it was back to shovelling. After some three miles of climbing beside a tumbling watercourse whose Gaelic name I won't even attempt, we came to the summit and burst through two short tunnels. For a scary moment it seemed highly unlikely to me that the tender would fit into the portals, but it did of course, though everything went pitch black and I learnt exactly what it was like to be a piston in a cylinder.

Daylight found us high above Loch Eilt, a beautifully slim and sinuous expanse of water which, by the time we had reached the other end of its three mile length, we were almost at water level with. Coasting downhill, it sounded as if there was a kettle drum group playing beneath the wheels. John had taken a breather and bellowed in my ear:

"To get from Fort William to Mallaig and back we need four

or five tons of coal, eight thousand gallons of water, and seven pints of Youngers!"

After the lonely station at Lochailort we began to climb again and Frank fiddled with the radio in the tender locker to change the channel. We ran through three more tunnels, which no longer unnerved me. Now I was a prince among thieves, an old hand, a card carrying member of the footplate fraternity. Well, not quite, but the excitement was contagious and I am attempting to relay it to you. Momentarily, the B1 began slipping on a wet curve. Bill wrenched the regulator back, then opened up again, regaining control. We passed Our Lady of the Braes, the famous white church at Polnish, skirted Loch Dubh and swayed across Arnabol Viaduct. Then we went volleying into the wet woods like an elephant charging through the jungle; roaring, whooping, swirling, thumping out a rhythm Keith Moon would have died even more prematurely for. Although a tarpaulin was stretched across the gap between the tender and the locomotive, there was little sense of being enclosed: it felt to me as if we were sitting on top of a coal wagon with only an umbrella for protection. My chest was soaked, but my back was roasting. With no cocoon of glass between me and the landscape, I was not watching a steamy scene on television, I was making love; violently!

From the footplate there was barely a second or two to savour the seaward view from Loch nan Uamh Viaduct. We plunged into two tunnels and began to attack the bank up to Beasdale.

"I'm winding the valve gear to 40%," Bill shouted, "if we get over the top at fifteen miles an hour we'll be doing well."

We did do very well, despite another bout of slipping; though the crew told me they'd rather run on wet rails any day than face the resistance inherent in dry track. On a line as hilly and curvy as the West Highland Extension six coaches is just about as much as the B1, powerful engine that it is, can manage. Paradoxically, the K1, a noticeably smaller locomotive, can manage seven, its tractive effort registering at 32,080 pounds against the bigger engine's 26,880. In steam days the K1s were in regular use of the Extension, whilst the B1s tended to work south of Fort William. At least this LNER duo are authentic engines for the West Highland, and with six maroon carriages behind us we presented a moving tableau which might easily have been mistaken for the daily scene forty-five years ago.

Beyond Beasdale Bill shut off steam to go down the bank. We squealed over Borrodale Viaduct and rumbled down through more drenched woodlands to Arisaig where we stopped and radioed June at Banavie for another token. Yachts were lying serenely at anchor in the harbour, but it was far too murky a day to see the sublime horizons of Eigg and Rhum. This little corner of Scotland fascinates me - but then they all do. During the Second World War it was a 'protected area', access being denied to anyone who didn't have an officially sanctioned reason for being there. No tourists in those days. The railway played a significant, if unusual, role in the training of Special Operations Executive agents who would use it to prepare themselves for blowing up railway lines in occupied France. A regular exercise involved the dropping of agents at Loch nan Uamh early in the morning, their mission being to 'derail' a train by placing explosives on the line in a cutting north of Arisaig. First they had to make their way over difficult terrain, then they had to set their charges without being seen, finally, they had to make for the coast and escape by boat: all in a day's work! Apparently the Czech trainees had a tendency to take things too literally, and once or twice almost severed the West Highland Extension for real. Other exercises included night raids on railway goods yards, and learning how to jump out of moving trains without hurting oneself too much. Gavin Maxwell, the gentle, otter-loving author of *Ring of Bright Water*, was apparently a locally stationed instructor in the deadly art of mortal combat.

Slowly, over the pointwork at the end of the loop, we pulled away, radioing Banavie again to confirm that we had passed the 'look clear' board. The railway swerves inland over the boggy glacial deposits of Mointeach Mor, the 'big moss'. We coasted downhill for a couple of miles, then began to climb again, our exhaust confidently barking through the woods. We had to pass over a level crossing to reach Morar. Northbound it's treadle-worked automatically, on the return trip the engine crew have to pull up at Morar platform and press a plunger to activate the barriers. We crept cautiously over the crossing at ten miles an hour and passed the hotel where Arnold Bax composed much of his Celtic-tinged symphonic music. It would have made a good soundtrack to a film of our journey. I caught a glimpse of the famous white sands, but on a grey day they lacked lustre. Morar was sacked by Government troops in 1746 in retribution for its Jacobite sympathies.

One small gradient to climb and then we coasted down into the terminus at Mallaig using the brake. John let the fire cool down. During the two hour sojourn in Mallaig he wouldn't want the engine blowing off steam and there would be some clinker to throw out to keep the firebox clean. Waves were lapping gloomily on the rocky foreshore. I felt sorry for those passengers who perhaps hadn't been to Mallaig before and were not seeing it at its best. At least, if they had my guide book, they would know where to find food and drink. It had been a pleasure and a privilege to work over the West Highland Extension with three dedicated professionals like Bill, Frank and John. Such is the camaraderie of railwaymen, I already felt I knew them well. We made various genuine promises to keep in touch. I stepped down on to the platform, just another member of the public again, and found my way out into the town with the crowd, determined to be first in the queue at the Carry Out.

By electric, diesel and steam traction I had travelled from London to Mallaig, from Euston Road to the Sound of Sleat. I had covered 619 miles in 15hrs 15mins. On Euston Road businessmen and bank clerks would be snatching a quick lunch, buskers and *Big Issue* sellers would be trying to make the price of a hot meal. The only busker in Mallaig was a wee boy sawing at a violin in the station lobby. I dropped 50 pence in his case, hoping that it went some way to helping him get what he wanted; though even if you were poverty stricken, you wouldn't want for much in a paradise like this. Then I went and said a quick hello to Sonia Cameron, the nice lady at the Boat

House, a harbour-side glory hole of gifts and outdoor clothing. In the harbour, Caledonian MacBrayne's *Lord of the Isles* was getting ready to cross the Sound of Sleat to Armadale on the Isle of Skye. I savoured my fish & chips from a brown paper bag. The rain hung like a net curtain over the smudged outline of Skye; sea the colour of prep school socks. Not so much the Sound of Sleat, more the Sound of Silence.

Useful Contacts

Caledonian Sleeper - Tel: 08457 550033

West Coast Railway Company - Tel: 01463 239026

Fort William Tourist Information - Tel: 01397 703781

Glenfinnan Station - Tel: 01397 722295

Mallaig Tourist Information - Tel: 01687 462170

The Boat House - Tel: 01687 462604

Caledonian MacBrayne - Tel: 01687 462403

"ROGART"

Remembering camping coaches. Frank Roach and the Highland Rail Partnership. The Inverness Sleeper. The Far North Line: Inverness to Rogart. Tutti Fruitti at Tain. sleep-erzzz at Rogart. The Far North Line: Rogart to Thurso.

Do you remember Camping Coaches? There was a time when barely a seaside siding, barely a dale or glen didn't boast one or two elderly carriages, pensioned off from the real business of rolling stock and converted to sleep various permutations of holidaymakers. This inspirational concept originated with the London & North Eastern Railway in 1933 and the other three-quarters of the 'Big Four' were soon proving that imitation is the sincerest form of flattery. Like all brilliant ideas, it was devastatingly simple. Obsolete coaches, converted to provide living and sleeping accommodation (including cooking facilities), were strategically sited at locations likely to appeal to holiday-makers. In common with the publishing of guide books, it was a subliminally effective means of increasing rail travel, for in

121

most cases holidaymakers travelled to the site by train and often used the railway for local touring as well.

Before the Second World War came along to spoil the fun, the best part of a hundred scenically placed stations in Scotland had camping coach facilities provided by the LNER and LMS. During the war many of the vehicles were used for 'emergency' accommodation. After it, they flourished again, until Beeching intervened and the railways reinvented themselves: no longer did they seemingly exist to provide a transport service to the general public and industry; henceforth they were to be a firm of chartered accountants. The big business of hotels and shipping, the more modest activities like luggage in advance, refreshment rooms, packed lunches, racing pigeon carrying, guide book publishing and documentary film making - fell foul of the 'bottom line'. Camping coaches were one of those victims. The last one in Scotland closed its doors on the unswept crumbs of its final campers in 1969.

It took an enterprising young couple from Bristol to revive the tradition. Frank and Kate Roach came upon the empty station at Rogart, on the Far North line, on a cycling holiday in the early 1990s and never looked back.

"We'd been living on a narrowboat at the bottom of the Caen Hill flight on the Kennet & Avon Canal near Devizes. I was teaching at a school for naughty boys, Kate was in organic horticulture."

This was Frank talking as he chopped wood, collected eggs, erected a sign, and made me a cup of tea before taking the evening train down to Inverness to catch the Caledonian Sleeper, at the start of a marathon twenty-two hour journey, with daughters Lettie and Felicity, to visit his parents in Cornwall. A busy man! Having come to the Highlands for a quiet life, he now finds himself Rail Development Manager for the Highland Rail Partnership, an affiliation of local authorities, enterprise bodies and rail businesses determined to maximise the role that rail can play in transport north of the Highland Boundary Fault. Their work is reflected in the fact that all year round Sunday services now operate on the Kyle of Lochalsh and Far North routes.

Frank has acquired an office in the old station building at Lairg, so more and more of the task of running the camping coaches falls to Kate. The week I'm about to describe was our second at Rogart. Serendipitously, Karen had booked one of the coaches for a holiday in 2000 and, because her husband, Richard, was away captaining his propane tanker on the high seas, we'd been invited along to fill some of the empty berths. There were seven of us in the end and we had one of the holidays of our lives. Our usually ambitious plans to range fully over a district, diluted every day. We became perfectly happy just to mooch about the station, soaking up the atmosphere of a country branchline. I had a morning ritual that year which I was looking forward to repeating. I would rise at six-thirty, make a cup of tea, take it out on to the platform and wait for the Safeway train to come along the glen, on its way to Georgemas Junction where its containers, loaded at Mossend from Safeway's distribution depot at Bellshill near Glasgow, would be transferred to lorries for the supermarkets at Kirkwall, Wick and Thurso.

In a perfect world all goods would go like this. On some mornings this year, the Safeway train hauled extra covered vans (VKA's to aficionados) conveying building materials for Dounreay and metal parts for a refrigerator manufacturer near Wick. Frank was ambitious to add to this traffic on the Far North Line. Already there are firm plans to collect timber from Kinbrace (overnight from a lineside loading bank to avoid the cost of siding provision) and deliver oil to Lairg. Frank is also keen to develop the sidings adjacent to his new office into a multi-purpose rail terminal, with the worthwhile aim of lightening the roads of juggernauts and greening the Highlands for a sustainable future.

In the good old days the railways would sell their camping clients an inclusive ticket covering both travel and rental. In 2000 we'd been faced with a tedious car journey from the English midlands, necessitating the expense of an overnight stay in the Scottish Borders. This time we caught the sleeper from Crewe and thoroughly enjoyed the experience, despite the need to stay up until midnight. In the morning we gathered in the well appointed lounge car, enjoying the Highland Main Line's journey through Kingussie, Aviemore and Carr Bridge, before reaching Inverness at eight-thirty. Highly civilised, until we came unstuck against the iron will of an uncooperative receptionist at the Royal Highland Hotel (née Station Hotel) who wasn't prepared to store our not excessive hand luggage for two or three hours, in return for the purchase of eight breakfasts at £8.95 a head. Costa's coffee shop came to our rescue, performing the same function with a friendly smile at a fraction of the cost. I don't suppose they'll thank me if I encourage you to imitate us, but until we create the kind of society where luggage can be stored for short periods without fear of terrorism - which is why there are no longer any Left Luggage facilities on Inverness railway station - tourists have to make their own arrangements.

Luggage difficulties apart, it was no kind of chore to wait two or three hours in Inverness for a connecting train to the Far North. Inverness is simply one of the most appealing medium sized towns I know, either side of the border. The station is centrally placed, so that you can quite literally be in the main shopping thoroughfares within seconds of leaving the concourse. After our coffee we separated into groups of specialised interest: the teenage girls, Tamar and Emily, making a bee-line for the shops, Jackie, Karen, Richard and Robyn heading for McDonalds, whilst Eden, my ten year old son and I repaired, as is our wont, to the nearest secondhand bookshop; he for the sports shelves, me for topography and transport.

Leakeys, on Church Street, is one of my favourites. It's housed in an old Gaelic chapel. After Culloden, wounded Jacobites were tended here until Hanoverian troops discovered them and dragged them out and shot them against the wall of the neighbouring High Church. Leakey's claims to be Scotland's 'largest' secondhand bookshop, an unnecessary vanity, because it's the quality of its stock which counts, and I seldom go away without one or two valuable new additions to my library. The gallery contains a cafe where you can flip through your new acquisitions over a plate of Orkney herrings if the mood so takes you.

But Eden and I had to join the others at the station in time for the 11.27. We walked quickly along the south bank of the Ness and back into the town centre where a lone piper was playing an unnecessary lament in the midst of such fine surroundings. With twenty minutes still to go, the 2-car 158 was already filling up. We managed to requisition eight seats in the first class section at the front of the train. The year before Frank had taught us that all trains north of Inverness are declassified. Keep that secret to yourself! The sleeper locomotive, 47733, was still waiting to go back to the depot for the day. A herring gull was sitting on the roof of the cab and didn't bat an eyelid when the driver fired the engine up and it was engulfed in a black pall of burnt diesel fumes.

A dad and his wee boy watched us out, wheels squealing round to Rose Street Junction. Highland Haulage were loading Safeway containers onto flats for the evening train back to Mossend. We crossed the River Ness where, just downstream, a coaster called *Border Jouster* lay at the quayside. Apparently oil and rock salt come into Inverness by sea, and timber goes out. It was good to see a little port busy with shipping. Later in the week I saw three small ships in the docks simultaneously. Behind the harbour, Kessock Bridge carries the A9 over the narrows which separate Moray and Beauly firths.

At Clachnaharry, the line crosses the Caledonian Canal by way of a swingbridge whose operation is controlled from a little timber signalbox. From my seat on the right hand side of the train I glanced towards the canal's exit lock down into Beauly Firth, and saw a yacht preparing to pass down into the freedom of saltwater. People were talking about how busy the train was for a Monday. The eight of us were lucky to be in close proximity. A man across the aisle from me was reading a hefty tome called *Vermeer & The Delft School*. Perhaps he'd just bought it in Leakeys. He had something from the Deutsche Grammaphon label on his personal stereo, and with his gold rim spectacles and wavy grey hair looked the complete aesthete. In contrast the woman across the table from me was filling in a puzzle book, and I was wondering where my next meal was coming from.

The tide was out in the Beauly Firth, exposing what in England would be called saltings, though I suspected the Scots might have another expression for it; other than 'bluidy mud' that is. A heron was hunched over the water's edge waiting for his lunch to come along. Across the neap water channel the Black Isle rose enchantingly to the heights of Mount Eagle. At the marshy head of the firth a girder bridge carried us over the River Beauly. Just as I'd been about to leave home, a fax had arrived from Railtrack to say that work on the re-opening of Beauly station was about to begin. It was one of Frank Roach's babies, part of his ambitions for an 'Invernet' commuter scheme. The £200k project for a 15 metre platform of innovative, low cost design was being funded by the Strategic Rail Authority, ScotRail, the Highland Council, Inverness & Nairn Enterprise and the Highland Rail Partnership. The original station had closed to passengers in 1960, but Beauly's population has increased since then, and as most of the new houses are within walking distance of the new platform, Frank was optimistic that passenger figures would be favourable.

If Beauly was getting a brand new station, Muir of Ord's looked in dire need of at least a makeover. Dereliction hung in the air, belying the pleasant resonance of the name. A big grey, asbestos clad silo was being demolished. I imagined it must once have been connected with the local whisky trade, in the days when the railways played a part in that business too. The Black Isle branch line ran from Muir of Ord to Fortrose. It opened in 1894 and was intended to run as far as Rosemarkie. The final passenger train ran in 1951 and the last goods train nine years later. The refreshment trolley came round, and I bought a breast of chicken sandwich advertised as containing less than 350 calories, because my wife had started drawing tactful attention to my girth; the rest of them, you'll recall, already having gorged themselves in McDonalds.

Two or three fishermen were standing waist high in the River Conon where Telford's once graceful road bridge has been replaced by a flat concrete and steel span. A black dog ran across a thistly field to bark us ceremoniously into Dingwall, a handsome Highland Railway station at the junction of the Far North and Kyle of Lochalsh lines. Later in the week I had to change trains here and confirmed this initial favourable response. It dates from 1882 replacing the original station opened twenty years earlier which traffic had outgrown. The booking hall was shut, but I peered through the windows into a spacious wood-lined public area. ScotRail seem prepared to take more care with their stations than some of the railway franchisees south of the border. One wing at Dingwall is occupied by a very pleasant looking tea room and craft shop, whilst, at the north end of the main platform, there's an 'all day' bar called The Mallard which seems to act like a magnet to townsfolk as well as travellers. The front of the station is overlooked by a big pink Free Church of Scotland kirk, and the space between hosts a poignant war memorial to the Seaforth Highlanders who fell at the Battle of Cambrai in the Great War. An extra memorial commemorates one John Meikhill of Nitshill station, killed on July 20th 1918, and I couldn't for the life of me work out why a Glasgow & South Western employee would be so remembered deep in Highland Railway territory. Whatever the reason, it seemed appropriate that the front of the station now incorporates a Christian bookshop.

Ross County's football ground overlooks the northern end of Dingwall station. We'd come down from Rogart the previous summer to watch them play Albion Rovers. We had two pies each. The train pulled away, then stopped almost immediately to effect a radio token exchange. Apart from the swingbridge cabin at Clachanharry, there are no signal boxes north of Inverness now, both the Far North and Kyle lines being worked by RETB. I watched the line to Kyle curve away through the opposite window over the shoulders of the Vermeer enthusiast, then turned my attention to Cromarty Firth as the train gathered speed towards another new road crossing, slicing miles off the railway's rival. But in landscapes as beautiful as these, speed is not necessarily of the essence.

The tide was making by Foulis Point. Suddenly the firth

seemed full of oil rigs. They looked surreally out of place in this inland anchorage. The next stop's Alness - later in the week I learnt it's full of displaced Glaswegians, and that some of them have brought less pleasant lowland attributes with them, like drug-related crime. Perhaps naively, I hoped that the landscape would, in time, rub off on them enough to eradicate such ills. Invergordon is another workaday community, chiefly remembered as a great naval base and the scene, in September 1931, of a two day mutiny caused by the threat of a reduction in naval pay. The Depression was at its height and the Government proposed cutting the income of all military personnel by 10%. Not a great deal where officers were concerned, but critical to the finances of other ranks. It's the maintenance of North Sea rigs that concerns Invergordon's seaward side now, whilst inland a huge distilling, blending and bottling plant dominates the scene. The Highland Rail Partnership's proposal for the provision of a rail link to serve these industries, has met with considerable local opposition. Nimbys, perhaps, are not a phenomenon confined to South-east England.

Cromarty, a lovely little town on the tip of the Black Isle, can be seen as the train leaves Invergordon. The last car ferry on the old road route to Wick plies between Cromarty and Nigg on the north shore of the firth. We'd driven home that way last year, thoroughly enjoying the brief voyage on the maximum of two vehicles vessel, our eyes peeled for the dolphins which besport themselves in these waters. Now, on a lengthy straight, the train was running very quickly, so that the second axle of each bogie was hitting the rail joints just a fraction of a second after the first, giving rise to a pulsating rhythm that any rock drummer would be proud of. They were haymaking with a tractor by Milton. The stations at Delny, Kildary and Nigg all disappeared from the timetable on June 13th 1960 - I wonder if it was a Friday! - but Fearn remains open, a worthwhile railhead for a scattering of small communities reaching up to Tarbat Ness. In the *Press & Journal* that very morning I'd read that one of my heroes, John Byrne, the Paisley born artist and writer - creator of the sublime television dramas *Tutti Fruitti* and *Your Cheatin'*

Heart in the late Eighties - was now living in Fearn and exhibiting at Brown's Gallery in Tain. I beat a path to that very door the next morning and admired his work, alongside that of Neil MacPherson and Gordon Brown, the gallery owner, promising to return with my cheque book should the sales of *Railway Holiday in Scotland* sufficiently enrich me. Apparently, if I'd been there in the afternoon, there would have been a good chance of meeting John Byrne face to face. "He'd have played you some of the songs from *Your Cheatin' Heart* on his guitar," Gordon had told me. I'm not sure I could have coped with the excitement.

Tain is an ancient and lovable town. It's Scotland's oldest Royal Burgh, a status which goes back to 1066, of much greater significance than some other event that year which took place south of the border. It squats on a low hill, and in the time the train calls at Tain station you catch an inviting glimpse of turrets and steeples which make it look like something out of a fairytale. The fact that it can support a classy art gallery tells you what sort of place it is. Back at the station - empty at the time of my journey, but due to be refurbished as a centre for the performing arts - I was drawn to the Gaelic version of Tain, Baile Dhubhthaich, reckoning that if I'd suddenly woken with a jolt as the train came to a halt, I'd be thinking I was in Albania or the Balkans.

Glenmorangie's famous and picturesque distillery lies beside the line on the northern outskirts of Tain. I am not a whisky drinker but I know a good malt when I see one. My only sadness is that, in common with many distilleries in the North-east of Scotland which stand alongside working railways, no use of rail is made for the inward carriage of ingredients or the outward logistics of the finished product. Further evidence of road's near monopoly of transport was just about to manifest itself. The Dornoch Firth road bridge dates from 1991. At the time of its construction it was seriously suggested that a dual purpose road/rail bridge should be provided and some ten miles of new rail route built to serve the area's largest town of Dornoch, rejoining the existing line south of Golspie. Had it come to fruition, half an hour could have been cut from the Inverness-Wick/Thurso journey time, and the railway would have been in a much stronger position to compete with coaches. At the time the cost was peanuts - £5.5m, half of which would have been put up by Common Market grants, but British Rail were unable to present a sound enough financial case for the project, and only road transport benefited from the new bridge. When I asked Frank what he thought about it he was sanguine.

"Some people accuse me of self-interest, living at Rogart station and working now at Lairg, but I don't believe time considerations are that critical. In any case, if some future initiative routed the railway through Dornoch, the inland route would make a great steam railway!"

Dead right Frank, I thought, and anyway what do those motorists do with the time they save? They park their cars and wonder what to do next, unable to define the difference between tourism and pilgrimage.

Glistening sands, oystercatchers reflected in glassy tide-abandoned pools, these are the railway traveller's dividend - who needs speed? Wanting to shorten the journey would be like wanting to abridge *War and Peace*. From the south bank of Dornoch Firth you can look due north to the Mound Rock, ten miles as the crow flies, thirty-five by train. Indeed, the thrusting firths and other natural obstacles serve to double the distance by rail from Inverness to Wick and Thurso. The eye tends to be drawn to the Dornoch Firth between Tain and Ardgay, but I always make a point of looking inland, between Easter and Wester Fearn points, at where the building of the railway on a causeway has obviously created a small loch. On the morning in question it had the sheen of satin. Three or four swans were asleep on it, their slender necks bent round on their backs, a visual realisation of *Swan Lake*.

On one of my boyhood Highland journeys we watched salmon being netted at Bonar Bridge. Its station is now called Ardgay, with the last syllable being pronounced to rhyme with 'guy'. I peered through the boles of platformside trees to an inviting prospect of rippling water, wondering if I was alone in being tempted to alight at each and every station. Culrain and Invershin stations are only thirty-six chains apart. The former is much the busier, being the point at which large numbers of backpackers detrain for the Youth Hostel housed in the impressive Scots Baronial surrounds of Carbisdale Castle. Between the two stations the line crosses the Kyle of Sutherland by way of the wrought-iron, lattice truss Oykel Viaduct. Of course it's best appreciated from below, a good reason for asking the guard to put you off at the request stop of Invershin.

It's a steep climb through Lairg to the 488ft high summit of this section of line. When it opened in 1868 it was known as the Sutherland Railway, and you will still see the intertwined initials 'SR' engraved on some of the stations' stonework. The train plunges into dense woodland, becoming luxuriantly wrapped in bracken and ferns which caress the carriages as they pass, throwing up fronds in abandon, like Mexican waves. We pulled into Lairg (from where the postbus runs, through the glens and faraway, to the *ultima Thules* of the north-west coast) and found Frank and his assistant, Alison Cavender, plus Conrad, a local lad from Rogart who helps out, all waiting on the platform. All that was missing was a pipe band. Frank was his usual ebullient self, and yet a self-effacing master at making everyone feel at home. Alison came and sat next to me and we got on like a 999 call. No one was in any doubt that the holiday had begun!

Lairg Summit lies a couple of miles beyond the station. Before you reach it there are panoramic views in a north-westerly direction towards Lairg itself and Loch Shin beyond. The summit marks the watershed between the rivers Shin and Fleet and, having been travelling north you suddenly find yourself travelling east. Strath Fleet is a little slice of heaven. We're in crofting country now and the emptiness of the upper valley gives way to a human landscape of houses and farms. We swayed into the loop at Rogart and there was much clambering to clear our bags and make for the door. Karen and I were staying on the train as far as Brora, where we'd arranged to collect a hire car from Russells Garage. The rest deposited themselves on Rogart's low platform. All the bags were placed on an old-fashioned porter's trolley and wheeled away by Conrad as the train pulled out with Karen and me smugly reflecting that the rest would have the responsibility of unpacking.

It was their most onerous duty of the week. While I worked, the rest disported themselves around Sutherland and Easter Ross and drank heavily. Frank and Kate are still receiving counselling for the number of bottles they had to take to the recycling centre at the end of the week. For my part I effectively became a commuter, disappearing north or south on the first train of the day, and returning, more often than not, on the last. As commuting goes it wasn't onerous. If I was going south on the 08.35 - a through train from Wick to Aberdeen - I'd have Alison for company. She and her husband John, a deep sea fisherman, had just moved from Edinburgh, but she already seemed well assimilated in the vicinity, happily chatting with small knots of locals who seemed to appear down from the hills to catch each train. It was refreshing to be in a neighbourhood where the railway mattered so much. Each time a train drew in was like a family gathering. Laughter and jokes flew thick and fast. Travelling back from Brora on our last day, having deposited the car, the driver and guard fooled Karen into believing that Rogart didn't qualify as a request stop on Fridays. One evening I returned from Dingwall with the sexagenarian Mr Mackay, who'd been to Inverness to have some stomach ulcers looked at. He took some delight in describing the length of pipe they pushed down his throat and other even more unthinkable elements of the technique involved. I was more comfortable with his shopping expedition to Burton's, the purchase of three shirts for the price of two and the making of a further appointment for the measuring of a bespoke suit, Mr Mackay being, and I'm sure he won't mind me saying this, of less than average height. It became apparent that he had missed the lunchtime train back on account of 'a wee dram'. A wee dram that had of necessity multiplied severalfold when he was forced to wait for the teatime train. More wee drams might have ensued had the catering trolley made an appearance. I had visions of Mr Mackay and me staggering off the train at Rogart singing *I Belong to Glasgow.*

At the beginning of the week the distaff side considered it necessary to drive over to Dornoch for the provisioning of our party. By the end of it they were coming round to the view that Rogart's post office stores dispensed all the necessities that civilisation offered. The 'Pittentrail Inn' also felt the benefit of our custom. Hector, the womenfolk assured us, had shed a good few pounds since the previous year, but the haggis, neaps & tatties tasted just as sublimely good. Richard even took to sloping off for a lunchtime pint while the rest's backs were turned, much to the chagrin of Tamar and Emily, who felt that a man should not be allowed to drink alone.

Frank and Kate's accommodation, marketed under the inspired name of sleeperzzz.com, consists of two ex Network South-east Mark II corridor first class carriages, a Class 127 multiple unit driving brake trailer, a single-decker bus and a fairman's trailer. We booked the same Mark II for the second year running. All seven compartments have been kept intact, four with double bunks facing their original rows of three first class seats, one as a dining room, one as a kitchen, and one in its original 3 x 3 state as a sitting room. Most of the compartments still feature Edward Pond's illustrations of East Anglian landscapes, a sure sign that this particular carriage must once have worked regularly out of Liverpool Street, to Kings Lynn, Norwich or Parkeston Quay. Seeing them again reminded me how Mr Pond's work used to be signed Edward in first class and plain Eddie in standard class. At either end of the carriage the toilets have been retained and showers added. Many of you will know that we have spent many years travelling the English canals, but no boat we ever had was as comfortable as this.

The railway vehicles are still on tracks in what would have been Rogart station's goods yard. Kate has transformed the old loading dock into a charming garden with lamps and benches. She has plans to turn the redundant signal box into a greenhouse and conservatory. Various old items of railway infrastructure add interest to the station platforms: a tablet catcher, a re-railer and the upturned sharpened point of one of the old timber piers from the original Ness Viaduct. The station building itself dates from the line's opening, but looks as if it has always been there: a farmhouse perhaps, appropriated by the Sutherland Railway; but of course this is just me being fanciful, it is simply the railway builder's vernacular sensitivity to the spirit of Strath Fleet manifesting itself. Not something we would necessarily be quite so good at now.

I went up to Thurso on a warm July afternoon, running out past the empty mills and the rotting sheep pens. Through the strath, past fields of freshly baled hay, the train sped on to The Mound, formerly the junction for Dornoch which lay at the end of an extremely picturesque branch; three miles of estuarial wandering beside Loch Fleet followed by a clifftop run past Embo to a dainty little terminus, whose booking office remains intact as an ice cream-serving cafe. The line was abandoned in 1960, by which time the motive power was curiously being provided by light-weight Western Region pannier tanks. L.T.C. Rolt and P.B.Whitehouse travelled over the line in the early Fifties, recounting their experience in *Lines of Character*. They'd breakfasted, on the way up from Inverness, in an inlaid veneer lined ex-Caledonian Pullman dining car which was shunted off the Wick train at The Mound to replenish its water and gas supplies before returning south and serving lunch to another set of hungry travellers. Rolt was delighted to find the Dornoch train being hauled by a Peter Drummond 0-4-4 tank, and I know the canal enthusiast in him would have responded to crossing Loch Fleet on Thomas Telford's causeway.

The First Duke of Sutherland's statue presides over Golspie like Christ presides over Rio de Janeiro, though in this case the figure is perhaps not held in such affection, for he was a bit of a tyrant when it came to replacing people with sheep, one of the worst perpetrators of the Highland Clearances. Karen and Robyn climbed Ben Bhragaidh to pay their respects, so to speak, and found the Duke with his head in the clouds, which is perhaps the kindest way one might describe him in life. My train ran into Golspie. The guard chivvied a backpacker off the train as if to say: "Go on, one foot in front of another, you'll be alright so long as the natives don't cook you for supper." It's hard to know what he was so nervous about, for according to the local web site: 'Golspie is an ideal centre for those wishing to get away from it all and offers an excellent base from which to explore the far North of Scotland'.

A steep 1 in 60 gradient delivers you out of Golspie and into Dunrobin Castle, a sweet little summer only request stop predominantly used by visitors to the not un-Disney-like seat of the Earls of Sutherland. The delightful, half-timbered confectionery box of a station was provided privately for the Third Duke of Sutherland who had been so supportive of the railway's march towards Caithness. His predecessor's statue watches protectively over it from the opposite side of the line. Once there was a tiny engine shed here to house his private engine, whilst I think I'm right in telling you that the Duke had special dispensation to drive locomotives along the line whenever the fancy took him; and apparently it often did. Scratch the surface of any omnipotent man and you're likely to find a simple soul who wants nothing more from life than to than to be a bargee or a bus conductor or a manufacturer - in a small way - of seaside rock. Peer through the station building windows and you will see a tantalising display of railway memorabilia and ephemera provided by a group called the Small Stations Society. Curious to learn more about their activities I telephoned the number quoted in one of the windows and found myself talking to Daniel Caitlin-Brittan, the well known television producer and director whose railway-loving alter ego is the General Manager of the society. He leases Dunrobin station from the Duchess of Sutherland for a peppercorn rent and occasionally flings open its doors to the public.

For the next fifteen miles or so the line is hardly out of sight of the sea and is often very close indeed. Brora is the next stop, a lively little town with lots of interesting industries under its belt, past and present. Mr Russell marked our card for us when we went to collect the car. A tall man, with an engaging Highland lilt in his voice, we sensed that little in Brora escaped his eye. Besides, his wife's the librarian, and nothing so much gives a town's character away as the books its inhabitants read -

or, for that matter, don't read. Mr Russell recommended we visit
Brora Heritage Centre. I delegated this mission to Jackie and
Karen and they returned much enthused with sheaves of local
literature so detailed that I could have devoted this whole chapter - if not the book - to Brora. Weeks later we received further
information on the mines from a lady called Jacqueline Aitken;
they are that friendly in Brora. Oh, and according to Eden and
Robyn, the beach is beautiful as well!

Brora's industrial past reads like a roll call of commerce. I was
particularly intrigued by its coal mining pedigree, 1529 to 1974
being the precise parameters of this activity according to a fascinating book on the esoteric subject by John S. Owen. It contains archive photographs of colliery headgear which make
Brora look like Rhondda on Sea. One doesn't necessarily need
to read between Mr Owen's lines to realise that coal mining in
Brora was rarely a profitable affair. In 1951, for instance, short-
ages of coal in London resulted in stocks being despatched to
the capital by rail. All well and good you think, but read on: the
coal sold for £2.50 per ton and British Railways charged £4 per
ton for carriage. In the last few years of its difficult life the mine
went in and out of liquidation. For a while it was worked as a
miner's co-operative. In the mid-Sixties a typical annual output
was in the region of six thousand tons, the respectable daily output of a modern mine in Fife. Towards the end the coal was
worked from drifts. Floods and faults and roof-falls, together
with a dwindling workforce, made the winning of coal a harder
and harder proposition. Labour was being drawn away to more
lucrative work on the oil rigs. The last coal was won in March
1974, shortly afterwards the mine's last owner suffered a heart
attack underground and died.

Brakes on for Brora station, I looked down and saw its little
harbour as the train crossed the river - 'the only drystone harbour in the north of Scotland'. At the end of the 16th century
salt pans were established here, the salt being used to cure the
herring. Coasters of up to a hundred tons used the harbour
commercially until between the wars, bringing better coal than
Brora could manage from Fife and returning with agricultural

produce. Nowadays a few locally based boats still fish for lobster and crab whilst dolphins, otters and seals swim about the river mouth. But the station buildings are empty and graffitied and in need, like 'Alan' in Deacon Blue's *Chocolate Girl,* of some 'gentle rending'. Time, I felt, for my friend Frank to be on the case.

The railway line leaves Brora, like the railway line leaves most Scottish towns, past a golf course. Ahead of you an entrancing series of headlands jut into the sea in diminishing chromatic intensity. When the last fairway is left behind the line veers round and makes the seashore its own. I saw oystercatchers and black-headed gulls on a lonely beach. *All* the beaches were lonely, devoid even of Man Friday footsteps. The motorists on the A9 were too intent on getting to John O' Groats for a souvenir to stop and feel the sand beneath their feet. I wish there was still a station at Loth, roughly halfway between Brora and Helmsdale, where you could get off and paddle in the burn that skips down from the inland hills, and watch the herons flap slowly across the point or commune with the cormorants who huddle on the black rocks like banquet waiters between courses.

The 158s are air-conditioned, but occasionally an obliging guard will open the top hopper window for you, and on such days you can smell the tang of seaweed along the coast. I would dearly have liked to get off at Hel-ums-dale as the locals call it, but the present timetable isn't always conducive to hopping on and off at whim. My train passed a southbound unit here, and for a minute or two the photographers and the smokers alighted to pursue their respective fetishes. I had held a pristine image in my head of Helmsdale on a hot summer's day with a Pickersgill 4-4-0 simmering at the platform between shunting duties. 21st century reality was more muted. Here was another station crying out for a new lease of life as a restaurant or a suite of offices or a counselling centre for chronologically challenged railway enthusiasts.

158718 thrummed in from the north and we got away smartly, turning our back on the sea, a cathartic landscape change. Apart from one or two minor dips and let ups, the driver now faced thirty miles of climbing from almost sea level to the County March Summit of the line, 708 feet high. Strath Ullie reminded me of the Conwy Valley Line in North Wales. A similar sense of emptiness, a clear-watered river rushing down a gravelly bed. The landscape grows lonelier and lonelier, as well it might, for you are now in the heart of clearance country where the sin of ethnic and commercial cleansing is not readily redeemed. If those occasional shooting lodges you see had a conscience, their neatly chamfered walls would blush with shame. The roots of this infamy - as so often is the case - lay in defeat, in this case the defeat of the Jacobite Rebellion in 1745. To ensure that there would never be another insurrection the Government in London took steps to eradicate all Highland status and tradition. For the next hundred years the Highlanders became effectively a politically and culturally disenfranchised race; commercially too, as landowners stepped into the vacuum to make profits from sheep farming and game. Does all this sound familiar?

There is evidence of earlier inhabitants as well, hut circles, standing stones and broches - or circular defensive towers - which hint at its prehistoric occupation. At Kildonan the down platform is trackless, but still supports a derelict timber waiting room. We didn't stop at the station but we did stop at the unprotected level crossing, blowing our horn circumspectly before proceeding. Progress in this increasingly featureless landscape can be measured by the yellow-painted mileposts on the down side of the line. Gnarled rowans and lofty pines lend some vertical relief to the horizontal moorlands. A line of electricity pylons seems not so virtuous. I watched a yellow dust road snake over a hill and saw some bee-keepers by Borrobol Lodge, beyond which the line curves to cross the Helmsdale River on a simple truss girder bridge. The diesel's horn echoed with infinite melancholy in the empty glen.

Tom Rolt fell hook, line and sinker for Kinbrace station in 1951: 'Its buildings were freshly painted and colour-washed, while flower beds along the length of its platforms blazed with colour.' Let us just say that the years have not been kind. We didn't even stop. With the Bannock Burn for company the train continued northwards under the pointed summit of Ben Griam Beg, desolation growing with every beat of the wheels. Rolt likened the landscape to a dark and stormy sea. Searching for a more powerful simile, I scribbled in my notebook that the emptiness was snow-blinding. A sequence of lochs only served to emphasise the isolation, they were like the oceans of the moon.

Miles and miles of eroded snow fences accompany the line, bringing home how vulnerable the railway has always been to drifting snow. As recently as February 2001 a Sprinter was snowbound near Kinbrace for six hours. Eighteen passengers, two ScotRail crew members and a CCG catering trolley operator were eventually rescued at 1am by two workers from the Borrobal Estate, who reached the stranded train on an ex Army Snowcat. A newspaper article quoted one passenger as saying: 'There was a great community spirit on the train. The crew kept our spirits up by playing cards with us and we all shared food and drink. The snow was horrendous, and at one point I thought we were going to be there all night, which was quite frightening'.

Forsinard is another place I would have liked to fit my schedule round. Next time, I promised myself, I'd eschew the delights of Thurso or Wick and get off here instead to visit the RSPB reserve and soak up the atmosphere of the Flow Country, as these peatlands are known. According to the leaflet 'regular weekly guided peatland walks tie in to train times' which, given the paucity of the timetable, is no mean feat of organisation. The same leaflet lyrically reminds you that 'the peat beneath your feet contains seven thousand years of history', and for a moment I thought I'd read that 'the Visitor Centre looks much the same as it would have done seven thousand years ago', but then I realised that it was the *view* which hadn't changed. Well, not if you pretend to ignore the station, which is only 127 years old, a product of the locally promoted Caithness Railway, built with the help of subscriptions from the Highland Railway and the Duke of Sutherland to the tune of £50,000 and £60,000 respectively.

In the foreground the dainty little signal cabin, and in the middle distance, the Forsinard Hotel, looked equally abandoned, but there were plenty of cheerful-looking kagoul-clad walkers in and around the Visitor Centre which occupies the former station building. Five more miles of ascent, most of it at a steepish 1 in 60, lead to the summit, marked by a signboard. Then through rocky cuttings the train rattles down into Altnabreac, a small halt in the depths of a big forest. Two hikers got on here and I saw the ruined base of an old water tower from steam days. When at last the forestry plantations receded, I was able to look back over my shoulder in a south-easterly direction to the 'sugar-loaf' summit of Morven.

Scotscalder station belongs to Daniel Caitlin-Brittan, whom we encountered back at Dunrobin, and who has beautifully restored it since purchasing it from British Rail in 1988 for an unspecified sum 'plus a pound for every mile it stood from Euston'. At certain times Scotscalder is available for let through the Small Stations Society as a holiday home, and is also the occasional venue for concerts in the Northlands Festival programme of events.

"Everyone has to arrive and depart by train," Mr Caitlin-Brittan explained: "and we serve a buffet lunch; I think we had about eighty people for some opera and folk songs on the last occasion."

Subliminally, the landscape conveys a sense that journey's end is impending. Over mosslands with bog cotton flapping in the wind the line runs into Britain's most northerly railway junction at Georgemas. Rolt and Whitehouse were enraptured to find one of the last Highland Railway 'Ben' Class 4-4-0s waiting to take the Thurso portion of the train. Portions are sadly now a thing of the past, perhaps the aspect of modern rail travel in Britain whose almost total absence I regret the most. Nowadays northbound Sprinter units on the Far North Line run to Thurso and back from Georgemas before continuing on to Wick, repeating the exercise on their way back south. Back in 1951 *Ben Alder's* crew invited Rolt and Whitehouse on to the 'swaying footplate' for the ride down to Thurso. They must have been in heaven. EWS's 66110 was waiting for us to clear the single line before heading south with the Safeway train. It was unbelievably good to see a working freight train this far north. If Georgemas can have goods trains, I thought, then why not Penzance, why not Aberystwyth, why not Scarborough? A lot of genuine people like Frank Roach are working on it, but there are times when they must feel that Sisyphus had a soft option.

Our driver swapped ends and we set off on the seven mile journey to Thurso, through small fields delineated by flagstone fences. The line crosses the River Thurso and drops down into the town past a cemetery on one side and cattle pens on the other. A small timber trainshed adds dignity to Britain's most northerly terminus. For no good reason I could define it reminded me of Roscoff in Britanny; only at Roscoff the gentlemen's facilities are open to female gaze and appraisal. A runround loop remains in place for works trains and occasional locomotive hauled excursions. The timber goods shed still stands and, suitably refurbished, would make a good venue for a small interpretive centre devoted to the Far North Line. Against the buffer stop, inside the trainshed, a mural depicts Highland Railway locomotive No.68 *Caithness*. Shame it couldn't have been preserved in real life. What do you do when you get to Thurso? My grandmother's second husband, Mickey, had the answer - 'walk 'til your hat floats'.

Useful Contacts

Inverness Tourist Information - Tel: 01463 234353

Leakey's Bookshop Tel: 01463 239947

sleeperzzz.com - Tel: 01408 641343

Highland Rail Partnership - Tel: 01549 402896

Royal Mail Postbuses - Tel: 01463 256228

Brown's Gallery, Tain - Tel: 01862 893884

Dornoch Tourist Information - Tel: 01862 810400

Lairg Tourist Information - Tel: 01549 402160

Helmsdale Tourist Information - Tel: 01431 821640

Tain Tourist Information - Tel: 01862 894089
Dunrobin Castle - Tel: 01408 633177
Small Stations Society: - Tel: 0208 969 0882
Brora Heritage Centre - Tel: 01408 622024
Russell's Garage, Brora - Tel: 01408 621356
Forsinard RSPB Reserve - Tel: 01641 571225
Thurso Tourist Information - Tel: 01847 892371

THE GOOD WIZARD

"KYLE OF LOCHALSH"

Why it always rains in Kyle of Lochalsh. Dealing with friendly fellow passengers. What happened to the Strathpeffer branch. The sombre slow movement. The lively finale. No fish trains on the Sabbath. The beauty of Loch Carron. The Kyle and Harrison Ford.

Every time I go to Kyle of Lochalsh it rains. This, I'm assured, is no coincidence, just an accurate reflection of the local climate. The hackneyed joke goes:

"If you can't see Skye it's raining, if you can see Skye it will soon be raining."

So when I think of The Kyle my head tends to fill with raining songs: Billy Bragg's *The Home Front*, 'And when it rains here it rains so hard'; Randy Newman's *Louisiana*, 'Clouds roll in from the north and it starts to rain'; Bruce Springsteen's *Downbound Train*, 'Now I work down at the car wash where all it ever does is rain'.

It was on a 'downbound' train that I left Inverness for The Kyle on a damp afternoon. It was a 'through' train from Aberdeen, and thus went through the interesting and, as far as Inverness is concerned, time-honoured procedure of reversing out of the terminus's south-facing platforms as far as Welsh's Bridge Junction, before proceeding, via the Rose Street avoiding curve, on its way to the north. It's a chore rendered easier by the use of diesel units with driving cabs at each end, but it does result in the (as far as I know) unique public address announcement: "Would passengers please keep the aisle clear of themselves and their luggage so as to allow the driver to walk through the train." Note how, at the 'sharp end', we are still referred to as passengers as opposed to, in prevalent business-school-speak, customers.

Of all Scotland's scenic rail routes, I think that the Kyle line is the most tourist conscious. For all its beauty, the West Highland still has a sense of purpose and commerce about it, whilst the Far North is usually perceived as being too austere and time-consuming for the average holidaymaker's sweet-toothed palate. The two and a half hour journey from Inverness to Kyle of Lochalsh falls within the modern tourist's attention span capacity; it's the equivalent of a Hollywood epic, or a football match which goes into extra time, our multimedia-battered senses can cope with it, just, especially if the trolley attendant is conscientious enough to appear down the aisle at fairly frequent intervals. The number of times that the Kyle line gets written about or televised confirms my theory. Michael Palin immortalised it in one of the BBC's *Great Railway Journeys* when he went there to collect one of the old light blue station nameboards. It's the 'Llangollen Canal' of railway rides, and no amount of persuasion on my part is going to divert most of you to Stranraer or Sanquhar or Shotts instead.

The damp afternoon was transforming itself into a grey evening. There was a melancholy feel about the cornfields bordering Beauly Firth. Low cloud veiled the hills on the Black Isle. The elderly woman opposite me was inclined to be chatty and I had to take a firm hand with her. Of course the travel writer is always on the look out for local colour. They desire nothing more from life than to bump into fascinating characters with stories to tell. Sometimes this enthusiasm even leads to a degree of 'creative' writing. But, by the same token, even the meanest hack must leave at least one eye open for passing extravagances in landscape.

You already know all there is to know about the line as far as Dingwall. The same fishermen were still up to their waists in the River Conon, the same black dog barking madly at Dingwall. I had armed myself with two contrasting books about the Kyle line: *Rails to Kyle of Lochalsh*, a weighty Oakwood Press publication, prodigiously researched and cogently written by David McConnell; and *The Kyle Line*, an inexpensive guide book from Famedram by Tom Weir written in the days of diesel locomotive haulage on the route, and thus nearly as nostalgic in its illustrations as the archive steam views proliferating in McConnell's book. Needless to say I would have liked to have been travelling in a compartment carriage with a 37 up front, or better still a 26, or - and we're getting into the realms of wish-list here, a Black 5, or - for heaven's sake Pearson - a Skye Bogie.

"Excuse me, I couldn't help noticing the book you are reading. My husband's interested in trains and I don't know if he's got that one. The chemist in Kyle has a good selection but he's always on the look out for new ones."

I don't need to tell you where that voice came from. I held up David McConnell's book for her to see.

"Ooh, that looks a good one, I'll have to tell him about it when I get home. I've been to Inverness for the fish," she added, pointing to an array of fish food tubs now displayed on her table. She displayed each tub in turn and named its contents. I wasn't paying enough attention to tell you what they were. Neither could I determine if the food was for fish in an aquarium or whether she single-handedly felt responsible for the upkeep of all the fish in the depths of Kyle Akin. Lesser men would have become embroiled in a deep discussion regarding tropical fish, but I am the master of the polite put down, and turned my head to look fixedly out of the window, as if suddenly focussed on the landing of an alien spaceship or a group of black magic worshippers about to set fire to a sacrificial pyre in a field close by the line.

In fact there *was* something quite interesting happening out of the window: a woman was grooming a llama and turned to wave at the train with a shepherd's crook. This seemed so surreal that I almost missed Fodderty Junction, or at least its scar tissue; Fodderty being the point at which a branch line once ran under the bare neckline of Knockfarrel to the pretty little spa town of Strathpeffer. This short branch, which carried passengers from 1884 to 1946, need never have been built at all if the Kyle route, as originally conceived, had not encountered the intransigence of one Sir William MacKenzie, the owner of considerable estates in the vicinity. The proposed route would pass within a quarter of a mile of his mansion, Coul House, and Sir William - who had hitherto professed to support the new line - insisted that were it to do so the line's promoters - the Dingwall & Skye Railway Company - would have to construct an otherwise unnecessary five hundred yard long tunnel to obscure the railway from his windows. How often one reads in histories of canal and railway construction of routes being significantly diverted at the whim of powerful landowners. By what ill-gotten gain, one wonders, did they, or their ancestors, acquire this land in the first place? In the end Strathpeffer Spa was bypassed, and a new route taken to the north, which resulted in a deep cutting at Raven Rock reached by a challenging climb of 1 in 50 from each direction.

Even the Sprinter felt the ascent, its underfloor Cummins engines groaning against the grade. A massive forestry plantation engulfs the line, shrouding it in mystery. In railway terms the summit is 458 feet above sea level, but Ravens Rock itself towers another 250 feet above the track. It reminds you of the North American Rockies. You wouldn't bat an eyelid if outlaws leapt on the roof of the train and held it up at gunpoint. I sensed the unit's relief as it crossed the summit and began the descent to Garve. Conifers gave way to indigenous and deciduous birch, rowan and pine. Under the overcast early evening sky the woods seemed exaggeratedly primeval, Amazonian in their opaque density. I expected to see goblins and wizards, but instead I read about them - well a wizard anyway - for near the beginning of David MacConnell's book he makes reference to a mid-nineteenth century book by Alexander Smith called *Summer in Skye* which recounts a conversation in which the railway locomotive is described as 'the good wizard of our modern day', and continues: 'its whistle scares away filth, mendicancy and unthrift; ignorance and laziness perish in the glare of its red eye'. I couldn't have put it better myself had I lived in the era for which I was patently earmarked, some muddle in the conception department obviously resulting in my arrival almost a century late.

Escaping from the woods for a while, the line runs beside the reedy margins of Loch Garve, turning north to the village of the same name. Little Wyvis loomed in the middle distance but big brother Ben (the awesome hill) was skulking behind cloud. There's a loop at Garve and two platforms. 158713 was waiting to pass us, travelling eastbound to Elgin. A railway was authorized in 1890 to run from here to the fishing and ferry port of Ullapool, but finance was not forthcoming and the project gathered dust in deed boxes before being formally abandoned three years later. Lines proposed but never built are just as tantalising as lines closed. The lover of train travel for train travel's sake can only speculate mentally what might have been, and in this instance wonder how it would have felt to steam over the unpopulated miles through Dirrie More and down to Loch Broom.

The line runs out of Garve on an embankment past a big hotel. We were bang on time and the train began to climb again towards its second summit at Corriemuillie. Coaches were overtaking us on the A835 but nobody on the train would have swapped places simply to save time. My 1947 edition of the *Railway Magazine's* book of *Gradient Profiles* tersely puts it that speed restrictions on the Kyle line are ' too numerous to warrant their inclusion'. Twisting through trees we came to the banks of Loch Luichart. The station of that name is a utilitarian brick building dating from a deviation constructed in 1954 in association with a hydro-electric scheme. Static caravans added to the lugubrious atmosphere of the present day, though I was intrigued to read in David Connell's book that Thomas Carlyle and Robert Browning had both used Lochuichart station when visiting Lady Ashburton of Lochuichart Lodge. One trusts not simultaneously.

My neighbour had bagged up her array of fish food and was now working through a swatch of needlework silks. Inadvertently I caught her eye. Fatal.

"One of my needlework pictures has been valued at over a thousand pounds," she confided.

"I try to get as many Scottish animals into each picture as I can. I had to unpick one recently because I'd made the moose to large to start with."

Were I Paul Theroux I'd take the mickey out of her and give her a funny name, but I couldn't be so cruel. She was just being friendly, if a tad self-absorbed, and goodness knows the British could do with lessons in friendliness, though travel writers should be afforded statutory immunity against such approaches. I must get a badge made to supplement my scowl: 'I am a travel writer, back off'.

A bridge carries the railway across the head of the loch and then you see the hydro-electric power station at Grudie. Then the line essays a course between two smaller lochs before reaching the isolated request halt at Achanalt. We didn't stop but my friend assured me:

"A Siberian husky lives here, with coat you can *sink* your hands into."

To my relief she then *sank* into a crime novel by Reginald Hill, absolving me of any need to talk knowledgeably about various breeds of dogs and the comparative depth of their coats. We passed a solitary goal and net in a high-grassed field - obviously, to paraphrase the Tartan Army's sung response when Estonia failed to turn up for a football match against Scotland in Tallin, there is 'only one team in Achanalt'. Wriggling free of forestry, the train came to Strath Bran, reminding me of the wide open landscape being crossed by a tiny, lonely train in *Out of Africa*. The trolley steward came round. His name was Charles Urquhart, and I hope he won't be offended when I tell you that he'd walk away with any Robin Williams look alike competition. He'd better not be, soon I hope he and his CCG colleagues will be selling my guidebook to the Perth-Kyle route.

Nostalgia oozed out of every pore at Achnasheen. Jackie and I got out of the much lamented observation carriage here in 1980, to stretch our legs while waiting for an oncoming train to pass. Fifteen years earlier, my parents and I had been put up on sofas in the lounge of the neighbouring hotel when there was 'no room at the inn', or seemingly any other inn for a radius of fifty miles. Queen Victoria was more fortunate. She arrived at Achnasheen by special train on September 12th 1877, alighting on to a tartan-carpeted platform, and by all accounts Her Majesty was most 'amused' by the scenery she had encountered along the mountainous course of the Dingwall & Skye Railway.

Mist clung, like a white silk scarf, to the shoulders of Carn Beag. Even on a day of brilliant sunshine, I thought to myself, the emptiness of this landscape might be intimidating. Its sheer lack of detail, of something to focus on, has the affect of making it mirror-like, inducing thought processes rendered recalcitrant by lack of use. What images there are have the simplicity of naive art: I saw a yellow cow beside a lonely croft and a buzzard ripping its prey apart on a fence pole. Life reduced to its essentials. I was reminded of the well-thumbed top of page 53 in my Penguin paperback of T.H.White's *The Goshawk*, 'One had to find out what things were not necessary, what things one really needed. A little music and liquor, still less food, a warm and beautiful but not too big roof of one's own, a channel for one's creative energies and love, the sun and the moon.' And a railway at the bottom of the garden, Terence, an estuarial view, and a secure place in the midfield of a veterans' football team.

Slowly, the train crossed the last summit at Luib, 648 feet above sea level, 31 miles from Dingwall and 32 from The Kyle. A bleak halfway house if ever there was one. In the relative absence of entertainment through the window I was dipping into *Rails to Kyle of Lochalsh*, admiring the wealth of archive photographs and discovering, for example, how the line in its early days had revolutionised the west coast fish trade and brought much increased tourism in its wake; how the London Midland

& Scottish Railway - the Highland Railway's successor after the 1923 grouping of the railways - operated two restaurant car trains from Inverness to Kyle of Lochalsh and bestowed on them the names The Hebridean and The Lewisman; and how the line assumed military importance during the Second World War, Kyle itself being given the secret identity of Port ZA, mines were stored at strategic intervals in sidings along the line and large numbers of service personnel were carried through what had become a 'restricted area'.

I must have fallen asleep. The train jolted to a halt at a wayside station and woke me in the process. The rain had misted the window but the station looked oddly old fashioned. There were oil lamps and, further down the platform, what looked like milk churns awaiting collection from a wooden trolley, flower beds and enamel advertisements. It was more like a preserved railway station than the basic bus shelter and bare platform of the twenty-first century. A lot of passengers seemed to be getting off and talking to each other excitedly. I felt compelled to follow them and see what was afoot, but I didn't want to get stranded. The stationmaster was ushering people through a wooden gate, a broad beam on his face. Somewhere in the distance I could hear a piper and what sounded like singing. I imagined it must be a wedding or something. The mist was really thickening. I stood by the door deliberating.

"Is that you Tommy?" someone called out of sight, and in response a man's voice questioned, "Fiona?", followed by a sudden surge of music from goodness knows what source. Thoroughly mystified, and not a little unnerved, I returned to my seat just as the doors slid shut and the train pulled away. I pressed my face against the window trying to see if this strangely unworldly station had a name. There was just enough light shining on a sign at the end of the platform to make out the last few letters '...gadoon'. And then I realised where we had stopped and why it did not appear in the timetable, and that there was nothing for me to make a song and dance about.

Overlooked by the Munro, Moruisghe, the Class 158 loped downhill, passing a big shooting lodge on the neighbouring hillside where there was once a platform called Glencarron at which prospective passengers were expected to operate a semaphore signal to stop the train. It brought into my mind a line from Buchan's *John Macnab*, something about Lamancha being fetched under cover of night by Archie Roylance from 'a station so remote that no one but a lunatic would think of using it'. When I was twelve I wanted to grow up into someone like Sir Archibald Roylance and marry a Janet Raden, 'an authentic creature of the hills and winds'.

We swayed through a cutting of rhododendrons. It was raining now, quite heavily, obscuring the view through the window just as it was beginning to get interesting again. Several commentators have likened this journey to a three movement piece of music, and I could see what they meant, it is just like a Sibelius symphony; No.3 comes closest. We'd just completed a sombre slow movement, now we were anticipating a lively finale full of lilting rhythms and memorable tunes. More rain-lashed woodlands led to Achnashellach and an isolated request halt in the trees. This is a stop likely to appeal to serious hill-walkers, for an old deer-stalkers path, called Corrie Lair, finds its way through the Coulin Pass to Glen Torridon. The Munros, Sqorr Ruadh (3,142ft - red peak) and Maol Chean-dearg (3,060ft - bald red head) are also accessible for those suitably equipped. On the north side of the line the trees came to an abrupt end on the banks of the River Lair which was in spate. Suddenly I found myself looking up a cleft in the flank of Sgurr a' Mhuillinn reaching right into the clouds like a stairway to heaven. At Balnacra a level crossing ushers the A890 over the line, the road, despite its A status, being merely a single lane with passing places; a bit like life itself.

The River Carron pours out of Loch Dughaill, making its way towards its eponymous sea loch. At Strathcarron station there's a loop and a siding and the temptation to alight and beg, borrow or steal transportation to the earthly heaven which is Applecross. A shop and information centre occupy the former station building and there's a sizeable hotel across the road, the sort of place where they are used to visitors arriving with the aggregate moisture content of a small reservoir. There was a slight delay as our driver walked down the platform to make use of the train's toilet. Steam engine drivers had bladders built from boiler stays. Now begins eighteen miles of perhaps unsurpassed beauty when all Britain's scenic railways are taken into account. Loch Carron makes its first appearance in subdued circumstances, introducing its eastern end as a mysterious expanse of mud, rock and seaweed. Herons flap across its upturned tree stumps like something out of a weird computer game. My neighbour began to cackle quietly to herself - at a passage in her book, I hoped - and men of less resilience may well have been unnerved.

The loch grows deeper and there's a request halt at Attadale. This might have represented the original end of the line, but in the event it was decided to push further west. A bridge carries the track over the little River Attadale, and then both railway and parallel road pass through a short avalanche shelter built when the road was laid in 1971 to by-pass the ferry at Strome, one of those road building projects, like the Skye bridge itself, which only serve to dilute the essence of the Highlands. The water in the loch was so clear I could see submerged, barnacle-covered rocks laced with swaying fronds of seaweed. I was doing my best to picture the scene on a sunnier day when the view, I had no doubt, would be scintillating. It would be like a Norwegian fjord, shipped lock, stock and barrel to Scotland's western seaboard.

A change of Ordnance Survey maps, several being required for this fragmented coast, points you in the direction of Strome Ferry, the terminus of the line for no less than twenty-seven years. Baulked by the sheer cost of completing the initially proposed route through the intractable rock which faced the southern shore of Loch Carron, the builders of the railway were content to stop short at a point where a small ferry plied between the shores of Loch Carron at its narrowest. Here a small port was constructed and a pier inlaid with railway tracks built out into the loch. The terminal platform was covered by an attractive timber train shed. Steamer services were instigated to

Portree on Skye and Stornoway on Lewis. It was even suggested, as the railway was being built, that fishing boats might be hoisted on to railway wagons and conveyed from coast to coast much faster than using the Caledonian Canal or making the arduous voyage round the top of Scotland, but although successful trials were apparently carried out, this innovative scheme wasn't pursued.

Strome is chiefly remembered now for a riot which took place here in 1883, the upshot of protests from devout Presbyterians concerning the working of fish trains on the Sabbath; a sub-clause pertaining to the Fourth Commandment clearly stating that fish trains were not permitted to run on Sundays until further notice from Moses. I apologise for flippancy, the riot was very real, over a hundred and fifty angry male protesters physically prevented railway workers from transhipping freshly caught fish from the steamers *Harold* and *Lochiel* into waiting railway wagons on the pier. Eight police officers arrived by special train from Dingwall to quell the disturbance, but naturally made little impact in the face of such a large and ugly crowd. The protesters finally dispersed on the stroke of midnight, the wagons were loaded and the fish train despatched, some twenty-four hours late. In due course ten Presbyterian ringleaders were arrested and tried, and though found guilty were granted clemency on account of their clear religious beliefs. Incidentally, the Sabbathians may have lost the battle, but in a way they won the war, because another hundred years went by before the first passenger train ran on the line on a Sunday!

My own memory of Strome goes back to the days when the vehicular ferry was still operating, before that new road was built around Loch Carron's southern shore. On an early summer evening the queue for the ferry must have stretched half a mile. We were all famished, but my father heroically stayed at the wheel, slowly progressing down to the jetty, while mother and I dined in the hotel. We even had time for dessert before rejoining him at the point of embarkation, mercifully equipped with a 'doggy bag'.

In the final analysis, the completion of the railway to Kyle of Lochalsh was forced on the Highland Railway by the rival North British Company's extension to Mallaig. Strome was never an ideal port, being difficult to work at times owing to strong tidal currents in Loch Carron. The threat of competition, so often the case in the history of commercial undertakings, became the spur to action. We reap the benefit of that over a century later, and you should remember this as you ooh and aah over the ravishing seascapes revealed at every bend. Silently I indulged in my fair share of gasps as the diesel unit wound around each rocky inlet licked by the salty tongue of the tide. Gasp, there's Applecross; gasp there's Raasay (where I onced docked briefly on the Portree boat to load cattle); gasp those must be the Cuillins; gulp, imagine being on this train when there's a fine sunset on an autumn evening. If you can bear to draw your gaze away from the sea, look quickly inland, where it is necessary to crick your neck to see daylight above the towering ramparts of rock. At Duncraig I saw boats beached in a rocky creek before being unable to resist the pull of the sea. On its sheltered shoreline, I recognized Plockton, made famous by its use in the BBC television drama *Hamish MacBeth*. Yachts were peacefully at anchor and a small cruiser was giving bedraggled tourists a trip round the bay.

Plockton's neat little station has been alluringly converted into a restaurant. It was very tempting to alight here and sample its menu. Through the rainy windows I saw diners lit by lamplight looking relaxed in obviously convivial surroundings. But I had a job to do, and had to suffer for my art, there being five more miles to go. On the way round to Duirnish I saw hay being dried on a flagstone fence. Tom Weir's little guide suggested there might be crofters strips to look out for at Drumbuie, but either they had bitten the dust or my eye wasn't accustomed to what to look for.

"Has that monstrosity come into sight yet?" my acquaintance asked with a sigh. At least we shared something, mutual scorn for the road bridge which effectively ridiculed Skye's island status; the *Skye Boat Song* being more topically correct nowadays as the *Skye Shuttle Bus Song*.

Reading between the lines you will perhaps have sensed my listless reaction to the central part of the journey. It would be churlish to be critical, and I am sure the weather played a big part in my subdued response, but I think I would have been more excited on a more appropriate type of train. Many people miss the observation saloon with its running commentary which ran on the line towards the end of the diesel locomotive era. However comfortable, however cost-effective, an air-conditioned multiple-unit designed primarily, one assumes, for inter-urban and commuter routes, is not the rolling stock to do justice to the Kyle line. See if you can get yourself on a loco-hauled excursion. The Scottish Railway Preservation Society come this way regularly. So - as you are about to see - does the Royal Scotsman luxury train, but you will need a better bank balance than mine to board it.

In any case, all the melancholia of the middle evaporated like Scotch mist on arrival at Kyle. I have always been captivated by the south-facing station on its pier head. It was 1974 when I first got here by train, hauled by a chuntering Sulzer Type 2 Bo-Bo diesel which dropped me off in the rain to catch the boat to Portree. Six years later Jackie and I sought shelter in the buffet, amongst sodden fellow travellers (sodden from rain or whisky? - it was difficult to differentiate) waiting to board the packet which ran on blue moons and martyr's days through the Sound of Sleat to Mallaig.

The long, low timber station building seems totally appropriate for its setting, an holistic response to the surrounding scenery. Better appointed now, in its red, white and blue paintwork, than at any time in my experience of it, the spit and sawdust buffet has been replaced by a smart seafood restaurant, whilst, a few doors along, a craft shop and exhibition centre is also headquarters to the Friends of the Kyle Line, an enthusiastic support group determined to maximise the railway's potential in the 21st century.

My friend went off to feed her fish and I imagined her next needlework composition would feature the small figure of a scowling, uncommunicative writer cowering under a giant stag in one corner. I strolled around the wet quay as the station quietly emptied in the dreich light of the damp evening. In the other platform stood the Royal Scotsman itself, suitably soberly dressed in its maroon livery, headed by its designated locomotive, 37401. Its pampered passengers were enjoying aperitifs at the bar. I peered enviously through the steamy windows like a stranger at the gates. I felt like the man in the joke who staggers through the desert increasingly desperate for water. He meets three camel trains whose drivers cannot offer him water but would gladly sell him a tie. At last he reaches an oasis with a smart restaurant, only to be told that they won't serve anyone not wearing a tie. I heard footsteps on the platform behind me. It was Harrison Ford. A brief flicker of recognition passed between us.

"Mr Ford," I said, "It's good to meet you, I thought you were brilliant in Peter Weir's *Witness.*"

"The feeling's mutual, Michael," he replied, a tad less swashbuckling, more man next door than in *Raiders of the Lost Ark.* "I've got all your books."

Useful Contacts

ScotRail Travel Centre, Inverness - Tel: 01463 239026

Kyle of Lochalsh Tourist Information - Tel: 01599 534276

The Royal Scotsman - Tel: 0131 555 1344

SRPS Tours - Tel: 01698 263814. www.srps.org.uk

The Skye Ferry - Tel: 01599 511302

TOKEN RESISTANCE.

"ELGIN"

Departure from Aberdeen in the Sixties. The railway town of Inverurie. A musical signalman and the station kiltmaker of Insch. The beautiful countryside of Bogie. Cairnie - a lost junction. Hero worship in whisky country. The Keith & Dufftown Railway. Elgin and Nairn - two interesting towns. Beyond the bufferstops at Inverness.

Thirty-six years ago I was a thirteen year old staying with my parents in the Station Hotel, Aberdeen; free for the day to explore the Granite City's railway hinterland. In the morning I chose to go to Inverurie. I can still hear the pyrotechnic departure of the North British Type 2 diesel locomotive, echoing through tunnels and cuttings and gardens on its way north. In those days Kittybrewster was a busy diesel depot. In 2001,

I discovered, it's a council depot with refuse carts parked where, back in 1965, there were rows of NB Type 2s, an ill-starred design built in Glasgow, which didn't last much longer than the steam locomotives they had been built to replace. Now, we men of a certain age and outlook miss them, and someone has even proposed building a working replica from scratch.

Then I hadn't noticed, or had perhaps simply not been socially enough aware to realise, how bad the housing was on Aberdeen's northern periphery. Now it looks so degenerate that I am surprised it hasn't been outlawed by a Brussels' directive. It's appalling enough to make me think that I am wasting my time. Should I be swanning about writing charming little travelogues when fellow members of mankind eke out so tragic an existence?

Dyce station did little to lift my spirits. It appears to take its cue from the surrounding mediocrity of industrial units drawn, 'nae doot', by the proximity of Aberdeen's airport. I was more interested in its former status as the junction for the Fraserburgh and Peterhead routes. Passenger trains ceased running shortly after I'd passed through behind that NB Type 2; freight lasted another fourteen years. Now the trackbed - and I'm sorry if I begin to sound like a press release here - has been 'imaginatively' converted into the Formantine & Buchan Way, 'ideal for an exciting and enjoyable day out for all the family'. Do you suspect apathy, or worse, antipathy? Not so, I think Sustrans is one of the most laudable organisations in the UK, and similar local authority makeovers of old railways deserve equal praise. It's just, of course, that I believe the lines should never have been allowed to close in the first place, and I hope to live to see the day the M9 is 'imaginatively' transformed into a bridleway.

But shaking off Dyce proved easy enough. Soon we were snaking along the banks of the River Don, through meadowlands grazed by herds of what, I trusted, were Aberdeen Angus. In a lineside field stood a monument to one Duncan Liddell, 1561 to 1613, former Rector of the Julian University in Rome and Physician to the Court of Brunswick. From Kintore, a branch used to run west to Alford through Tillyfourie and Monymusk, station nameboards to die for. Apart from the fact that the terminus now houses a transport museum and a short length of narrow gauge railway, I know little about the line, and sometimes it's best that way; you can let your imagination work overtime. In my May 1950 *Bradshaw*, on Scottish Region table No.220, no trains at all are shown; a ghost line if ever there was one.

There's a big paper mill on the outskirts of Inverurie, but rusty sidings illustrate that rail freight is no longer considered a viable option. I can't remember much about Inverurie in 1965, except that I dropped a ten shilling note onto the track and had to surreptitiously leap off the platform to salvage it. The railway workshops, headquarters of the Great North of Scotland Railway's engineering activities, must have still been in operation, but with the blinkered, number-collecting outlook of a thirteen year old, I missed the chance to do them justice. Now I was about to make amends, for waiting to meet me on Inverurie's down platform was Jimmy Brown, former Supplies Officer of Inverurie Works.

Jimmy had arranged for us to have a look around part of the workshops which had been bought out of railway ownership when Inverurie closed on the last day of 1969. Cruickshanks occupy the former wagon shop, where they make control relay panels for use in high voltage sub-stations. Mike Sinclair showed us round. I was struck by the latent ambience of railway activity. In an odd sort of way the premises were more redolent of the past than if they had been deliberately transformed into a museum. We wandered about under the high ceilings, with their serrated north lights, not ideal for a modern workshop and the devil to heat in the winter. Mike showed us a lathe that Cruikshanks had bought as part of their purchase which they still occasionally use. Similarly a big Vaughan overhead travelling crane, which once would have been used to lift whole wagons, remained in working order. A notice pinned nearby reads: 'The Railway Executive - Safe working loads for chain slings'. In the panel shop the rails are still embedded in the floor. I only had to close my eyes to imagine the workshop filled with railway wagons. Jimmy, of course, would be feeling this much more than I. He showed us some storage racks made in his time from scrap timber and steam locomotive boiler tubes. Outside Mike and Jimmy showed me where a large traverser had once stood to give the rolling stock easy access into the shops. Sadly the well has been infilled with rubble and lorry trailers are parked on it now.

On retiring, Jimmy (who once played in a Glaswegian dance band) became something of a freelance writer, self-publishing several books of reminiscences concerning his days as a railwayman, his wartime experiences with the Royal Naval Patrol Service (Harry Tate's Navy), his time as an Excise Officer, and as a sub Post Office owner. He has a fund of stories from all these lives and regularly writes for Scottish newspapers and magazines. He's a born raconteur and I could have listened to him for hours. He drove me up to his house for a cup of tea and introduced me to Margaret, his wife. They met at the railway works when Jimmy was transferred to Inverurie from Glasgow in 1963. She had been his typist.

"I tell people that I was her boss and she used the typewriter. Now it's the other way round, she's the boss and I use the typewriter!"

While Margaret rustled up some tea and biscuits, Jimmy showed me some of his treasures. One was the brass figure of a fox of the kind which adorned the splashers of Gresley's 4-4-0 'Hunt' class locomotives.

"It's not off one of the engines," Jimmy admitted, "but the mould somehow ended up at Inverurie so I had half a dozen extra ones cast!"

There were many perks, it appears, attached to the job of Supplies Officer. Jimmy waved his arm around the living room to show me coffee tables, book cases and display cabinets which had been the skilled efforts of the Inverurie carpenters. I was surprised that the upholstery of Jimmy and Margaret's suite didn't bear the initials LNER. I was shown whistles and ticket clippers, and books and photographs, one showing Jimmy's brother, Frank, a St Rollox driver on the footplate of a Standard Class 5 with Caprotti valve gear, another showing his father, a

Caledonian Railway carter, with a pair of horses and a wagon at Gushetfaulds goods station circa 1914. Jimmy is a third generation railwayman, his grandfather having been employed at St Rollox works.

Margaret comes from a railway family as well. Her grandfather, James Gregor, was stationmaster at Inverurie for many years. Jimmy told me a wonderful story about Margaret's grandfather as we drove back to the station to catch my train. Apparently the Great North of Scotland Railway provided Lord Kintore of Keith Hall with a private waiting room for his personal use. The water closet, however, with due railway parsimony, was accessed by a penny in the slot device. One day his lordship was 'caught short' without the necessary penny for the slot. Margaret's grandfather 'lent' him a penny. In due course the penny was returned in the shape of a silver dish with the penny mounted in the middle bearing the inscription: 'A Friend in Need is a Friend Indeed'.

Inverurie's present station dates from 1902. It looks impressive from the approach road and the interior has been beautifully restored. The wood-panel-lined waiting room, enhanced by archive photographs in frames, wouldn't look out of place in a gentlemen's club. Jimmy and I peered through the glass of Lord Kintore's now empty private room, marvelling at the quality of the woodwork, wishing that some appropriate use might be made of it now, railway travelling dignitaries with the status to acquire their own private waiting room being in short supply in these democratic days.

Leaving Inverurie, past sidings gratifyingly full of wagons being loaded with timber, and under the benign gaze of a big timber signal box, from which the signalman on duty always seems to give a cheery wave, those with a trained eye for such things will see the trackbed of the five and a bit mile branch to Oldmeldrum curve away to cross the River Urie, perhaps noting that there still appear to be some stubborn piles remaining from what must have been the railway's bridge across the river. Barely a couple of miles further on (having passed another monument - this one commemorating a 15th century battle) yet another old railway vanishes off into the countryside, this one was the Inveramsay, Turriff and Macduff, a thirty mile byway to the north coast. Again the station names are heavenly; to hear them announced must have sounded like a psalm:

"This is Inveramsay, this is Inveramsay,
change here for Wartle, Rothie-Norman,
Fyvie and Auchterless."

Mary Queen of Scots planted a thorn tree at Pitcaple Castle in 1562. Her great-grandson, Charles II, danced beneath its boughs eighty-eight years later. So thick were the 'thorn' trees now, that I couldn't see the castle from the railway at all. Perhaps we were going too fast, perhaps I was enveloped too deeply in the comfortable Turbostar's Business Class upholstery, perhaps I was hypnotised by the telegraph poles, an almost obsolete facet of railway signalling in the twenty-first century, one of those things which disappear without us noticing. I blinked and missed the Mill of Durno too, or maybe my attention had been caught the in the opposite direction, southwards to the multi-summited Bennachie, the 'hill of breasts'! All I can tell you is that the countryside really is glorious: pristine farms, sleek cattle, neat crops, the sort of almost too perfect landscape that adorns table mats and chocolate boxes.

Insch is the smallest town still to have a station on the Aberdeen to Inverness line. The old Shell guide actually calls it a village, and goes to some trouble to describe outlying antiquities, uninterested in the pretty wayside railway station on its periphery. Thank goodness, then, for the Insch Connection, a small museum housed in the station itself which celebrates the village and its railway in a thoroughly entertaining manner. One of the trustees is John McFarlane, who also happens to be one of Insch's signalmen. John it was who built the fine OO scale model of the station which takes pride of place in the museum.

"It shows the station as it would have been in the 1930s," John told me over the telephone between trains. "We try and ring the changes with the rolling stock to show different periods. At the moment we've got a B1 in black with five British Railways 'blood & custard' carriages. Children love it when it moves slowly out of the station."

Like me, John is one of those 'Scots' upon whom fate has thrust an English accent. Unlike me, however, John wears a kilt to work, in the McFarlane tartan naturally. Everyone in the Highlands seems to have two jobs, and as well as being a signalman, John composes classical music, a recent piece being *Gelert*, a fifteen minute long composition for voice and clarsach concerning the legend of the Welsh dog charged to look after its master's baby son. Away hunting, the master has a sudden vision of his son covered in blood, gallops back, is greeted by the dog whom he immediately slays, only to find the baby safe by the body of a wolf killed by the faithful dog. John has worked at Insch box for seventeen years and, even over the telephone, his enthusiasm was infectious. A traditionalist at heart, he obviously enjoys working on a line still using semaphore signalling.

"I must tell you, though, that Railtrack are just replacing the distant signals with colour lights, and I don't mind a bit, I had about a mile of wire to pull to work those!"

Other modernisations are appreciated too. Insch signal box dates from around 1860 but John told me it had been refurbished last summer and the opportunity taken to put in a toilet.

"So we don't have to run down the platform anymore," he laughed.

He can, however, just nip down the platform to have his kilts made, for Insch railway station is pretty unique in being the home of a kiltmaker. Muriel Jonassen moved into the station in 1997 after it had been refurbished. She occupies the former Ladies waiting room and learnt her trade at the Keith Kilt School. The Gordon is a favoured local tartan. Her customers hail primarily from in and around Insch but she has made kilts for people as far away as America. Sometimes her location at the railway station has unforeseen advantages.

"I've had people waiting to catch a train to Aberdeen to go and buy a kilt, see I'm here and not bother to get on the train," Muriel told me. "It's endlessly entertaining here. You should see folk's faces when they come in expecting to buy a ticket but find a lady sewing instead! We have won the 'Most Passenger

Friendly Unmanned Station Award' twice, which might seem like a contradiction, but I don't think so. We're proud of our village and the village is proud of its station."

Heartwarming stuff! And, moreover, just as it should be if communities would recognise the 'shop window' value of their stations. Also, if I ever need a kilt making I know where I'll go and how I'll get there for my fitting sessions!

For five miles west from Insch you are on double track, what in modern railway jargon they call a 'dynamic loop'; that is, one where trains can pass on the move. A striking tower overlooks the line about a mile out of the station, on the north side. This is the surviving remnant of the Castle of Dunnideer, a medieval tower on a prehistoric rampart. In the 13th century it belonged to Sir John de Balliol, whose wife, the Lady of Galloway, founded the Oxford college in her husband's memory. The dynamic loop has a 'wee burn' for company, its banks thick with meadowsweet in late July when I passed by. I had a flashing glimpse of an old station building, its name 'Wardhouse' still resplendent in gilt lettering on the glass window, in Great North of Scotland Railway fashion, above the booking hall. There's an abandoned station at Kennethmont as well (of timber construction) where the loop ends under the watchful eye of a signal box. We came to a halt here, the semaphore signal horizontally barring our way while, on the up line, the corresponding red and white arm was at forty-five degrees, heralding the passage of a train. In our air-conditioned cocoon it was not possible to hear all the birds of Banffshire and Aberdeenshire, 'mistier and mistier', but it was pleasant to be at peace for a moment in such congenial countryside. Presently, 158725 swished by Aberdeen bound. Its 'home' signal dropped and ours rose, seconds later we were away, crossing the point by Teacher's Distillery, rusty sidings *de rigueur*.

The landscape was as well-upholstered as my Turbostar, I might go as far as writing, luxuriant. Two people waved contentedly from their veranda, surrounded by big fields of barley for all that whisky. The fall and rise of the telegraph wires, the four beat rhythm on the rail joints, the variegated greens of field and hedge and wood left me in a trance. Forget the modernity of the rolling stock, this *feels* like a traditional railway. A well-honed Yellowlees aphorism came into my mind, something about the Aberdeen-Inverness's unique combination of a sense of heritage with a sense of relevance.

The train went spinning downhill overlooked by sensuously bare summits - Tap o' Noth, Hill of Kirkney, Hill of Collithie. Farms in the valley of the Water of Bogie are called the 'Mains of this', the Mains of that'; a foreign language. Due north past Gartly, another gilt-edged forgotten station, and now the Water of Bogie has become the River Bogie: buzzards wheeling over woodland and cattle impervious to our progress. Under Clashmach Hill we came to Huntly, greeted by a small signal cabin and some sidings which actually look used. On this occasion only a solitary EWS covered wagon was in residence, though I know for a fact that timber is loaded here. The two-platformed station is neat and features a new booking hall with reconstituted tiles for its roof. The town lies to the west, laid out in a grid-iron pattern in the 18th century under the patronage of the Gordons.

Downhill, again, with the River Deveron, crossed by a viaduct after two or three miles, as it meanders away on its journey to the sea at Banff. A tributary, the Isla, takes its place; how the railway builders relied upon their river valleys. The Isla flows southwards, so we must be climbing. Climbing to the ghosts of Cairnie Junction, long lost nodal point of the Great North of Scotland system. Here, at an island platform out in the wilds, the train from Aberdeen would be divided into three, one portion going directly forward to Inverness as we will, a second to Elgin via Keith Town and Craigellachie, the third (most romantically) on a long coastal hike, calling at places - too numerous to list in their entirety - like Tillynaught, Portsoy, Portknockie, Findochty, Buckie, Port Gordon, Spey Bay and Urquhart, before arriving at Elgin the best part of an hour after the Inverness direct portion had passed through.

Cairnie must have been tantamount to a train-watcher's paradise. The 1950 timetable is Byzantine in its complexity. I can pore over it for hours, perplexed by its diversity, entranced by its footnotes. In *Trains Illustrated* July and August 1956, W.A.A. Bremner wrote about the Aberdeen-Inverness route's contemporary operating practices, tantalising me now with talk of fish vans being attached to passenger trains, coal going into distilleries, animal fattening by-products coming out, the Cairnie portions being run as full trains on Winter Saturdays when Aberdeen were playing at Pittodrie. The current Ordnance Survey's Landranger Map 29 doesn't even name Cairnie, there's nothing there *to* name, just the merest hint of a trackbed swerving north-eastwards through the trees before you cross the boundary between Aberdeenshire and Moray.

There was a station at Grange as well, and a loop to the coast line to facilitate through working from Keith. You know you're closing in on Keith when you start seeing small mountain ranges of stacked (but empty!) whisky casks in compounds beside the line. A passing loop is inconveniently sited east of the station which was V shaped with bays facing east. Here the Great North of Scotland handed over to the Highland; here I got off to meet a hero. He was left high and dry by the diminishing, post departure crowd, obviously the man who had come to meet me, though we hadn't met face to face before. He was George Behrend, author of *Gone With Regret*, the best book ever written about the Great Western Railway; a cast iron nominee for the best book ever written about a railway, anytime, anywhere.

I paid homage to George in *Coming Up With The Goods*, hardly expecting to receive a telephone call from him out of the blue. It was, how can I put it, like getting a call from Beethoven to say he was glad you liked his Fifth Symphony. Furthermore he was nice about my book, the hero had become the fan. Thereafter we had spoken regularly on the telephone, but not, until this moment, met. I was in two minds whether to go down on the platform saying "I am not worthy, I am not worthy," or not. In the end I just shook his hand. It emerged that he had arranged a whistlestop tour of the emergent Keith & Dufftown Railway, and a meeting with its Managing Director, Peter Bradley.

We drove along the B9014 in George's car. On page 75 of the third edition of *Gone With Regret* it says, of a road in the Forest of Dean: 'There are so many bends one can never look at the scenery'. Sound advice that the author, thirty-seven years after writing those words, appeared to have outgrown. Not finding anything to cling on to, I clung on to myself as bend succeeded bend and George pointed out the Keith & Dufftown's picturesque passage through Strathisla and Glen Fiddich. He harmonised this sight-seeing with personal reminiscences interspersed by an engaging sequence of chuckles. I learned of his first encounters with the Great Western at Highclere on the Didcot, Newbury & Southampton line at the age of three in 1924; of his school years at Marlborough, where he memorised bus timetables and made jam; of Oxford, where he gained an MA Hons. with a thesis on the Area Bus Agreement of 1913 (buses being his second love); and of his time with the 8th Army in Egypt, Libya, Tunisia, Algeria, Greece and Italy. Of Anglo-German descent (with family origins in the Electorate of Hanover) he farmed in Hampshire before moving to Jersey in 1956 (prior to immigration being restricted to the wealthy) and married in 1960. In the Channel Islands he wrote - sixteen titles, mostly of railway interest. Either side of the Second World War he formed a long friendship with Benjamin Britten, with whom he worked at Glyndebourne and the Aldeburgh Festival.

All of which brought us to Dufftown, deep in Whisky Country, but also soon to be better known in railway circles as the headquarters of the Keith & Dufftown Railway, an eleven mile remnant of the Great North of Scotland Railway's circuitous Elgin to Keith route. I stood on Dufftown's solitary platform chatting to Peter Bradley while George went off to talk to some chums. Stabled beside us was one of the line's two Class 108 diesel multiple units, this one in Network South East red, white and blue, the other in good old BR green.

"The station at Keith Town is being rebuilt as a close replica of the original, which was unusual in that it was on two levels," Peter told me.

"The entrance was on the upper floor with access from the

town, and you descended to the platform. The last passenger train ran on May 6th 1968, but the line stayed open for grain to the distilleries until we took it over in the early Nineties. So, effectively, it has never closed. The Northern Belle excursion train used it from 1984 until 1991."

A white Highland Terrier was keeping a watching brief on our conversation, as if ready to interrupt tactfully should Peter get any of his facts wrong; facts being, in the best railway circles, as highly valued as rhetoric in political ones.

"Manning's going to be our biggest problem," Peter continued. We rely on volunteer labour, and until we become better known, it's difficult to attract enough interested parties."

It was interesting to see a small private railway at an early stage of its operational existence. Peter and I went back into the Booking Hall where someone was painstakingly applying paint to the raised letters of a salvaged nameboard. In preservation, no job is too small, no commitment unvalued. George was in the Ticket Office with two old buffers, obviously in their element, born again railwaymen who ask nothing more from life than to be able to serve on a branchline.

"Best of luck with the new railway," I said, and meant it.

We drove back via Drummuir, which entailed reversing down narrow lanes and pulling out from narrow gateways on 1 in 4 gradients. I won't say I was hysterical, that would be putting it too mildly. George was remembering some of his foreign travels - chocolate & cream trains in France which made him feel at home. He wrote the first of the *original* Railway Holiday series published by David & Charles in the Sixties. It was set in France, and is a continuous source of inspiration to me. He also wrote *Railway Holiday in Switzerland* which I enjoyed because it took the reader to Murren, in the Bernese Oberland, and Jackie and I had stayed there twice in the days before the children came and we could afford to indulge ourselves. His latest book is *Pullman and the Orient Expresses*, a massive, self-published tome which reveals his encyclopedic knowledge has not been diluted by the passage of time. He moved to Morayshire, for his wife's sake, in 1990, but she died of cancer two years later and he now leads, I sensed, a somewhat solitary existence on the coast, in a Station Road which no longer leads to a station.

He took me back to Keith, where we had a quick look at the Town station in the throes of being rebuilt. On the platform at 'the junction' I handed him a bottle of Petit Chablis, having read between the lines of *Railway Holiday in France* that his tipple is wine; an irony not lost on him in the sea of whisky he finds himself surrounded by. My train came in after a slight delay, it had been held in the loop while a late-running Aberdeen train went by. That tongue-tied vacuum which invariably overtakes people - both the leavers and the left behind - on railway platforms rendered us inarticulate. Only as I boarded did George start to speak again, but his words were lost in the shutting of the doors. Caught behind an old woman who wouldn't sit down, I didn't even have the chance to return his wave.

In Highland Railway territory now, the train pulls away from Keith past the whisky bonds of Chivas Brothers; Fort Knox security for Scotland's gold reserve. It is no coincidence that so many distilleries stand beside the railway in this part of the world, the railway was vital to business in the 19th and for much of the 20th century. Bit by bit, however, road transport got the upper hand in the Eighties and Nineties. A fascinating little book called *Rail Freight in Moray*, written by Ron Smith, a mutual friend of George and mine, frustratingly reveals how all this traffic ebbed away. The last whisky contract by rail was from Keith to Dalmuir and was ultimately lost through indifference and far from customer friendly operating methods. Ron's book reads like the Retreat from Moscow as, in addition to whisky, fertilizer, grain, container goods, salt, coal and military traffics have all been lost to rail in the North-east of Scotland. In 2001 the only freight traffic north of Aberdeen that goes by train is timber.

The line runs west past two more distilleries - Glentauchers, which is visible from the railway, and another, Singleton of Auchriosk, which isn't. There are many woodland interludes and a big hill called Ben Aigan. An old station at Mulben is encountered, then the train dashes downhill to cross that most sumptuous of salmon rivers, the Spey, on a big box girder bridge. The old Highland Railway station buildings remain in domestic use at Orton and Orbliston. The last passenger trains stopped to pick up at both of them on December 7th 1964. Photographs of both of them in more innocent times are reproduced in Gordon Stansfield's small but beautiful picture book *Banff, Moray & Nairn's Lost Railways*, one of a series by Stenlake Publishing. Going off at a tangent, I can't resist drawing your attention to my favourite picture on page 23, a wet August day at Tillynaught in 1956 which perfectly distils the essence of a country junction. Orbliston was a junction station too, for a three mile branch to Fochabers, closed to passenger trains in 1931, though still used by freight for another thirty years. Fochabers is a fine Georgian town chiefly known nowadays as the home of Baxters Soup. Wouldn't it be nice if one day the branch was relaid to serve their Visitor Centre, both for the import of tourists and the export of soup. From the map there appears to be little impediment!

I got off at Elgin to look for my marbles. I felt as if I was walking into a French town. Seagulls provided a soundtrack, rose bushes provided scent, lime trees provided shade. It seemed a supremely civilised place, and I was going to visit the Cathedral until I discovered, at the Tourist Information Centre, that it's a ruin. Not that I have anything against ruins, some of my best friends are ruins of their former selves. The High Street is spacious and pedestrianised and I would have gone into the Greek doric temple of St Giles if it hadn't been shut for renovation. Spiritually thwarted, I retraced my steps to the railway. Elgin once enjoyed the luxury of two stations, linked - in a manner immediately reminiscent of Manchester Victoria and Exchange - by a lengthy common platform. The westernmost station - the one still in use - belonged to the Highland Railway, the other to the Great North of Scotland company. Ironically, it is the most architecturally imposing of the two stations which has closed, an elaborate Scots Baronial pile which would have served some laird admirably at the head of a deer rich glen. Thankfully it has survived as office accommodation, mostly of a municipal nature, and no one seems to mind you exploring it, and discovering for yourself that the astonishingly ornate and imposing Booking Hall remains intact, right down to the ticket window barriers. More sadly, the GNS station is adjoined by acres of rusty sidings dominated by a huge yellow coloured container lifting device, but until we learn again the art of bringing rail freight back to small towns like Elgin, dereliction rules OK. The Highland Railway station building met an even worse fate. It was demolished and replaced by a modern structure which looks as though the architect was working late one night on a health centre and got the blueprints transposed. Unable to bear any more, I went into the adjoining ASDA for a refrigerated sandwich.

No sooner have you left Elgin station than the train pulls up again. This is for the driver to receive a good old fashioned token from the signalman at Elgin West. Tokens remain in use as far as Nairn, and are exchanged at Forres. The line crosses the River Lossie and finds itself in a flat landscape: so many north flowing rivers, a relatively unusual phenomenon in Great Britain. Alves was the junction for a branch which led to Hopeman via Burghead. The overgrown track has been retained to serve a maltings, but it is obviously a long time since it last functioned thus. A curiously isolated classical style church overlooks the junction. I have written before (*Pearson's Railway Rides - Cotswolds & Malverns 1994*) of the affinity between country stations and parish churches: 'wheezing organs and wheezing engines, hymn numbers and platform numbers, leaking roofs, rotting timbers and dwindling practitioners'; whilst, along with musicians, men of the cloth often evince more interest in railway matters on average than people in other walks of life.

The ruins of a Cistercian abbey overlook the railway as it skims Kinloss, better known nowadays for its RAF base. Woodlands make it difficult to see much of the mud and sand expanse of Findhorn Bay. Findhorn rang a bell with me, and then I remembered that Mike Scott (he of The Waterboys and *Whole of the Moon* fame) had recorded his accoustic album *Bring 'Em All* In at the Findhorn Foundation, a spiritual community founded in 1962 and now developed into an ecological village as well. It sounded just the sort of place I could do with - if only I had the time! The Findhorn Railway didn't have much *time*, lasting (as far as passengers were concerned) just nine years from its opening from Kinloss in 1860.

I saw Forres Mechanics football ground, a tower (commemorating Lord Nelson) in the trees on Cluny Hill and the signalman exchange tokens as the train ran into Forres. But what I couldn't see was Sueno's Stone, a 23 feet high, thousand year old monument to the victory of the Norseman Sweyn over King Malcolm II, which would just have to wait - like much else in life - for another day. Forres used to be a 'triangular' station, with platforms on all three sides. (Quiz question - how many other fully platformed triangular stations can you name in Britain? Three scores high, four and you're brighter than me!) Those on the west-south curve served the original route between Inverness and Perth via Dava and Aviemore, opened in 1863 and considered a main line until the direct line through Carrbridge was completed in 1898. If Forres station was still fully intact I couldn't have resisted further exploration, but all that's left is one platform with rails beside it and a low brick building of what I'd guess to be Sixties vintage. An elderly couple of military bearing were meeting someone off the train. The distaff side peered excitedly up and down the carriages, but the poor old buffer looked as if he'd been in too many battles to know, still less care anymore, who he'd come to meet.

Ragwort and rosebay willow herb flourish where busy sidings once lay. The train gathered speed past potato fields then roared across the River Findhorn on an unusual viaduct with high wrought-iron plates which obscure the view. It dates from 1858 and is the work of Joseph Mitchell who is said to have been inspired by Robert Stephenson's tubular bridges in North Wales. Mitchell was a Forres man who'd worked with Thomas Telford on the Caledonian Canal before following in his father's footsteps as a road engineer. By the middle of the 19th century he had his finger in a number of railway pies and he has left a legacy of particularly fine bridges - fortunately none of the rest are as difficult to see over. His grandson was quite good at engineering as well, his name was Reginald and he designed the Spitfire fighter plane that saved our bacon in 1940. Brodie Castle (seat of Brodie of Brodie whose family has owned land in the vicinity for ten centuries) is open to the public, but the neighbouring station closed to passengers in 1965 (and now offers bed & breakfast instead) so visitors must arrive by road. Forestry occupies much of the low-lying landscape now, but this is reputedly the 'blasted heath' where Macbeth and Banquo met the three 'weird sisters' on their way to King Duncan's court at Forres.

If I was conscious of Nairn at all - other than as the surname of my all time favourite travel broadcaster and writer Ian, and the home of David St John Thomas, railway writer and founder of one half of the David and Charles publishing house - I would have been hard put to place it on a map. In railway terms it had been well known in recent years as the spot where the signalman or woman had to cycle madly along the platform between the two boxes to effect the passage of trains. Alas, this delightful ritual ceased in April 2000, a victim - in common with many other quaint railway practices - of modernisation. The station building, located on the lengthy up platform between the two now boarded up signalboxes, is a handsome Highland Railway stone built affair, two end pavilions parenthesising a long canopied centre. It reminded me of Dingwall. On the down platform, there is an elegant timber waiting room which apparently housed until recently an exhibition of railwayana. One thing puzzled me, at the eastern end of the station both platforms and their attendant running lines are carried across a road and the girders on each platform appear to have been cast in different foundries: one by Westwood Baillie & Co of London, one by Alex Findlay & Co of Motherwell; nothing like competitive tendering is there!

While I had my nose up against the window of the timber waiting room a young Spanish couple came over the footbridge and asked me, in pigeon English, if it was the correct platform for Inverness. It would have been once, of course, but nowadays, where feasible, trains in both directions use the platform with the main station buildings on it, mostly in order to save the signal man or woman's legs as they come out of their hidey hole in the office to give or receive the token from trains going to, or coming from, Forres. Suspecting that the subtleties of railway operation would get lost in the translation, I led them over to the platform edge and pointed down at the rusty track. They shook their heads in a confused manner and re-crossed the bridge to seek further information in the booking hall, probably under the impression that I was suggesting that in Britain the done thing to ensure trains stop at wayside stations is to stand on the track.

After recommending a suicide pact to the young Spanish tourists, I walked into town, a Mr Hulot figure trailing chaos in my wake. Nairn seemed a jolly little place. Everyone walks slowly, a sure sign of contentment, but when you've only ninety minutes between trains, spurts of speed become a necessity. I evolved a penguin-like technique of overtaking in rapid stacatto strides, and turned a few heads I can tell you. I hadn't expected so likeable a town, let alone one with a seaside resort tacked on one end, and an award winning beach to boot. In Harbour Street I came upon the intriguing premises of the Piccolo Press. A small back room is devoted to exhibits of elderly printing machinery, the sort of equipment, I'm embarrassed to say, that I was all too familiar with at printing college in the Seventies. I was transported back to days of patiently fitting packing behind letterpress frames to ensure an even density of print, to aching limbs after hours picking metal characters from a wooden case; capitals at the top, the origin of the term upper and lower case. But it was the firm itself that I found most noteworthy, for they are the last die-stampers left in Scotland, and one of a rapidly dwindling number of printers anywhere in Britain still using the letterpress technique. Luckily, the owner, Tim Honnor, a former Commander of submarines, was in. Refraining from the obvious conversational gambit - which I'm sure he must have heard a thousand times - of asking if I had the honour of meeting Mr Honnor, I explained my Scottish railway journey and my interest in printing. He responded warmly, appraising the brevity of my visit with naval precision, and thrust a handful of samples and company profiles into my hand. Reading them at home I was fascinated to learn that Piccolo Press have found a niche market in providing embassies and consulates around the world with high quality stationery such as engraved invitations and business cards. While I was there Tim showed me a map of the world hung on the office wall with a red spot for every customer. Few capitals are unspotted, most suffer from a positively contagious rash.

On the way back through town I was tempted into Ashers Bakery, my eyes lighting on a devilish concoction known as bean and potato pie, essentially a Scots meat pie with a layer of baked beans crowned by a piping of mashed potato. An inspired combination, it reminded me of the baked bean and corned beef pie I'd discovered in the West Yorkshire town of Mirfield on my canal travels in the mid-Nineties. There, in a corner shop, I'd been served by a girl with a smile I had likened to that of a Pre-Raphaelite angel. In Ashers it was the freckly face of a Minnie the Minx which smiled so warmly at me over the counter.

Nairn County's football ground overlooks the railway at the west end of the station: Inverurie Loco, Keith Town, Elgin City, Forres Mechanics and now Nairn County; I felt as if I was on a football odyssey rather than a railway one. The sea disappears behind the Carse of Delnies as the train speeds west on the last lap to the Highland capital. If you concentrate you may catch a glimpse of the overgrown earthworks of a branch that led from Gollanfield Junction to Fort George, and which lost its passenger trains in the middle of the Second World War. Fort George is an 18th century redoubt built at the behest of George II to ensure that there was no repeat of the Jacobean rebellion after their defeat at Culloden. The B9006 which crosses the railway today is a former military road which led to the fort. Gollanfield was the scene in 1953 of an alarming head-on collision between an eastbound passenger train and a westbound goods. Three of the four footplatemen involved were killed, and the passenger locomotive, a 1920 built, Caledonian Railway 4-4-0, was damaged beyond repair and cut up on the spot. It was a Forres based engine, No. 54481.

A British Midland plane was landing at Inverness Airport. They had probably flown from London in the time it had taken the train to run from Elgin. I looked beyond the runway to where the Moray Firth was glinting like quicksilver in the evening light, the Black Isle an intractable isthmus in the distance. The line from Perth leapfrogs over the Aberdeen route on the outskirts of Inverness, before merging half a mile further on at Millburn Junction. 66110 and 37416 were in the goods yard. A cheeky little shunting engine was propelling sleeper carriages towards the station. Beyond the bufferstops there was only one place to go. I had forgiven (if not forgotten) the Royal Highland Hotel its indifference to my luggage-encumbered family. Its tradition, its architecture, its calming presence, the mounted stag's head in the foyer, the rippling laughter of the monied classes, the formidable plumbing in the toilets, the Japanese coach parties queueing to be served dinner from the white damask table-cloths of the Wallace Room: all mitigated against its uncooperative outlook. In essence I was grateful to sink into the deepest armchair I could find with a pint of 'Eighty Bob'. An elderly group at the next table were speaking in Gaelic. The angels had had their share of the malt. Behind the bar, Robbie deferentially asked me what I'd be having. The time of my life, I suspected, the time of my life ...

Useful Contacts

Inverurie Tourist Information - Tel: 01467 625800

The Insch Connection - Tel: 01464 821354

Keith & Dufftown Railway - Tel: 01340 821181

Elgin Tourist Information - Tel: 01343 542666

The Findhorn Foundation - Tel: 01309 690311. www.findhorn.org

Forres Tourist Information - Tel: 01309 672938

Nairn Tourist Information - Tel: 01667 452753

Piccolo Press - Tel: 01667 454508

Ashers Bakery - Tel: 01667 453206

"DALWHINNIE"

Climbing out of Inverness towards Culloden. The 'rout' of Moy.
Wartime on the Highland Railway. No connection at
Aviemore. Monarch of the Glen Country. Druimuachdar
Summit and the Pass of Killiecrankie. What to do in Pitlochry
and Dunkeld. The distillery at Dalwhinnie. Teatime in
Aviemore. The River Findhorn and its viaduct.

Is it just me, or do Druimuachdar & Slochd sound like a firm
of Inverness undertakers? And would their slogan echo good
old British Rail's 'We make the going easy ...?' Though I have
my doubts about '...And the coming back'. Then again they
might be whisky makers, or butchers or the management duo of
some shinty team. But naturally my well-informed readership
will already know that Druimuachdar and Slochd are the two
major summits that the Highland Railway had to cross to make
their direct line from Perth to Inverness. I had decided to
explore the line on an out and back basis, starting at Inverness
and alighting where my fancy took me on the day. Trains run
more or less every two hours in either direction, so if you go
station-hopping like me you can manage a couple of hours

wherever you choose to get off, just an adequate amount of time to explore a town or village on first acquaintance.

I had a comfortable seat with table in a Turbostar for the first leg of my journey. It pulled out exactly on time. The overnight sleeper's carriages were being propelled through the washer by a fussy little shunter painted black like the obsequious character 'Diesel' in the Reverend Awdry's *Thomas the Tank Engine* stories; simple tales which it took an astute businesswoman, Brit Allcroft, to turn into a multi-million pound, world-wide commercial success. I am waiting for her call. Further along Millburn Yard a Class 66 stood at the head of some cement wagons, presumably waiting to form the afternoon EWS 'Enterprise' service to Mossend. We passed an old distillery which has been converted into a restaurant, went under the dual-carriagewayed A9 approach to the Kessock Bridge, skimmed the muddy edge of the Moray Firth, crossed the Aberdeen line and began to do some serious climbing, more than twenty miles of it to get us from sea level to the summit at Slochd, 1,315ft up in the mountains. Even in a modern lightweight, aluminium-bodied Adtranz Turbostar, with 422hp engines beneath each of the three cars' floors, there was work to be done to get up long sections of 1 in 60 gradient. The line runs in a great horseshoe curve to make the ascent easier, embracing Culloden's field of tears in the process, and crossing the River Nairn on a massive sandstone viaduct of no less than twenty-eight arches. The viaduct is 600 yards long, the arch over the river being twice as wide as the rest and looming 128 feet above the water. Construction, in the 1890s, bankrupted the original contractor.

As so often in the highlands, the weather couldn't decide what to do. The cows were lying down, waiting for it to make its mind up. The conductor reminded me of Gary McAllister, he took my ticket with the same curving aplomb of the great midfielder's free-kicks. Beyond Culloden (sometimes known as Nairn) Viaduct the sense of approaching wilderness intensified. Bald moorlands alternated with massive forestry plantations. Near Moy the train, which had had a brief breather from climbing, was forced to proceed carefully across Aultlaslanach Viaduct, the only timber built bridge on a Scottish main line, a method of construction forced on the railway's builders by the boggy nature of the ground it stands on, nature confirmed by the presence of meadowsweet in the ditches below.

Lloyd George may once have used its waiting room, but that didn't stop Moy - together with many local stations between Inverness and Perth - from being closed to passengers in May 1965, a direct victim of the Beeching Report. The passing loop was reinstated in 1979 when there was a surge of traffic over the line in connection with the North Sea oil boom. Moy was the scene of the famous 'rout' in 1746, when a large body of Government troops searching for the 'Young Chevalier', were turned back by the local blacksmith and four other men, whose wild Highland yelps from the woods were sufficient to convince the Hanoverians that a much larger force was mustered against them. Bonnie Prince Charlie himself was quartered at Moy Hall with Colonel Anne Mackintosh, a spirited female supporter of the cause whose husband, Angus, was a captain in the opposing ranks of the Black Watch. Not long after the rout, when Angus was captured by the Jacobites near Dornoch, Princes Charles sent him back to his wife on the understanding that 'he could not be in better security or more honourably treated'. Anne is said to have greeted her husband with the words: 'Your servant, Captain', whilst her husband replied, 'Your servant, Colonel'; obviously a man who knew his place in the marital chain of command as well as the military one.

Strathdearn funnels the Funtack Burn towards its confluence with the River Findhorn. The grey whisky bonds of Tomatin herald another loop and another lost station, the platforms still intact, but the brick-built signal box boarded up. My father arrived here one December midnight in 1941 and found only the signalman on duty. Anyone of my Dad's generation will tell you that, throughout the war years, far more time was spent travelling about the country on secondment than actually fighting the enemy. On this occasion he was endeavouring to get from the Orkneys to Llandudno to go on a radar course. No official transport being available, he had hitched lifts on a trawler and an army truck to get this far. The signalman took pity on him and stopped the next southbound train in order that he might negotiate a lift. It was a goods train and he rode in the guard's van his 'ears almost falling off' throughout the freezing night. It was not until he alighted at Perth the following morning that he learnt that the train was carrying *mines*. To regain his composure he breakfasted at the Station Hotel, past caring that the restaurant was reserved for the exclusive use of officers.

My father's adventure apart, the Highland main line really had to reach deeply into its resources during the two world wars. The north of Scotland was a militarized zone during both emergencies which only authorized personnel could penetrate. Tourism died a temporary death during both wars, but passenger figures increased dramatically as the railways carried troops and workers in vast numbers. During the First World War the Highland Railway increased its passengers by 50%, goods rising by an incredible 102%. Given that the vast majority of its route miles were single track, you can imagine what a feat of organisation and operation this took. A feature of both conflicts were the naval specials between London Euston and Thurso, a journey of over seven hundred miles, accomplished in twenty-two hours. As well as the mines my father encountered, another massive traffic developed in pit props of all things. Traditionally sourced from Scandinavia, they could naturally no longer be brought in by sea from occupied countries such as Norway. Luckily the Highlands offered an alternative source, but it all added extra traffic to the already almost grid-locked Highland main line. Seventy-five extra trains a week needed providing to cope with this extra traffic flow alone. At first the complicated marshalling of these timber trains took place at Inverness, Forres and Perth, but they were soon jammed tight as the number of wagons outnumbered the siding space available. In response all timber trains were worked to Grangemouth where more capacity was available for the sorting and assembly of trains destined for the south. Wartime histories are full of generals and strategists and military victories and defeats, but they won't tell you that the wars were equally won by the Highland Railway and the LMS with their pit prop and sea mine specials.

South of the site of Tomatin station, the line launches itself spectacularly over the creaming waters of the River Findhorn on one of Britain's most graceful viaducts. Consisting of nine steel spans, supported on slender masonry columns, it is 143ft above the river and curves at a radius of half a mile. Impressive as this data is, it fails to convey the viaduct's beauty in its peerless riverine setting. I first saw it, I'm abashed to tell you, when speeding across the neighbouring A9's pale concrete imitation of a viaduct. Love at first sight, I went back to see it close up, falling at once for its high mottled piers and lattice girders, lying on the Findhorn's grassy banks in wait for the sleeper, the resultant, moonlit photograph reproduced on the cover of this book.

One of General Wade's 18th century military roads finds its way to Slochd over the adjoining brow of a bare hill, but the railway and the A9 make a more cautious approach, conserving their resources for the summit, whose crossing must have been greeted with prayers of gratitude and relief by enginemen in the days of steam. Lineside surfacemen's cottages are still in domestic use. Through rocky cuttings of great desolation the line commences its descent, passing the stony flanks of Carn nam Baintighearna on which the face of a soldier is said to be discernible.

With a leap and a bound we crossed the Dulnain and arrived at Carrbridge - variously spelt as one word or two - waiting in the platform loops for a northbound Sprinter to pass; 158713, its dot matrix destination screen showing Kyle of Lochalsh. Carrbridge station building is of timber construction, but follows the Highland Railway style of wings either side of a canopied central section. From my map I read that the prominent mountain to the east was Craiggowrie, not high enough to be a Munro but still impressive.

So well known in tourist circles now, Aviemore was little more than an inn on one of General Wade's military roads before the railway arrived in 1863. And, even then, it was not until the opening of the direct route to Inverness over Slochd, and the rebuilding and extension of the station to cope with its new significance, that a resort of any size began to develop. The 1892 station encountered today is a symphony in timber, beautifully maintained, its diversity of use - booking hall, restaurant, sports equipment hire outlet, estate agent and last, but far from least, steam railway terminus - ensuring a bustling liveliness for much of the day. With its cream and red colours and curvaceous figure, it's quite unlike any of the other handsome, but dour Highland Railway stations. More than anything, it reminded me of the candy floss effect of Troon.

Journeying down from Inverness, I had been trying to marry the Strathspey Steam Railway's timetable with ScotRail's, to see if I could manage a quick return trip to Boat of Garten. But I couldn't make it work, not without spending more time in Aviemore at the expense of other places I wanted to visit. Even on the way back, the 14.53 from Perth was shown as arriving in Aviemore at 16.29, a tantalising nine minutes after the last train of the day to Boat of Garten, which didn't even bother to come back. Still, I have it on good authority that it's a very worthwhile ride, offering panoramic views of the Cairngorms, and one which is due to be extended in the not too distant future.

Eliminating a steam train ride from my list of possibilities, I elected to get off first at the next station down the line, Kingussie, where the Highland Folk Museum has one of its twin venues. On the way there the line skirts Loch Insh, a centre for watersports, and the neighbouring Insh Marshes, an RSPB nature reserve of considerable importance. I remembered Sandy Barclay and Andy Clarke telling me - when we travelled along here one misty morning on the Safeway train for *Coming Up With The Goods* - that the railway along the marsh had been built on a raft of sheep's bladders. In the distance the Cairngorms stayed sullenly behind a curtain of cloud, refusing to come out and play.

Kingussie was as quiet as a monastery. I'd stepped off the train at a pleasant station of obvious Highland parentage. At the northern end of the two platforms a signal box oversaw a level crossing, whilst semaphore signalling protected the loop. The

booking hall was well appointed, the waiting room was deco-
rated with old railway publicity paintings of Scottish scenes, the
toilets were clean and the station master seemed a convivial soul,
treating enquiries from the travelling public with the good
humour of an elderly prep school teacher; besides *Iron Road to
the Isles* was prominently on sale at the ticket counter, so
they obviously know a good thing when they see one at
Kingussie station.

Apparently I was in *Monarch of the Glen* country. It's not a television programme I can claim to have seen very often, and
being only an occasional viewer the plot - always assuming there
is one - has somehow eluded me, but the scenery transcends
such complications, as it did for the programme's creator and
writer, Michael Chaplin, when on a train trip along the
Highland main line in 1968, he'd first fallen under the spell of
Kingussie's location. All this, and that Kingussie doubles for the
fictional town of Glenbogle, I learnt from a leaflet picked up at
the Tourist Information Centre housed in the Highland Folk
Museum, less than five minutes walk along a road of quiet stone
houses from the station.

It proved a charming little museum. In the grounds - which
border the railway - I discovered a preserved smoke house built
of corrugated iron in which salmon would be cured by dint of
lighting a peat fire beneath the structure. Beside the smoke-
house stood some stachle stones which would be used to form
the base of a corn rick, ensuring sufficient ventilation. Moving
on, I came upon a clack mill, so called because of the noise the
machinery would make as it was turned by water power. In
pride of place, however, was the Black House, a typical 'long
house' from the Isle of Lewis which would have been used
simultaneously for the shelter of both crofters and their animals.
Inside a lady in period costume, with the hint of a South African
accent, was explaining to a couple of visitors the rudiments of
18th and 19th century lifestyle in the highlands and islands. We
all agreed that, idyllic as the past often appears to be, this was
not a lifestyle that any of us could contemplating embracing.
There were indoor exhibits as well, and an interesting, though

as yet not properly displayed, collection of farm machinery.

"You should go and see our other venue at Newtonmore," urged the lady in period costume. "It's on a much bigger site and there's a lot more to see."

Another time, I thought, knowing I'd be back to research my forthcoming guide to the line. Kingussie is regarded as the capital of Badenoch, but being by-passed by the A9 now, it seems a peaceful spot. The local tourist leaflet explains it better than me: 'Kingussie, capitale del Badenoch, e' situata vicino al fiume Spey, circondata dalle montagne del Cairngorm e le montagne del Monadhliath, nel cuore dell'alta Scozia.' Comprendes? In a side street I found a prize-winning butchers called Hamlett & Gow, famous apparently for their home made haggis. In no position to sample that particular delicacy, I made do with a mutton pie, and 'estupendo muy bueno' it was too. Walking back to the station I encountered Elton John and Bernie Taupin. Well, I couldn't actually see them, but I knew they were up there, if you see what I mean, because somebody was on the roof of a house and prodigious quantities of moss were falling down into the street, and suddenly I began to have a funny feeling inside ...

The next train south was a four car 158. At Newtonmore I saw some of the other exhibits of the Highland Folk Museum, what looked like a working farm, and I felt it was a shame that more trains didn't call at the nearby station's single platform, so that visitors could travel between the two venues by rail. Call me a visionary if you like, but perhaps one day they might even provide a vintage Highland Railway replica train to shuttle between the Kingussie and Newtonmore sites.

We began climbing in earnest again, 1 in 90 through Glen Truim, waves of moorland under Creag Ruadh. I saw again a little dual-arched bridge over the Truim where I'd attempted to photograph the down EWS 'Enterprise' freight running through the narrow glen against a picturesque backdrop. Everything went well, the train was on time, the sun was out, the water rippled. Then, as I pressed the release cable, a gust of wind blew the tripod over, the back of the camera opened, and the masterpiece was spoilt. The moral is, if you're doing photography in the Highlands, whatever the time of year, batten down the hatches!

Whenever I'm on the Highland main line, I always look out for the pretty whitewashed distillery at Dalwhinnie, its copper-topped pagodas seeming to gleam and wink as I pass, whatever the light. Perusing the timetable once again, I reckoned I could fit in a visit to the distillery on the way back. Meanwhile, however, the train was continuing to charge Druimuachdar, flashing non stop through Dalwhinnie station where the down 'Enterprise', largely consisting of cement wagons on their way from the Blue Circle works near Dunbar to Inverness, was waiting by the signal box for us to clear the single line. It was good to see working freight on the line, but once again I only needed to glance at the neighbouring A9, busy with juggernauts, to realise that much more could be done to carry freight through the Highlands by rail.

Leaving Dalwhinnie, with the track now double as far as Blair Atholl, you catch a glimpse to the west of Loch Ericht, a deep chasm in the mountains, almost fifteen miles long. Under the very noses of the Boar of Badenoch and the Sow of Atholl, two bare mountain tops either side of the County March, the railway breasts the highest main line summit in Britain, 1,484 feet above sea level. The Ordnance Survey map calls this the Pass of Drumochter, a phonetically anglicized sop. In railway circles we stay true to the Gaelic, Druimuachdar. If I had had a geologist with me (Barbara Streisand, reprising her role in *What's Up Doc?*, would have been admirable) I could relate to you, in fascinating detail, what all the rocks are. The only other occupant of the first class compartment was a politician, going through the minutes of his last meeting and the agenda of his next. I knew he was a politician because only MSPs, Americans, and travel writers benefiting from the abundant largesse of ScotRail use such undemocratic facilities as first class now. I was able, without looking, to differentiate between the minutes and the agenda by the aural characteristics of each sheet of paper's flick; one contemptuous, one apprehensive.

185

Dalnaspidal station was another victim of the May 1965 purge. Now it's just a lonely level crossing leading to a shooting lodge. In steam days, being close to the summit, it was the point at which banking or assisting engines would discreetly retire, leaving the train locomotive to its own capable devices. If you're quick, to the south-west you'll get a tantalising glimpse of Loch Garry, gleaming like antimony in its fold in the heather, before the train rockets down the 1 in 70 to Struan, cocking a snook at the frequently caravan-stymied traffic on the A9. The crenellated bridge at Struan is notable for crossing a road bridge, and the river beneath it, simultaneously.

It was sunnier to the south of Druimuachdar, and coming down from the barren mountain tops into the fertile glen felt like returning to a hot bath at the end of a long hike in the hills. There are crumbling platforms in the undergrowth where Struan station stood, but most of you will be wondering what the pointed peak is which looms ahead. Ben Vrackie is the answer, but first you come to Blair Atholl, which once had an engine shed for the bankers. The line singles here, and always has done, to negotiate the confined Pass of Killiecrankie. In deference to the Duke of Atholl, Joseph Mitchell went to some pains to design a viaduct and tunnel portal which would harmonise with the dramatic setting of the ravine. An excited correspondent for the *London Illustrated News*, writing only days after the railway opened in 1863, described the setting thus: 'one has scarcely time to admire the crags, the varied foliage, the precipitous sides of the ravine, and the black abysses through which the river cleaves a way'. The same holds true today, only greater degrees of vegetation obscure the view even more, and there is no longer a station at which to alight and see if you can emulate the giant leap of a soldier escaping from the battle fought here in 1689, scene of the death of 'Bonnie Dundee', aka Graham of Claverhouse, the Jaocobite supporter of James VII. It's just a bit sad that Killiecrankie station is no longer open to provide access to the National Trust for Scotland's admirable visitor centre.

Piltlochry is the quintessential small, traditional, Scots resort.

So cosy it cloys, well almost, but keeping enough of itself back not to be overwhelmed by tourism. You can visit a distillery, gain entry to the hydro-electric power station, watch the salmon leap up their ladder, attend a production at the Festival Theatre, go to a Highland Gathering, hire a rowing boat on Loch Faskally or shop 'til you drop in the souvenir and clothing emporiums. In the face of such choice, and being infamously poor at decision making, I contented myself with lunch in Cafe Biba, Canadian pancakes with maple syrup, then walked - or rather, swayed - across the suspension bridge over the Tummel, thereafter lingering by the salmon ladder in vain for a relative of Salar to pass. I liked the station as well, architecturally and ambiently it's a coherent part of the town: the main stone built building on the up platform being typical of Highland Railway practice, with crow-stepped gables and Scots tudor styling; the cricket pavilion like waiting room on the down platform being linked by a lattice footbridge cast by Hanna Donald & Wilson in Paisley. Waiting for the next southbound service, I paced the length of the platform, passing an ornate, cast-iron drinking fountain (doubting if it functioned anymore for the quenching of thirst) and stood by the semaphore home signal until it rattled upwards to herald my train. Don't fall into the trap of thinking that time spent on stations is wasted. Country stations are like country churches. Railways and religion may leave you cold, but there is a spirituality inherent in both which you should allow to rub off on you before you rush off to your next pressing engagement.

The road and the railway rush out of Pitlochry like gangsters on a getaway. Only the River Tummel's calming influence, and the balm-like forested flank of Ballechin Wood prevent further bloodshed. Blood should have been shed when Beeching closed the branch line from Ballinluig to Aberfeldy. Why did we so often give in so easily? Eight miles and fifty-nine chains of Tayside rhapsody ripped up for a few paltry thousands. Railway writer and publisher David St John Thomas 'did' the branch in 1963 and described the journey in *Double Headed*, an inspired father and son collaboration. The single coach train was hauled

by what Thomas called 'a two-year-old express-size diesel locomotive' (probably a Birmingham Railway Carriage & Wagon
Co. Type 2) and the guard was happy to talk of local history and
point out famous fishing reaches on the way. Even the timetable
might be made pliant, it appeared, if Thomas wanted to have a
quick look round Aberfeldy. When he got back to Ballinluig he
watched the branch train leave again, without a single passenger
on board. So what? Lack of passengers doesn't necessarily equate
with lack of worth. If no one passes on the country road that I
live by for hours at a time, does it mean it should be closed to
the public? If a book isn't borrowed from a library for a year or
more, should it be burnt? I closed my eyes at Ballinluig, not
being able to bring myself to look at the scars. Smokey Robinson
wrote a song for how I felt: *Tracks of My Tears*.

The railway crosses the Tay at Dalguise upon a superb, low
slung, lattice-girder viaduct supported by three sets of orna-
mental piers, the inspired product of Joseph Mitchell's drawing
board: to crenellate or castellate, that is the question. Dalguise
House is an activity centre now, but it was regularly rented by
Beatrix Potter's father for summer holidays in the late 19th century. The Tourist Board are understandably keen to cash in on
the Beatrix Potter connection. It is thought she was inspired to
write *The Tale of Peter Rabbit* whilst in Dunkeld, and that her
childhood holidays in the vicinity influenced much of her writing and illustration. Neil T. Sinclair puts her Perthshire visits in
a railway context in his admirable book *The Highland Main Line*
(Atlantic 1998), quoting from her journals the description of a
journey from Perth to Birnam.

Readers of *Coming Up With The Goods* will know that I experienced some difficulty recalling the plot of *Macbeth* on the day
of my A Level Exam. Virtually all I can ever remember about
Shakespeare's 'Scottish Play' is the bit about the wood moving
from Birnam to Dunsinane. I was equally inept with *Hamlet* at
O Level. In class I was singled out to explain Shakespeare's use
of the metaphor.

"Ophelia and Hamlet," I replied with relief and certainty.

"Would you care to elaborate, Pearson?" said the master,

scenting the opportunity to ridicule a usually less than forth-coming pupil.

"Ophelia and Hamlet," I insisted, "they must have met afore the play started."

Looking out for commandos disguised as trees, I got off the train at Dunkeld & Birnam station. It's a tidy walk across the Tay to Dunkeld, but the day had brightened up, and a big blue sky filled with cotton wool clouds beamed down on me as I strolled across Thomas Telford's lovely stone bridge of 1809. Upstream, two fishermen were casting their lines from a boat into the wide river. Mentally, I wished them 'tight lines' and entered Dunkeld, 'one of Perthshire's gems'! I saw no reason to pick holes in the propaganda. I admired the Atholl Memorial Fountain, the 'Little Houses', and the Cathedral, part ruin, part parish church. Sadly, I did not have time to go on any of the numerous signposted walks in the vicinity, but I did pick up a leaflet describing them from the Tourist Information Centre, and promised myself I'd try one or two of them one day.

To all intents and purposes, the Highland Main Line contin-ues to Perth, though in actual fact its junction with the Caledonian Railway was at Stanley, eight miles to the north. It was lunchtime, however, and rather than use up valuable time running down to Perth for the sake of it, I caught the next northbound train from Dunkeld, a man with a mission, to visit a distillery!

I had made a mistake in not buying anything for lunch in Dunkeld. The train was full and its incumbents had already emptied the catering trolley of anything more meaningful and sustaining than biscuits and crisps. I salivated at the contents of an American family's picnic in the bay ahead. They were replete with 'chips' and cookies and candy bars. One of the boys was so full he had to answer a call of nature, returning white of face to tell his Mom that there was *no* washroom!

I saw things I had missed on the way down: the hydro-elec-tric power station at Linn of Tummel; a better view (from the left hand side of the train) of the Pass of Killiecrankie; Blair Castle's whitewashed and turretted towers; the visitor centre at the Falls of Bruar. Moreover, the sun had moved round and the classic Highland scenery of Glen Garry positively glowed in the new angle of light. I swear there was a cheeky gleam in the eye of the river plashing down its rockpools in the glinting, dancing sunlight. I wanted to pull the emergency lever, leap from the train with my rod and creel and land a brace of brown trout for my missed lunch.

Two backpackers left the train at Dalwhinnie. One was going to spend a couple of days hill-walking across the flanks of Ben Alder to Corrour on the West Highland line, twenty-two miles away. The other was going half a mile to the distillery. No prizes! The temperature felt a good ten degrees lower in Dalwhinnie than Dunkeld. As I walked along the road to the distillery, a playful little wind came whipping off the mountains, snapping at my legs like a bad-tempered Jack Russell. But there was a lark singing above me, the sunshine made the mead-owsweet gleam like vellum, and there was no need for directions - I could smell the alcohol.

The distillery at Dalwhinnie was opened in 1898, a major consideration in its choice of site being the transport opportunities offered by the Highland Railway. That didn't stop it going into liquidation within a few months. Doubtless investors could be equally accused of short-termism a century ago. Under new ownership, however, it managed to survive initial difficulties, actually passing into American ownership until Prohibition caused it to be re-sold back into Scots hands. Five owners in thirty years illustrate the difficulties of the whisky business. In 1934 the distillery burnt down. Four years later it had hardly resumed production, before wartime restrictions on the use of barley closed the distillery yet again. Post war there was something of a revival, though modernisation inevitably eroded some of the traditional working practises, like the production of malt from barley on site, coal firing of the machinery and, in 1969, use of the railway siding. Nowadays just seven people are engaged in the making of Dalwhinnie's distinctive 15 years old malt: 'Pre-dinner dramming of the highest quality', according to *The Original Malt Whisky Almanac*.

I thoroughly enjoyed my tour of the distillery; me, five Spaniards, a German, two Italians and a nice middle-aged couple from Basingstoke. We saw the gleaming copper stills; we heard about the 'head', the 'heart' and the 'tail'; were made familiar with the origin of the phrase 'grist for the mill'; discovered about 'the angels' share'; and learnt that Dalwhinnie keeps its whisky in secondhand American bourbon casks, which will be used up to four times before being turned into charcoal for barbecues; not a bad end for a seventy year life. I wanted to know what the kiln-like structures which peep over the rooftops of most distilleries are called, and Marie, our good humoured guide, told me they were pagodas. Yet I wasn't far wrong in thinking of them as kilns, because, in being used to dry the barley, they functioned in the same way as Kent and Herefordshire oast houses, albeit sadly no longer, the maltings having ceased production, the barley being bought in from specialist maltsters now. At the end of the tour we were all given a 'sample', a none too subtle sales technique which nevertheless had me reaching for my wallet, not that I'm a whisky drinker, but I reckoned a bottle of the stuff would enliven Yellowlees's office-bound routine.

It was just a small sample, not even a 'wee dram', but the walk back to the station seemed both warmer and less far. Save for a pair of house martins chattering to each other as they skimmed over the bog grass, there was utter silence at Dalwhinnie station. The sun was warm on my knees, and a peaceful, post-distillery-tour kind of calm filled me with well-being. My peace was disturbed, but not unpleasantly so, by a Liverpudlian and his grandson who were cycling from Land's End to John O'Groats.

"It'll take us three years," he told me with ill-disguised pride. Which I thought was rather on the slow side until he added: "That's in stages of course."

They weren't cheating. The grandson's spindle had worked loose, so they were train-hopping to Kingussie where they knew there was a bicycle shop where it could be repaired.

"We'll just have to come back to Kingussie and start the next leg next year," sighed the Liverpudlian who then sprang into a vituperative rant against farmers and foot and mouth and the compensation they acquire.

"If you were running an engineering business and something went wrong, either with the manufacture or the market, you wouldn't get Government compensation would you? Not that I've anything against farmers, it's just that they've had it too easy for too long."

Fortunately, before being called upon to give an opinion (and I'm not entirely sure what that might have been) the train came in, coming to a halt at Dalwhinnie's up platform which most trains, other than the down sleeper, seem to use. A 158, well-filled, it rumbled out past the signal box, returning to single track. I saw the distillery's rusty and overgrown siding and wished that some financially acceptable case could be made for making use of it again. Examples of a new generation of MPV (multi-purpose vehicles) units have been developed which would be ideal for lightweight freight. Essentially they are the freight equivalent of a Sprinter, and if marketed effectively could take many non-bulk freights off the roads in cases where the cost of a single wagon and attendant locomotive cannot be justified. I think it was Trix who brought out an attractive OO scale model of a whisky grain wagon in the Sixties. I had two or three on my model railway, and ever since I have felt it appropriate, and altogether desirable, that the ingredients of whisky-making and the finished ambrosia should make its way around the country by rail.

The train cantered down Glen Truim. The sky was darkening over the Monadhliath Mountains. There was going to be no golden evening in the west. We crossed the River Spey on a box girder bridge I hadn't noticed in the morning, and this time I was sitting on the right side (literally) to see the gaunt remains of Ruthven Barracks, half a mile to the east as the train slowed for Kingussie. In the local patois they say 'Riven'. Ruthven by name, riven by history, for the site's tempestuous history goes back to the 14th century when it was a stronghold of the Wolf of Badenoch. It last saw fighting during the Forty-five and was captured by the Jacobites. The survivors of Culloden rallied here in the hope of carrying on the fight, but a disillusioned Bonnie

Prince Charlie ordered them to disperse.

The marshes at Insh looked sombre and mysterious in the fading light. Two thousand acres of them belong to the Royal Society for the Protection of Birds. There are hides and a two mile waymarked trail. I could think of nothing nicer to do with a day than take the train to Kingussie, visit the Highland Folk Museum, Ruthven Barracks and the RSPB Reserve, then round it all off with a pint or two of one of the locally brewed Iris Rose beers at the Royal Hotel. Dash it all, I might even be tempted to paddle a Canadian canoe from Kingussie down to Loch Insh and make a weekend of it.

Aviemore was not looking its best under cloud. I always think it needs sunshine to sustain the illusion that you're in a Swiss ski resort. It was teatime and the shops were shutting, the last steam train had puffed off in the general direction of Boat of Garten, and it was too late in the day to consider hiring a mountain bike, or enrolling for an evening class in feng shui. The long main drag was heaving with holidaymakers. It was hard to find a Scottish voice to eavesdrop on. Germans, Americans, Spanish, Japanese, Scandinavians; all the world had been sold a package tour to Aviemore, and now they wanted to know what to do with themselves. They should have read the small print, and the small print should have said that Aviemore is primarily a 1960s development - when the railway was enjoying its heyday there were just two hotels here, a line of railway-workers houses and a man doing Harry Lauder impressions. Architecturally, Aviemore has the look of a mountain resort in the Yukon, and much of the gold rush mentality too. It should not be mistaken for a traditional Scottish town like Dunkeld or Pitlochry, and once you make that distinction you will avoid disappointment. After walking up and down the main road (and there is basically only *one* road) twice I found myself fighting the urge to go round Tesco. My mother always told me I lacked moral fibre. Years later I realised that that was why she started giving me bran flakes for breakfast. And actually Tesco was fascinating, in a sociologically experimental sort of way, because it was full of foreign nationals moving slowly up and down the aisles in a trance-like state of fascination with the brand names - just the sort of way we entertain ourselves when we're abroad. If you analyse it, we could probably eliminate all this business of tourism, catering and leisure, and go straight from the airport to the nearest retail park.

Healing balm was available at the station - though, don't misunderstand me, not from vending machines. I had to source it from within, make myself spiritually at one with the angels in the architecture. It wasn't difficult, Aviemore really is a beautiful station, the irony is that it doesn't harmonise with the modern community on its doorstep. If there was such a thing as a station transfer market, they ought to do a straight swap (no financial adjustment necessary) with Keith or Elgin where new buildings don't comfortably equate with the old-fashioned towns they serve.

It was a relief to catch the 18.51 Turbostar (170418) back to Inverness. Through conifer plantations it ran to Carrbridge where we crossed with a southbound Class 158. There's a passage in Josephine Tey's posthumously published crime novel *The Man in the Queue*, in which the Inverness-born authoress describes her hero Inspector Grant on board the night sleeper's morning journey down into Inverness: 'and so with a rush, the train took heart on the down grade, to fields again - wide fields in broad straths and little stony fields tacked to hillsides - and lochs, and rivers, and green countryside.' Unfortunately her editors did her the disservice of not correcting her gaff of having it depart from King's Cross; by the 1950s, only Euston sent a sleeper train to Inverness. Not that I'd ever take issue with Ms Tey, for her mostly out of print crime novels are wonderfully written and plotted works, far out-plotting and out-syntaxing the Christies, Sayers and Allinghams of the genre.

The setting sun peeped out just long enough to caress Findhorn Viaduct with its ochre rays. I pressed my face against the window and watched it curve towards me, wishing that either I had the driver's view or a window I could drop and look out of; not daring to ask for too much, like cinders in what's left of my hair. Two girls waved at the train from little grey houses on the hillside at Tomatin, and I signalled back, feeling like the 'old gentleman' in *The Railway Children*. A tractor was whisking hay beneath Culloden Viaduct, and smoke curling up from the chimney pot of a stone cottage beside the Nairn. I drank in the darkling scene, treasuring the day's end play. In the middle distance the Moray Firth lay luminescently at peace, a wider invitation to an altogether bigger picture, and one, perhaps, that only the reliable Messrs Druimuachdar & Slochd would be able to help me with when the time comes.

Useful Contacts

Highland Folk Museum - Tel: 01540 661307.
www.highlandfolk.com

Beatrix Potter Exhibition - Tel: 01350 727272.
www.birnaminstitute.com

Blair Castle - Tel: 01796 481207. www.blair-castle.co.uk.

Perthshire Tourist Board - Tel: 01738 450600
www.perthshire.co.uk

Dunkeld Tourist Information - Tel: 01350 727688

Pitlochry Tourist Information - Tel: 01796 472215

Strathspey Steam Railway - Tel: 01479 810725

Aviemore Tourist Information - Tel: 01479 810363

Bothy Bikes, Aviemore - Tel: 01479 810111

Loch Insh Watersports - Tel: 01540 651272

Kingussie Tourist Information - Tel: 01540 661297

Hamlett & Gow (Butchers) - Tel: 01540 661212

Dalwhinnie Distillery - Tel: 01540 672219

Fastening the Central Belt.

Early morning exploration of Glasgow. An open-top bus tour of Stirling. The Bo'ness & Kinneil Railway. Princes Street Gardens. The Bathgate Line. Cycling Route 75. Rogano.

If the comedian Tony Hawks can hitch hike round Ireland with a fridge and write a bestseller about the experience, went my thought process, then encumbering myself with a bicycle for a train journey back and forth across Scotland's Central Belt should be child's play and might just embellish my sales figures. It wasn't just a mercenary consideration, I would need the bike later in the day. But for the time being it was a cumbersome companion, something needing to be somehow infiltrated into the right-angled, guards-van-less confines of Turbostars and Sprinters; although ScotRail seem to be making a better fist of providing cycle space than many other train operating companies. On the Far North line they even lay on a shadow road van service to take the overspill during the summer months. Trains and bicycles should be the bedfellows of sustainable transport, more bike hire facilities need to be laid on at strategic railheads as in Holland and Germany and, ideally, you should be able to hire from one station and deposit at another.

Bright September mornings don't come much better than the

one I had woken up to. Mother Nature was stripped provocatively to the waist and massaging liquid gold into the shoulders of the statues on George Square. I had been for a loosener down by the Broomielaw, finding myself en route amidst the poignantly truncated approach viaducts to St Enoch's fondly remembered station; reading, on an abandoned bridge support pier by Central station, that 'All Greatness Stands Firm In The Storm'. I had breakfasted on an Americano at a pavement cafe. Pavement cafes in Glasgow! Are they getting soft? It felt 'guid' to be back in the City after sating myself on all that Highland scenery. It was tenements after crofts, it was Partick after Pitlochry, it was auld claithes and porridge, and I loved it. On the concourse at Queen Street I wheeled the bike between incoming hordes of commuters like a war correspondent foolishly making for the front against a tide of retreating soldiers. It felt as if I was a visual metaphor in a French art house film, but to the commuters whose ankles got bruised on my pedals, I probably looked like a right plonker. The 08.40 Turbostar was heading for Aberdeen, but I was only going as far as the first stop, Stirling. Pedants might argue that I was straying away from the Central Belt right at the start of the day's itinerary, but I have a reasoned argument in response. It goes like this - 'drap deid'.

The Turbostar went effortlessly up Cowlairs bank. The neighbouring high rises looked like Lego in the brittle light, though I doubted if life in Sighthill is as perfect as life in Legoland. On another day, on another, photographically based book, I would have been revelling in the opportunities created by the autumnal light. The train picked up speed along the route of the original Edinburgh & Glasgow Railway of 1842 which, apart from the notorious incline at Cowlairs, was laid out for high speed running on a flat, level plane. What visionaries these Victorians were. By Bishopbriggs, three miles out, it was shaking off the city's tentacles. Rosebay willowherb's purple blooms were dwindling and the railway cuttings losing their perennial splash of colour. The sidings at Cadder were overgrown and bereft of wagons. Campsie Fells formed the northern horizon as we came to Lenzie, a suburb of Kirkintilloch. Lines once splayed off north and south, but you have to look closely to see their scars in the landscape. Until 1951 you could reach Aberfoyle from here, thereafter a commuter service embraced Kirkintilloch until 1964; since then the housing schemes have burgeoned and Beeching's pessimism and parsimony have left them short-changed. Even at the outset, the Edinburgh & Glasgow Railway knew when it was on to a good thing by promulgating the 'villa trade'. The line to the south originally belonged to the Monkland & Kirkintilloch Railway, opened as early as 1826 to the unusual gauge of 4ft 6ins. Just after leaving Lenzie I spied yet another ruined asylum, the Central Belt seems full of them. Was it something in the water, was it something in life's raw-edged intensity that filled these gaunt edifices with the deranged and despondent? This one, the Woodilee Hospital, was built in 1875 for 'pauper lunatics'. Ouch!

Where the line crosses Luggie Water, the trackbed of a loop line from Coatbridge passes beneath a girder bridge to join the main line. The density of railways hereabouts must have been bewildering. Now there are just wastegrounds colonised by sil-ver birch, the boles of which gleamed intensely in the sunlight. There were outcrops of coal between Lenzie and Croy. Only bings remain. The last working mine closed in 1968. From Croy you can see Clyde F.C.'s Broadwood Stadium; they call them-selves the 'Bully Wees'! Jackie and I picnicked at Croy in the early Eighties when the trains were push & pull worked by Class 47/7s, and in the time it took us to eat our ham rolls we saw *Greyfriars Bobby*, *Lothian* and *Lady Diana Spencer*.

The Forth & Clyde Canal came into view across the laptop of the businessman at the table opposite me, revelling in its new found navigability. A much older linear phenomenon, the Roman's Antonine Wall, parallels the railway to the south. At Castlecary the railway crosses the A80 by way of an impressive eight arch viaduct. In the early days of the railway stage coach-es carried passengers from Castlecary station along the turnpike to Stirling. The former Caledonian line from Motherwell passes beneath the North British route and the two railways are linked by a chord between Greenhill's Upper and Lower junctions. The quarter-hourly express shuttle services between Queen Street and Waverley continue eastwards through Falkirk High. Trains for Stirling and beyond curve northwards, skirting Bonnybridge, passing beneath the canal and negotiating the west face of a triangle of lines at Carmuirs to reach Larbert. Traditional signal boxes and semaphore signaling proliferate, creating the impression of a railway time warp. In the old days there was a double triangle of lines leading to a branch running westwards to Denny and the Kilsyth & Bonnybridge Railway. Bring me my chariot of fire, bring me my non-corridor lavatory composite, bring me my knife-grinder's concessionary return to Colzium.

Beyond Larbert the old Caledonian main line strikes northwards to reach Stirling. The Central Belt and its industrial overtones are left behind. The Ochil Hills become prominent on the north-eastern horizon. You sense the Highlands and, I daresay, if the windows could be opened you might be able to smell them too. Across a freshly baled cornfield I saw a well restored tower house in the vicinity of Plean. There used to be a station at Bannockburn and I flippantly wondered if Robert the Bruce benefited from special party rates in assembling his force of five thousand there in June 1314, though knowing the Caledonian Railway's parsimonious reputation I somehow doubted it.

Stirling Castle and the Wallace Memorial lend a certain fairy tale character to the approach to Stirling. Small forests of semaphore signals add to the appeal. The impressively large Middle signal box should strictly speaking have been put in a museum years ago, but Railtrack Scotland's dwindling resources have been diverted elsewhere. Similar cashflow problems have put back the project to re-open the line through to Alloa for passenger trains. I extracted my bike from the designated cycle accommodation adjacent to the disabled toilet and alighted at Stirling's exuberantly styled station which dates from 1913. It is the work of James Miller who also designed the likes of Weymss Bay and Troon and, as a colleague of Yellowlees had recently remarked, looks like a seaside station also. Brushing the sand from my shoes I secured my recalcitrant metal companion (at my own risk) in the cycle rack and went for a brief stroll through the town's pleasantly pedestrianised thoroughfares before returning at ten o'clock to the Guide Friday bus stop outside the front of the station.

There are those (my nearest and dearest amongst them) who pour scorn on open top tourist buses, but I've always found them an excellent way of effecting a rapid introduction to the places they patrol. Guide Friday's Stirling service operates every forty minutes, and the round trip from the station takes an hour and twenty minutes. If you have time at your disposal you can alight at one or another of the interesting ports of call en route but, as usual, I had a hectic day ahead of me and only had time for the round trip. Nevertheless I thoroughly enjoyed the experience, even if the breezy weather made sitting on the top deck feel like going for a flight in the exposed cockpit of an early bi-plane.

The bus set off in a southerly direction, heading for the Bannockburn Heritage Centre. The driver was called Robin and the courier Diane, a feisty little red head who I kept expecting to break into the chorus of *Shout*. On the way out of town Diane pithily brought her audience of two up to pace on the Battle of Bannockburn. In 1313 Stirling Castle was in English hands, but under siege. Bruce's impetuous brother had made a chivalrous agreement with the governor of the castle that should the garrison not be relieved by an English force before the following Midsummer Day, it would be surrendered to the Scots. In effect this became a challenge to Edward II who turned his back on his war with France to make a show of strength against the Scots. Edward marched north with a well drilled army of twenty thousand cavalry, bowmen and foot soldiers. Bruce waited for him with little more than a quarter of that amount, mostly spearmen on foot. With a finely tuned sense of timing, the opposing forces took their places two miles south of Stirling, on Midsummer's Eve. The English, as always, were full of confidence bordering on arrogance. Edward half expected Bruce to retreat into the hills beyond Stirling, it would, he reasoned, be ridiculous for him to charge a force four times as big. That it was such an obvious course not to take, gave the Scots a huge element of surprise. At first light the Scots came out of their hiding places in the woods and attacked the English before their cavalry could be mounted. Chaos ensued and the English, for all their organisation, simply disintegrated. Many were drowned attempting to flee across the River Forth or the Bannock Burn. One of the most famous military victories of history was claimed by the Scots, something so rare that, to this day, in sporting contests, the Scots draw inspiration from Bannockburn before, nine times out of ten, facing up to a Culloden of a defeat.

If Edward II and Robert the Bruce were on the tour bus today they'd find their battleground occupied by hotels and car rental offices. The Saltire unfurls itself limply in the breeze over the Borestone, traditionally Bruce's command post, and a statue of the great Scottish king on his horse reflects on how history has cheated him. 'Browse in the shop and enjoy coffee or lunch in the attractive cafe', is what we are exhorted to do today, no more 'taking o' the ure', no more charging out of the trees to rebut the tourist buses, perhaps a more pernicious enemy than cavalry.

Cheerfully, Diane commentated on the run back into Stirling, past St Ninian's steeple, the church itself having been absent-mindedly blown up by the Jacobites in the 18th century. We ran through the town centre, seeing with fresh eyes the first floor architecture, still characteristically Scots above the everyday plastic fascia of the chain stores. We stopped to pick up extra passengers at the Tourist Information Centre and the Stirling Story visitor centre, then made our way out of town again, crossing the River Forth on a bridge built by Robert Stevenson (the writer Robert Louis Stevenson's father) in 1831. Nearby stands the old bridge, a picturesque medieval packhorse structure with large cutwaters. It was the first time I had seen it, yet it struck a chord and I experienced an inexplicable sense of *déjà vu*. Then I remembered that a print of a painting of the bridge had adorned our sitting-room when I was young, something my father had acquired early in his printing career. Diane was explaining that an even earlier wooden bridge had spanned the Forth, and that it had been the scene of another famous battle, when William Wallace had got the better of the Earl of Surrey hereabouts in 1297. I knew I should have paid more attention to *Braveheart*, but had found it difficult to take Mel Gibson in the role of William Wallace seriously, as I kept expecting him to transmogrify into Martin Riggs in *Lethal Weapon*.

The bus ran out to Bridge of Allan, passing black Scots cattle in a field of thistles and negotiating a level crossing over the main line to Perth. My fellow passengers and I learned of R.L. Stevenson's boyhood holidays in this little spa town and of the success of its brewery. We paused at some traffic lights and I reflected how odd it was to watch strangers going about their daily routine in the street below, feeling slightly superior, like another David Attenborough doing a documentary on the lives of a long lost species of ant-eaters. Stirling University opened in 1967, Scotland's eighth. We drove through the campus, much to the amusement of the students, who at their innocent age probably think they'll never be seen dead on an open top tourist bus. Wanna bet? A new National Swimming Academy is taking shape in the grounds which once formed part of the estate of Airthrey Castle. One more trip, I reckoned, and I could take over from Diane, blindfold!

All the time, we had been creeping up on the Wallace Memorial, a striking tower erected in 1869 by public subscription. I always like to read about monuments erected by 'public subscription'. What faith they had in posterity then. Can you imagine it happening now? The doorbell rings and someone's standing there asking if you'd give them money to put up a statue of some popular figure or other. The trouble nowadays is that popularity equates with vulgarity and they'd be seeking monies to fund a statue of a pop star, or a game show host or a National Lottery winner. Two hundred and forty six steps will take you to the top of the tower and Diane did her best to fill us with enthusiasm for the ascent, regarding me (for I was the only one who didn't rise to the challenge) with the jaundiced eye of the superior athlete.

It was rather disconcerting being left alone on the top of the bus with Diane. I felt like the only person in a pub who'd turned up to listen to a Lulu revival artiste. We ran down Alloa Road and along the A91, both of us clinging to our respective piece of handrail like seasick passengers on the deck of a cruise liner in a typhoon. Grimacing into her microphone, she regaled me with Wallace's fate after being captured in 1305, describing in lurid detail his hanging, drawing and quartering in London's Smithfield, and how Edward I - that popular figure north of the border, side-splittingly known as the Hammer of the Scots - had caused his limbs to be sent to various Scottish towns and cities, *pour encourager les autres* nae doot.

We came back into Stirling, called at the Tourist Information Centre again, then climbed up cobbled streets towards the castle, passing statues of Robert Burns, Rob Roy, Campbell-Bannerman (Britain's Prime Minister 1905-8) and Stirling's most famous son, Mel Gibson. It was a bumpy but fascinating ride. We growled uphill past the flamboyant High School of 1888 (now a hotel) and the Old Town Jail, arriving presently outside the castle itself, drawing level with ranks of tour coaches lined up outside its walls, and it crossed my mind that their arrival would have seemed far more menacing to the castle's beleaguered 14th century inhabitants than any siege.

In due course the bus dropped me back at the station and I retrieved my bike. The 11.35 to Edinburgh had started back at Dunblane and was formed by a Class 158 unit with provision for bicycles towards the centre of the train. I retraced my steps to Larbert, scanning an old one inch map on the way, noticing for the first time that there had been considerable coal mining activity in the area and a corresponding network of mineral lines. Another interesting looking line had been a branch which ran - across a swing bridge spanning the Forth - to Alloa through Airth and Throsk; I would have loved to have heard its services announced over the tannoy at Buchanan Street in a thick Scots burr, it would have been like listening out for the next train to Urth, Ayr and Warter.

On Larbert's up platform a plaque commemorates the men of the Royal Scots Leith Territorial Battalion who left here for Gallipoli on May 22nd 1915, but got no further than

Dumfriesshire, being victims of arguably the most appalling crash in British railway history - Quintinshill. What a poignant irony, to be heading for embarkation at Liverpool, to stare death in the face on a Turkish battlefield, only to die in a field less than a hundred miles from home. When a roll call was taken after the collision, only 67 of the 485 soldiers who had set out from Larbert were able to stand up and be counted; 214 of them were dead. At ten minutes to seven in the morning the troop train had collided with a local which had been placed on the up line to allow a late-running overnight express from London to overtake it, both the up and down loops at Quintinshill (a mile and a half north of the border at Gretna) already being occupied by goods trains. Barely a minute later the express ploughed into the wreckage. At five o'clock that evening the Royal Scots survivors were taken by train to Carlisle where a large but suitably subdued crowd was waiting in deference to the disaster. The soldiers did not walk or stumble dazedly out of Citadel station, they marched.

At Larbert Junction the train veered sharply east, affording me a glimpse of the Falkirk Wheel taking shape on a nearby hillside. It will be an astonishing landmark, proof perhaps that inspirational engineering skipped a century, although I can't help feeling that its significance will transcend its function, that of conveying pleasure boats through a 78 feet disparity in the levels of the newly restored Forth & Clyde and Union canals. Inspiration may have had to have been reinvented, but one might also argue that nowadays we save our greatest feats of civil engineering - the Millennium Dome, the London Eye, pedestrian bridges over the Tyne and the Thames, the Falkirk Wheel - for purely frivolous purposes.

An EWS train of empty coal hoppers passed us at Camelon, and then I saw the Forth & Clyde Canal go under the railway by a ladder of locks. In the canal's heyday there was a swing-bridge at this point to enable high-masted vessels to pass through. Falkirk Grahamston's modern station is more handy for the town centre than Falkirk High. A mile east of here a freight only branch curves away in a north-easterly direction to serve various depots at Grangemouth. The railway reveals wide views of the Firth of Forth, Longannet power station's high chimney being the dominant landmark. Skirting the parkland of Callendar House the line reaches Polmont Junction where it joins the route of the original Edinburgh & Glasgow Railway. Polmont station is an attractive stone built original dating from the mid 19th century. For a mile or two the Union Canal parallels the railway on an embankment to the south. At Bo'ness Junction there is a connection with the Scottish Railway Preservation Society's Bo'ness & Kinneil preserved line. This was to be my next port of call, so I made ready to leap off the train with my bicycle at Linlithgow, the next stop. First, though, the train had to cross the Avon Viaduct, a 26 arch structure listed as an Ancient Monument, and then pass close to Linlithgow Palace, an even more significant Ancient Monument, on its high level approach to the town.

Linlithgow is an historic town, a Royal and Ancient Burgh, and Mary Queen of Scots was born in the Palace here in 1542. So it was with a feeling of suppressed cultural denial that I ignored its symbolic attractions and pedalled furiously down the A706 to Bo'ness where I had an appointment to keep with Peter Howell, Senior Stationmaster on the Bo'ness & Kinneil Railway. It was a quiet afternoon, towards the season's end and in the absence of crowds, the station exuded a peaceful, timeless branchline feel. So it came as some surprise to me to learn that the station at Bo'ness which visitors encounter today never existed in working days. It has been formed by an amalgamation of preserved buildings from other sites: the station offices came from Wormit at the south end of the Tay Bridge; the train shed is from Haymarket and dates back to the opening of the Edinburgh & Glasgow Railway; the signal box is of Caledonian design and stood at Garnqueen South Junction near Coatbridge; and the footbridge belonged to the Highland Railway and spanned the platforms at Murthly on the line between Perth and Inverness. I asked Peter where the imposing engine shed was from and he admitted with a laugh that it wasn't an original at all, more a pastiche, though the window frames had come from the old Glasgow & South Western locomotive

depot at Corkerhill, Glasgow. This hotchpotch of railway architecture gels remarkably well, and I think even an informed
purist would be churlish to object to the marriage of so many
styles. It's atmosphere which counts, and the Bo'ness & Kinneil
Railway oozes with it.

Peter and I were getting along very well. He was an
admirable guide. Mind you, he should know his stuff, having
been the stationmaster for sixteen years. He hails from North
London and is a retired plant pathologist. I didn't get to the
bottom of what a plant pathologist does, but I did learn that the
source of his railway enthusiasm was the Great Eastern line out
of Liverpool Street and, that if he had had to rely on his wartime
experiences in Great Western territory, he probably would never
have become a railway enthusiast at all. As he took me on a con-
ducted tour, Peter explained how the Scottish Railway
Preservation Society had come to put down its roots in this
windy setting on the edge of the Firth of Forth.

"The SRPS is forty years old. We were looking around for a
suitable line to preserve. We looked at Callander, but the good
folk of Callander didn't want dirty steam engines back on their
doorstep. We were the original instigators of the line at
Aviemore, but at the eleventh hour the bulk of the membership,
who were largely based in central Scotland, felt it was too far
away. So we started looking again for a central Scotland option.
One of the curiosities of Beeching was that the demolition contractors got to work within *days* of each line closing. It was as if
they were desperate to make sure the clock couldn't be turned
back. We began fund raising to save the Alloa to Dollar line but
British Rail were asking for three thousand pounds a month as
a retainer, and the regional boundary changes of 1975 meant
that it was difficult to secure local authority funding. We ended
up here in 1979 with the help of the Central Regional and
Falkirk Council. It was good timing, we got a lot of help from
the Manpower Services schemes and made rapid progress."

Just then we heard a toot on a whistle and the train came into
sight, an industrial tank engine trailing three Mark 1 carriages in
its wake. Peter had arranged for me to do the next round trip to

Birkhill, travelling out on the footplate and back with the guard. The engine was called *Lord Roberts*, and it had been built by Neilson Reid & Co at the Hyde Park Works in Glasgow in 1902. I was introduced to the footplate crew: Inspector, Stuart Sellar; trainee driver, Stephan Kay; and fireman, John Marson. As soon as the engine had run round its train and coupled up we were on our way. *Lord Roberts* is a right hand drive locomotive, and I stood on that side of the cab, immediately behind Stephan. As we puffed out of Bo'ness, Stephan explained his connections with the SRPS.

"I've been interested in trains since I was about eleven years old. I was Chief Executive with Inveresk, but I retired from the paper industry. I've done quite a lot of driving out in Poland, but here I'm just working my way up from the bottom again."

We were steaming slowly beside the waters of the Forth. I could see the picturesque village of Culross directly across the firth. A small tanker was heading upstream towards Grangemouth. A woman was walking a West Highland terrier along a path beside the line. I had recognised Stuart Sellar from a television programme. He's well known in railway circles for his collection of self shot cine films showing steam in the Fifties and Sixties. He had been a professional railwayman, but I didn't get the chance to ask him in what capacity. Beyond the request stop at Kinneil the line curves inland, passing beneath the main road and beginning to climb at 1 in 45. *Lord Roberts* was working hard against the grade. John shovelled coal furiously into the firebox. I looked ahead through the big round spectacle at the track ascending through the woods, enjoying the sensation of a locomotive hard at work.

Presently we came out of the trees and ran between cornfields, a welcome breeze blowing across the footplate. Suddenly the track splayed into a loop and we were drawing into Birkhill, a small station located in a cutting. Passengers can alight here and visit a preserved fireclay mine or simply go for a walk in the neighbouring woods of oak, ash, hawthorn and rowan exploring for eyebright and birdsfoot trefoil. As the locomotive ran round once more I chatted to John Marson, discovering that he had also been a professional railwayman, beginning his career in 1960 as a cleaner at Tilbury, later becoming a fireman at March. Curiously, he had regularly worked on one of the SRPS's preserved locomotives, the Standard Class 4 tank No. 80105 when it operated on the London, Tilbury & Southend line. In the later stages of his railway employment he'd been involved with the Freightliner services to and from Stranraer and was able to bemoan with me the complete absence of rail freight to and from that port now.

From the cacophony of the footplate I went to the cloistered calm of the guards van, where Ian Barrenger was waiting to tell me all about a guard's duties on a preserved line. Ian is an Essex man by birth, but met his wife while he served in the Royal Navy at Rosyth and he's been a postman in Lothian for thirty-seven years.

"People don't always realise," he told me matter-of-factly, "that it's the guard who's in charge of a train, not the driver. I arrive about an hour before the first train is due to leave. I sign on and then check the stock. Make sure there's oil in the axle boxes; check the connections for the steam and vacuum pipes and the buckeye couplings. Then I go over the train and make sure it's clean. When the engine backs on I have to look at the vacuum gauge for the brakes, then go along to the last carriage and take the pipe or 'bag' off to check the vacuum there. I've also got to make sure that everything's in the guards van: a spare 'bag', tools, a ladder, chocks, a fire extinguisher, track circuits and a spare screw coupling."

All the train crew on the Bo'ness & Kinneil Railway, and the vast majority of other workers as well, are volunteers, and I marvelled at their professionalism and commitment. Running a preserved railway is not like running a car boot sale. It's an unpaid version of the real thing, and the travelling public trust you in exactly the same way; perhaps not fully appreciating the dedication that goes into providing such a service. Ian told me how he had recently had to remonstrate with a member of the public who was trying to cross the line at the level-crossing at Kinneil while a fair was on. The man, who was accompanying two small children, apparently had no comprehension of the danger he was putting himself and the children in by trying to cross the line when the gates were shut against him for a train to pass. That Britain's preserved railways have such a marvellous safety record is down to the vigilance of men like Ian much more than the care of the general public. Playing at trains? Do Celtic and Rangers *play* at football?

Back down the hill we trundled to Bo'ness. The last service of the day was due to be diesel hauled: primarily to give the engine crew time to dispose of the fire, but also because a new generation of railway enthusiasts enjoy the sight of old diesel classes, no longer in everyday service, working along the line as well. Stephan and John took *Lord Roberts* off to the engine sidings while Stuart went to fire 27001 up, a classic Birmingham Railway Carriage & Wagon Co Type 2 design dating from 1958. I stayed with Ian, working my passage by carrying the tail lamp from one end of the train to the other and proudly fixing it into place on what had again become the rear of the train. I would have liked to travel up the line again on the diesel, but time was pressing and Peter wanted to show me over the running shed and the Scottish Railway Exhibition collection.

No one who's ever been a trainspotter can really resist a running shed. As soon as Peter had led me over the cindery tracks, I was back in my early teens, stealing into some smoky motive power depot or other, half excited at the numbers there for the taking, half fearful lest some officious foreman might unceremoniously eject me by the seat of my corduroy pants. Most trainspotters are born poachers and old habits die hard, I was shocked to find myself in the act of jotting down the numbers of the locomotives within. But then again, you're probably dying to know what they were! So here's a list:

419, a Caledonian Railway 0-4-4 tank of McIntosh design built at St Rollox, Glasgow in 1907.

"This is our flagship," Peter remarked, "and it's a sobering thought that it has spent a third of its life in preservation."

65243 *Maude*, a North British engine dating from 1891 and named, not after the lady who Tennyson invited into the garden, but after the First World War military figure.

44871, a Stanier Black 5 whose claim to fame was that it worked the last leg of the 'Fifteen Guinea Special' at the end of steam in August 1968. We had met before, because my father had driven me up to Rainhill to watch the train go sadly by. No one there that day could have possibly foreseen steam's second coming in the preservation era. The other mainstay of the SRPS steam fleet, the Standard tank 80105, was away on loan to the Caledonian Railway at Brechin, whilst, secreted away in another shed, was the Gresley 4-4-0 *Morayshire*, sole survivor of a handsome class of locomotive much associated with the LNER lines in central Scotland, and perhaps due to steam again within the not too distant future. Ironically, Bo'ness had been used as an assembly point for withdrawn steam locomotives in the days before the preservation movement began to flourish. Many LNER designs now either extinct, or extremely rare, were marshalled here before being sent to the breakers. Their loss is immeasurable.

From the running shed, Peter and I found our way to two huge exhibition halls at the rear of the site. They contain a fascinating collection of rolling stock and associated railwayana. Far too many items to catalogue here, but I suppose pride of place must go to the North British 4-4-0, *Glen Douglas*, one of the famous quartet of pre-Grouping locomotives brought back into steam in the Fifties for excursion work. It looked rather glum sitting lifelessly inside the exhibition hall, and Peter agreed with me that it ought to be brought back to working order, if only a sugar daddy would materialise. Similarly some vintage examples of rolling stock, the GNSR Inspector's Saloon of 1898, once used by Royalty on the branch to Ballater, and the Highland six wheeler dating from 1909, a regular on the Strathpeffer line. Proceeding along the ranks we found a fish van, a salt wagon, a gunpowder van, and a Lancashire & Yorkshire Railway tank carrying wagon from the First World War; each humble vehicle telling a story of Scottish transport and industrial history. It's a wonderful assembly, and the SRPS deserve much praise in bringing it together under one roof, but

I felt like an animal research activist, and wanted to liberate them all.

I didn't so much pedal furiously back uphill to Linlithgow, as laboriously. Three miles seemed like thirty and I was glad to be back on the train again, slumped by a window seat and heading for Edinburgh. The Union Canal and the M9 motorway keep the railway company like security guards. The landscape is largely agricultural, with hints of former coal mining activity here and there. I got a glimpse of the Forth road bridge, but not its more illustrious neighbour. A long sequence of rocky cuttings leads to Winchburgh Junction, at which point the coal trains from Ayrshire to Longannet veer away from the main line. In quick succession, a tunnel and a golf course and a castle and a bing send bewildering messages to the brain. Niddry Castle has associations with Mary Queen of Scots. The viaduct over the River Almond is the most impressive on the Edinburgh & Glasgow line. It is half a mile long and has thirty-six arches. It precedes Newbridge Junction and the Bathgate line, a route I would be following later in the afternoon. The lost stations of Ratho and Gogar no longer delay trains hurtling towards Edinburgh, but they do sound like characters from Shakespeare's 'Scottish' play. Some sort of public walkway seems to have been established on the trackbed of the Corstorphine branch, which closed its doors to passengers in 1967. Then come Murrayfield and Haymarket, those hallowed names to generations of rugby and railway fans; twin religions with an inevitability of disappointment and denial built in to them.

I found somewhere to leave my bike on Waverley station's Platform 1, and went for a stroll in Princes Street Gardens to stretch my legs. A piper was playing at the top end of the Waverley Bridge, from which open top buses were making frequent departures for a tour of the 'Athens of the North'. With all Edinburgh's considerable charms to choose from, I lay on the warm grass beneath the Scott Monument in the forlorn hope that some of his literary inspiration would rub off on me. (I expect you feel the same way). I am guilty of not knowing as much of Sir Walter Scott's output as I should, though I can reel off the names of W.P.Reid's sublimely elegant class of 4-4-0s first introduced in 1909: *Lady of Avenel, Laird o' Monkbarns, Kettledrummie, Cuddie Headrigg, Jingling Geordie, Peter Poundtext, Wandering Willie*; an inspired choice of locomotive names whose bearers I never had the good fortune to encounter. I have often thought that other authors' literary characters or titles would make ideal names for railway engines. I am surprised the Great Western didn't mine Quiller-Couch; or the South Eastern & Chatham, H.G.Wells; or the London & South Western, Thomas Hardy; or the North Staffordshire, Arnold Bennett; or the Metropolitan, Conan Doyle: *True Tilda*, *The Potwell Inn*, *Jude the Obscure*, *Anna of the Five Towns* and *The Solitary Cyclist* would have been marvellous engines to ride behind. Similarly, in more modern times, I always felt that the London Midland Region missed a trick when they didn't name the West Coast electrics after characters in Beatles songs: it would have been good to arrive at Lime Street and find *Lovely Rita*, *Eleanor Rigby* or *The One and Only Billy Shears* at the head of the next train to Euston.

The 16.18 to Bathgate manifested itself as a Strathclyde red & cream coloured Class 156, the sort of diesel unit where you hang your bicycle from a lofty hook and leave it dangling in a most ungainly way. It makes room for more bicycles if it does nothing for their self esteem, but I wonder how longer it will be before some clever train operating company has its commuters hanging vertically to combat overcrowding. I didn't choose the best of seats. No sooner had I made myself comfortable in a tabled bay of four, than a suited youth sat opposite me and began dosing himself with extra strong cold capsules. He was snorting and sniffling from every orifice, and looked as if he should not have been out at all. Jackie always warns me about travelling by public transport. Ideally, she'd like me to go through a decontamination unit each time I come home. This guy compounded matters by opening a packet of cheese and onion crisps and getting out a copy of *Lord of the Rings*, so there were three good reasons for not sitting opposite him. Five when you consider that he was half my age and had twice the amount of hair on his head. I was just about to get up pointedly and go and sit elsewhere when a woman came and sat beside me and I was stymied. Not that I could have found anywhere else to sit, for as the train pulled out it was strictly standing room only for any latecomers.

The Bathgate line is a success story. It re-opened in 1986 following thirty years of passenger train absence from Bathgate. My full to standing train is typical of its popularity. But how did all these people travel before the line re-opened? Or didn't they travel at all? Both questions are pertinent. Reinvigorated railways regenerate economies, it's a simple equation. The wonder is it takes such an eternity: so much market research, so many engineering reports, and all that fiscal agonising, before we set about re-opening a railway. Yet, invariably, they prove successful. So why does it take so long?

Such trains of thought brought me once more to Newbridge Junction and the divergence of the Bathgate branch from the main line to Glasgow. The year after the Bathgate line re-opened, the Railway Development Society published a slim guidebook to the railways of Scotland, part of an enjoyable series covering the whole of Britain; yet a series, one senses, which met with public indifference. John Yellowlees contributed a piece about the Bathgate line which he had modestly sent me prior to my journey. 'The mastery of the railway pioneers is well demonstrated in the magnificent view which the Bathgate train now affords of Grainger and Miller's superb 1842 Grade A listed Almond Valley Viaduct. On passing several modern industrial premises, the Bathgate line has its own Grade B listed viaduct over the Almond, Birdsmill, after which a much more modern structure takes the line again across the M8'. Quite so, Yellowlees, would that you had been with me to spice the facts with your dry sense of humour, you poor, office-anchored thing you.

The line crosses the Union Canal, and I caught a glimpse of a placid ribbon of water winding through the fields towards Broxburn. People had said, kindly, that I should be writing a guide book to it, but quite honestly I don't think it would be viable. After twenty years of canal guide publishing I know the habits and mind set of pleasure boaters better than most. The majority of them like their canals scenic and not too heavily locked, and though it pains me to say it, I don't think the newly restored canals of central Scotland will ever become as popular with holidaymakers as their counterparts in central England. But it would be wonderful to be proved wrong!

The line is double track for the first three or four miles. The train rumbled slowly over the down line's jointed track and a Class 158 slipped by Edinburgh bound. The mileposts count the distance from Glasgow via Airdrie, even though - as we shall see - the line no longer remains intact beyond Bathgate. Singling, and with shale bings to the south, the line reaches Uphall. Judging by the number of vehicles in the car park, this is a popular railhead. The train, however, didn't empty noticeably and we proceeded through a sub continent of industrial estates and business parks to Livingston North. If Uphall had held little attraction for my fellow passengers, Livingston (Scotland's fourth new town) proved quite the opposite. Even the one-man, virus-carrying, disaster zone got off, having fulfilled his daily quota of contaminations. You see, I had penetrated his disguise, he was one of these people that pharmaceutical companies impregnate with germs and send out into the community to drum up business. There, the investigative journalist in me has blown the lid off a public fiasco. If anything happens to me, you'll know why, but I'd just like to point out that my bank manager has access to the complete dossier.

A nature reserve and a golf course shadow the railway's approach to Bathgate: I don't know who was having the more fun; the newts or the golfers. I was preparing myself mentally for the next stage of the journey, a sixteen mile bicycle ride along the Bathgate to Airdrie Railway Path & Sculpture Trail, an integral part of National Cycle Route 75 managed by Sustrans. My preparations consisted of a sequence of breathing exercises passed on to me by a friend of mine who'd been in the Tour de France. He hadn't actually put his name down for the event. In fact, he'd been on one of those Cycling for Softies holidays, and had happily been riding along a tree-shaded French by-way one afternoon, wearing a rather fetching new yellow jersey his mother had bought him from the Wakefield branch of Marks & Spencer, when ...

Bathgate station is a single platform interchange with the local buses overlooked by Lidl and Argos. It is not on the site of either of the original Bathgate stations, Upper and Lower, nodal points of a complex network of North British secondary lines by which one could travel to such diverse locations as: Morningside (the industrial village in Lanarkshire, that is, not the uppercrust Edinburgh suburb); Glasgow Queen Street Low Level (via Airdrie); Coatbridge by way of Slamannan; and Manuel for Linlithgow and Bo'ness. The line I was going to shadow to Airdrie closed to passengers in 1956. Now its route is recognised as something of a black hole in public transport terms, and West Lothian Council, in conjunction with Strathclyde Passenger Transport, are keen for the railway to be reinstated at some point in the future. In the meantime, they see the provision of a connecting bus service as a worthwhile stop-gap and plan to petition the Strategic Rail Authority to secure funding for the project.

I cycled along Whitburn Road to find an access point to the railway path. As soon as I left the road behind I felt - just like the Four Tops all those years ago - as if I was in a *Different World*. The pathway's tarmac surface ran behind the backs of houses before escaping into the fields. It passed under the A801 as I cycled beside a herd of Belted Galloways. At frequent intervals one comes upon specially commissioned sculptures which reflect the route's origins and enhance the modern landscape. The first one I encountered was a giant 'keyhole' which you have to cycle through. It was difficult not to think of *Alice in Wonderland*, certainly a childlike innocence prevailed upon me, and I found myself pedalling along pretending to be a J39 with a bumping, swaying train of coal wagons behind me. Possibly this explains why people walking their dogs ran shrieking away over the fields as I approached them. For a while after one or two of these disturbing encounters I pretended instead to be a late forty-something on a purple and orange coloured ladies mountain bike, though with little noticeable effect on the reception passers by afforded me.

From time to time the tarmac left the trackbed and detoured around some obstacle or other: here a carbuncle like coal bing, there a close encounter with the water table. Baffling micro-ecologies of heather contrasted with acres of bog grass. Enigmatic buildings staked their claim on the landscape: old bothies; the crumbling edges of old platforms; a peculiar concrete structure that may once have been an air raid shelter, or the entrance to a small drift mine, or the foyer for a parallel universe. By Blackridge I toyed with the idea of leaving the route and going in search of a fish supper, but something told me I might not necessarily find one, and would therefore waste precious time. So I pressed on, coming upon a big worked out quarry face, and seeing the course of an old mineral line curving southwards into a sea of desolation. This was not a star-studded Central Belt, I reflected, but a well worn one; an altogether surprisingly remote buffer zone between the huge conurbations of Edinburgh and Glasgow.

Soon I was passing from West Lothian into North Lanarkshire, a very real divide between East and West. A rabbit ran out in front of me as his forefathers might have run out in front of a train. Beyond the overgrown timber platform which had been the remote wayside station at Forrestfield, the line began to run alongside Hillend Reservoir. What Burns called 'Westlin' Winds' blew across the water, trailing some rowing boats at anchor in their wake. A lonely angler stood thigh high in waders a few yards out from the bank. He and his ilk had undoubtedly inspired the Calor Fishermen sculpture nearby. Two middle aged women on horses passed me with a friendly wave. I came to the village of Caldercruix. There was a paper mill here once, served by the railway, and my old Ordnance Survey map showed another mineral line striking northwards into a region of mine workings. Now the place is quietly residential. Children were out playing after tea. Some teenage girls were giggling by the church, past which the cycle route is signposted to avoid a flooded cutting. It began sharing its course with the North Calder Heritage Trail, a waymarked trail stretching from the Summerlee Heritage Park at Coatbridge to the Caldercruix Countryside and Nature Park.

I cycled on, under the Moffat Hills which rise to over 800 feet, on the last lap; tired and thinking of my supper. The pathway was busier. Folk were coming out after their high teas. Several cyclists passed me, and more people on horseback. Dogs began to be a problem, too busy following scents to be wary of approaching cyclists. Their owners just look askance at you, as if it were you and not their dogs who were out of control. I passed Plains and drifted down the last mile into Drumgelloch, grateful to see the catenary gleaming in the evening light as I approached the single platform, siding-like terminus. It had taken me 105 minutes to cycle the 15 miles; Frank Roach would approve, I was sure. I had ten minutes to wait for the next train to Glasgow and leant gently against a lamp-post, soaking up the sounds of the housing estate: barking dogs, the tinkling tune of an ice cream van, an impromptu game of football on the grass.

When the train came in, several people stayed on it. I couldn't believe they'd come out to Drumgelloch for a scenic ride. I could only assume that they had arrived early at Airdrie and got on it rather than stand about waiting for it to run out to the terminus and return. It was formed of two Class 320, 3 car electric units; one in orange, one in cream and red. I found room for the bicycle in the centre car of the leading unit and sat down happily for the twenty-eight minute ride to Queen Street Low Level. Soon after pulling away, I saw Airdrieonians impressive new stadium, unaccountably called Shyberry Excelsior - sometimes it pays not to know. Airdrie station is somewhat less well-appointed, consisting of an island platform and a couple of sidings overlooked by a modern in design but derelict signal box. The track doubles and crosses a viaduct into Coatdyke. Then comes Coatbridge Sunnyside, which seemed an appropriate name on this sunkissed evening. We skimmed the Summerlee Heritage Park (which I would liked to have visited had it still been open this late into the evening), passed under the old

Caledonian Railway main line from Motherwell to Perth and proceeded towards Glasgow, pausing at a string of suburban stations whose names became increasingly blurred, and which would defy the most well-informed railway enthusiasts in a quiz: Easterhouse, Garrowhill and Shettleston, where are they now? Near Carntyne you can see Celtic's massive football ground on the southern horizon. Bellgrove is the junction for the City of Glasgow Union line which curves round to Springburn. The station of the same name is followed by a two hundred yard long tunnel and High Street Junction, forming a link across the Clyde and access, in the old days, to St Enoch. Beyond High Street station the line plunges underground. I was back, full circle to my point of departure; I had fastened the Central Belt.

To celebrate, I repaired to Rogano, a Glasgow institution since the 1930s, treating my famished inner man to a well chilled bottle of Orvieto, tomato soup, smoked haddock wrapped in bacon on a bed of mashed potato mixed with chives, and one each of all the sweets on the menu; at least, that's what I asked the waitress for, but she assumed I was joking, and made me make do with just the most exquisite sticky toffee pudding. On arrival, I had sensed the staff were somewhat nonplussed by clientel who appear bearing haversacks with bicycle pumps sticking prominently out of them, but they did me proud nonetheless. Gradually my fellow diners' conversation became louder and - from where they were sitting - their jokes funnier; their insight fathomless. The world spun on its axis. I assumed the aloof demeanour of a literary lion and read extracts from H. V. Morton's *In Scotland Again* to myself over coffee and biscuits; recognising in a moment of blinding insight, followed by disillusion, that he was really the Bill Bryson of his age. Roganos to Drumgelloch, Stirling to Bathgate, the secret is to live life not so much to the extremities but to the parameters, to the 'here be dragons' of medieval mapping. I paid the not inconsiderable bill with a notional advance on my royalties. Sometimes you just have to kick the ball and chase after it.

Useful Contacts

Guide Friday - Tel: 0131 556 2244. www.guidefriday.com

Stirling Tourist Information - Tel: 01786 475019

Bannockburn Heritage Centre - Tel: 01786 812664

Stirling Castle - Tel: 01786 450000

The National Wallace Monument - Tel: 01786 472140

Falkirk Tourist Information - Tel: 01324 620244

The Bo'ness & Kinneil Railway -
Tel: 01506 822298. www.srps.org.uk

Sustrans Scotland - Tel: 0131 623 7600

Summerlee Heritage Park - Tel: 01236 431261

Rogano - Tel: 0141 248 4055

EAST COAST EXIT WOUNDS.

BERWICK UPON TWEED STN.

The Granite City. A clifftop railway ride. Not getting out at Montrose. Arbroath Smokies. The land of golf. Dundee and Fife again. Crossing the Forth Bridge. An expedition to Bill Douglas Country. The final journey, Edinburgh to Berwick-upon-Tweed.

Aberdeen was going to work and I was ending my holiday. Both sets of participants looked as glumly grey as the Granite City's baronial edifices. The bars by the harbour were open for business before many of the shops, and I acquired visual evidence confirming its reputation as a hard-drinking city. Hard-drinking and hard-living if the housing (and I use the term generically) I had seen at Kittybrewster was anything to go by. The harbour is just a block away from the station. It gleamed like mother of pearl in the wishy-washy early morning light following a night of rain. P&O's *St Sunniva* was at berth pending its next foray to the Shetlands. Farther down the quayside sundry coasters and North Sea oil industry related vessels added activity to the scene. Access to the docks was refreshingly lax, all too often in my travels around the British coast my innocent curiosity has met the brick wall of security-conscious authority. We are an island race, we should be at liberty to inspect our docks and harbours with a Nelsonian eye.

Access to freight depots can be problematical too, so I had to linger on the perimeter of Guild Street's once imposing goods yard with its massive warehouses which emphasise so eloquently the sheer volume of freight which the railways formerly handled in cities such as this. Pip Dunn had written a piece in *Rail* about Aberdeen's current freight operations by EWS. Each weekday two freight trains arrive from the south and one returns. The commodities brought in include cement, coal, china clay and oil for Aberdeen itself, with limestone and pipes being worked to Montrose and Laurencekirk respectively. Timber from Huntly and Inverurie is carried back. Not a huge portfolio, but one which EWS would dearly love to expand and the introduction of an express logistics service, using the company's Spanish built, 125mph Class 67 diesel locomotives, will undoubtedly add prestige and, who knows, profit. The sword of Damocles hangs over Guild Street in the shape of the spectre of redevelopment. Being a prime city centre site, its value to Railtrack is greater in real estate than railways. I took snap shots for posterity of the goods warehouse, a line of brightly painted EWS mega box wagons exuding confidence within its pigeon haunted gloom. 'Keep Out', warned a hastily erected notice board, 'Dangerous Roof'. The danger, I reflected, lay not so much in the state of the roof, as in the state of mind which gives property development priority over transport.

Goods yards are not the sort of installation most holidaymakers make a bee line for, and neither has this been the sort of book to endear itself to aficionados of the obvious. Like a private eye I have followed my own hunches and made my own entertainment in the process. Boarding a Turbostar to Edinburgh with heavy step, I prepared myself for the last rites run down the coast to Berwick whistling Simon Nicol's plaintive guitar instrumental *End of a Holiday*. How much could I fit into this last day, I wondered, as the train pulled out past Clayhills Depot where the Aberdeen sleeper engine, 67021, was stabled for the day. A little bit further on I saw the poignant remains of Ferryhill engine shed. The last time I'd seen it, in 1965, there had been a Gresley V2 on the turntable, 60824 if my memory is as good as it used to be. If nothing else, my misspent trainspotting youth gave me a numerically retentive memory. Even now I remember my credit card numbers by identifying them with railway engines, though I find myself needing to refer to the cumulative deficit of the Baltic states to remember exactly how my bank account stands.

From Ferryhill the Deeside line ran to Ballater, a 43-mile journey of considerable scenic appeal regularly traversed by the Royal Train carrying its blue blooded occupants to and from Balmoral. How their stock had fallen, was revealed in 1966 when the line was abandoned. A country convinced that it wished to remain a monarchy in perpetuity would surely never have countenanced such a closure. In the early days of the line the management had erected grandstands for spectators at passing stations so that the paying public could cheer the Royal Train's progress.

The Turbostar crossed the River Dee and the line arced eastwards around the base of a big hill to find its way south along the clifftops. A succession of deep clefts make the coast look as if someone has attacked it with a cleaver. They have characterful names like Doonies Yawn, Long Slough and Altens Haven, and you can look down into them and see the waves disintegrating on their basalt flanks like glass splintering in an explosion. Out at sea a cruise liner and a trawler appeared like maritime manifestations of Landseer's 'Dignity & Impudence'. In the narrow strip of land between the cliffs and the railway, ruined farm-houses suggested that this had never been an easy environment to eke a living from.

Portlethen station was re-opened in the Eighties to serve the neighbouring community burgeoned by the oil business. For three or four miles the line drifts inland, negotiating rocky cuttings, the grade switchbacking with the contours of the land. Beyond Newtonhill the sea returns. From one particular curve I could see right down the coast, a succession of headlands; it reminded me of the sudden glimpse one might fortuitously gain down a beautiful woman's neckline, tantalisingly brief but memorably rewarding. Other men might be more enraptured by the gorgeous golf course on the headland at Garron Point offering treacherous tee shots over rocky coves. It would prove an expensive round for me, many balls being lost to the view, shanked into the sea. I would be more at home on the nineteenth, propping up the bar of the elegant wooden clubhouse.

A high curving viaduct carries the line into Stonehaven, or rather away from the centre of this attractive harbour town and through its western suburbs. If you know what to look for you might just see the impressive remains of Dunnottar Castle on its headland a couple of miles to the south-east. Even to the untutored eye the panorama is a particularly fine one. In 1965 I was ill-temperedly marooned on Stonehaven station for two hours having booked a return ticket from Aberdeen to enjoy some steam haulage, only to have made the mistake of using diesel-hauled Edinburgh services in both directions rather than the still predominantly steam worked Glasgow trains. In hindsight I might have enjoyed the English Electric Type 4 traction I experienced that day if I hadn't just watched Stanier Black 5 44704 steam out of Aberdeen ahead of me, first stop Laurencekirk! There wasn't a lot for a thirteen year old to do in Stonehaven but kick his heels on the platform and read the *Melody Maker*. Back then I was impervious to the architecture, its Italianate styling, its circa 1850 origins, its long, canted awning on the up side supported on elegant iron brackets.

Les temps perdu - by 1965 I hadn't read *Sunset Song*, Lewis

Grassic Gibbon's poetical account of Chris Guthrie's progress to womanhood in a rural community on the Howe of the Mearns. Its language is often more sinuously rhythmic than D.H.Lawrence, more sensuous too; shocking, in fact, when the novel first hit the bookshops and the *Paisley Express* labelled it 'close-packed filth'. They should see us now, those outraged newspapermen of 1932 whose morals would leave them islanded on higher ground than the foothills of the Grampians outlined through the train window in the distant west. A visitor centre in the village of Arbuthnott celebrates Grassic Gibbon's life and works, but it is miles from any railway station. Even Laurencekirk has gone from the passenger timetable, its timber station building a ruin, though pipes from Hartlepool are delivered by train to the adjoining goods yard whose pointwork is controlled from a classic Caledonian signal cabin.

Soft yellow cornfields framed the railway. Contemptuously, the Turbostar overtook the traffic on the A90. We crossed the North Esk, which separates Angus from Aberdeenshire and came to Kinnaber Junction, or rather the point at which it used to be. This was the famous finishing tape for the 'Races to the North' of 1895, the nightly contest to get the respective Caledonian and North British services from Euston and King's Cross to Aberdeen by the West and East coast routes which joined at Kinnaber, the North British having running rights thence over the Caledonian to Aberdeen.. At the beginning of July that year the London & North Western and Caledonian companies announced that their 8pm departure from Euston would reach Aberdeen at 7.40 am the next morning. So intense was the rivalry with the Great Northern, North Eastern and North British railways, who operated along the East Coast, that within two months, the timing for both routes had been reduced by roughly two hours. Public safety became sublimated to public relations. The best East Coast time, achieved on the night of August 21st-22nd, covered the 524 miles in 520 minutes. The following night the West Coast partnership travelled their slightly longer 540 miles in 512 minutes, after which sanity prevailed.

Nowadays there is no longer a sleeper service on the East Coast Main Line but the fastest daytime train operated by GNER takes 420 minutes. Don't let anyone tell you with a sneer that railways have not progressed over the last hundred years. To all intents and purposes Kinnaber lost its junction status in 1967 when the through route to Perth via Forfar closed (a year after the last Gresley streamliner had hauled its last Glasgow-Aberdeen 'Three Hour' express) though goods trains trundled along the increasingly overgrown track to Brechin for another four years. Once there were eleven junctions between Kinnaber and Stanley, a whole hinterland of branches reaching out to termini like Blairgowrie, Alyth, Kirriemuir, Edzell and Brechin. How many volumes would this book have stretched to if Scotland's railway system was intact? Yet, nowadays only the preserved Brechin to Bridge of Dun line remains of that once so intricate network.

Some maltings with a high silo overlook the lost egress of the Forfar line. Rusty sidings make mockery of political lip service to environmentally sustainable transport. In France the silo would still be rail-linked, even if it lay at the end of a twenty mile branchline and not on a main line with three passing freight trains per day. I would dearly liked to have got off the train at Montrose. The big expanse of water to the west of the station fascinated me. This is Montrose Basin, three square miles of tidal estuary at the mouth of the South Esk, a haven for migrant and resident wildlife alike. At high tide the basin looks like an inland sea, at low tide a desert of sand. A more than usually high timber fence on the down platform somewhat ironically masks the view of the basin from trains at rest in the station. According to the tourist bumph the town, with its 'exceptionally wide High Street', is worth seeing as well. The modern station building did little to whet my appetite however, it bears an uncomfortably close resemblance to the neighbouring supermarket for my taste.

Limestone from Thrislington in County Durham makes its way by rail on a fortnightly basis to Montrose. Thus I had a one in ten chance of seeing the sidings to the south of the station occupied, and for once statistics, contrary to Mark Twain's belief, did not lie, the tracks were innocent of container flats; moreover, it was apparent that some years had passed since freight last disturbed the dust in the big timber goods shed at one end of the yard. The unsung, single track, South Esk Viaduct, beautifully portrayed in EWS's 2001 Calendar by Lynn Patrick of the National Railway Museum, carries south-bound trains out of the station precincts, and, if you can tear your gaze away from the basin, there are views of the harbour. I effected a quick Wimbledon like shake of my head and saw three coasters at berth, framed by an interesting concrete road bridge which reminded me of one at Rhyl of all places.

By the time the line re-doubled, I had two songs on my mind: Ben Watt's *The Night I Heard Caruso Sing* and Ricky Ross's *Homesick*. Do you need me to tell you why? I would rather just commend Everything But The Girl's *Idlewild* album to you, and Deacon Blue's eponymous *Homesick* and give you the satisfaction of self discovery. Against the broad artist's brush-stroke sweep of Lunan Bay the train made its way south-wards. A few hardy souls were making the most of the British Summer on the wide expanse of creamy-coloured sand. I saw two ruined keeps which spoke of more violent times. Briefly we had the Lunan Water for company, meandering idyllically through set-aside fields of thistles.

I could contain myself no longer, and alighted at Arbroath. Drawn by the aroma of smoked haddock, I made my way to the harbour, discovering a hard, lorne sausage sort of town, gristly to the naked eye but tasty enough once swallowed. I found myself in the 'Fit O' the Toon' amongst low-roofed, grid-like streets. Squeezing through an alleyway I came upon the harbour in the act of being dredged by a small vessel called *Coquet Mouth* registered at Newcastle. There is something rather satisfying in watching a dredger at work, a subconscious cleansing process akin to one's ears being syringed. I imagined the little ship fill-ing its hold with mud and dumping it out at sea, only for the tide to bring it back again, and envied the captain his self-per-petuating contract.

But there was no time to beat about the bush, one doesn't leave Bakewell without a tart, one doesn't leave Melton Mowbray without a pork pie, and one doesn't leave Arbroath without some 'smokies', so I sought out the nearest fishmonger, and my nose led me to the backyard premises of M & M Spink on Marketgate. I sought reassurance from the proprietor that the fish might be packed in such a way as to minimise the risk of unpopularity on the remaining trains of my journey. I seemed to recall an Arnold Bennett short story in which a cheese is carried on a train with dire results. The effect of smoked haddock on a hot day, air-conditioning notwithstanding, could be devastating. I had reckoned without modern vacuum packaging. There would be "nae bother, nae problem" I was assured, as four large fishes had their heads sliced off and their long brown bodies enveloped in plastic. The fishing was, "not what it was", I was lamentably informed, but the fish were "locally caught, nae doot" and I found that comforting in a world where Mallaig Kippers can be caught off the Canadian coast and still pass the Trade Descriptions Act.

There is more to Arbroath than the 'smokies'. With much more time at my disposal I might have inspected the Abbey (scene of the 1320 declaration of independence from England and hiding place of the Stone of Destiny stolen from Westminster Abbey in 1951); gone for a ride on Kerr's Miniature Railway; visited the Signal Tower Museum (where the town's fishing history is celebrated along with that of the Bell Rock lighthouse, eleven miles offshore); or watched a game of Second Division football at Gayfield. What I actually did was beat a hasty retreat to the station and spend the remaining minutes of my time in Arbroath admiring railway architecture, recalling that the early Arbroath & Forfar Railway was notable as being built to the unusual gauge of 5ft 6ins, and that its engine drivers wore white coats which it was their responsibility to wash spotless every weekend. The curiously shaped, yet substantial stone building beside the station may well have been the A&F's original engine shed. It would be nice to think so, and in doing so, picture the white-frocked drivers preparing their trusty mechanical steeds for the next run to Forfar.

170417 came thrumming round the bend under the cantilevered signal box and pulled to a halt at the curved up platform. Its driver was not wearing a white coat, but he looked smart enough in his ScotRail uniform and tie. The lattice home signal was raised and the Turbostar attacked the visible gradient, the last adverse grade faced by southbound trains before fifteen level miles of coastal running to Dundee. I stored the smokies surreptitiously on the luggage rack. Just to be on the safe side Spinks had given me a plain white carrier bag to hold them in: "So nae one u'll know it's full o' fish." It was, as Bruce Springsteen might have put it, a *Brilliant Disguise!*

Rising above the rooftops of Arbroath's southern edge, I saw the football stadium, Kerr's Miniature Railway, the beach, a paddling pool sans paddlers and miles of caravans in which, I presumed, thousands of would-be holidaymakers were cowering from the bracing onshore winds, munching Tunnocks tea cakes whilst perusing the *Daily Record*. Three brave forty-somethings were trying to recapture their youth in the goalmouth of a municipal football pitch. Envy crept up behind me, I wanted to be out there with them in the wind, landing delicate chips on their Bobby Charlton partings. Other men who would be boys were playing golf on the Artisans' course where 'subtlety (sic) positioned bunkers and fast links greens have made rough unnecessary'. An Alsatian was running through the long, unkempt grass between the railway and the sea. A gang of crows was jay-walking through some yellow ragwort. On black rocks jutting out of the water guillemots were playing contortionist tricks with their rubbery necks. At Elliot Junction the up and down lines still diverge to accommodate the long lost island platform, but there is barely trace of the line which wound its way through Arbirlot and Cuthlie to a branchline terminus and a quarry face at Carmyllie.

The railway enters 'Carnoustie Country', heartland to all intents and purposes of the game of golf. Milksop of a son, it was a sport I could never come to terms with. I lacked the necessary levels of concentration. Two good shots followed by three bad ones, and par was a figment of my imagination. The other, more accessible, Pa rarely rebuked me. We can share enthusiasms with our children but must never impose them on them. If Eden shows more interest now in football than trains I can only be glad that he has an all-absorbing interest in life in an age when so many seem to lack any. The course at Carnoustie itself is said to date from the 16th century. The Open was first played on it in 1931, and several times subsequently. The likes of Henry Cotton, Ben Hogan, Gary Player and Tom Watson have all triumphed here. In 1953 Hogan outrageously played his shot across the bunkers on the sixth on all four rounds. My dad would have found that fascinating. I - even though no more than a year old - would have had my eye turned inland to catch a glimpse of *Sugar Palm* or *Pearl Diver* or *Irish Elegance* on the adjoining railway line. The open was last held at Carnoustie in 1999. Forty-five thousand spectators arrived by train; seven hundred of them alighted from one Virgin service alone. One golf mad ScotRail manager was given good news and bad news: he would be seconded to Carnoustie for the duration of the tournament, but he would not be allowed to leave the station!

Four footnotes in the timetable separate Carnoustie from Broughty Ferry. Four wayside halts called Golf Street, Barry Links, Monifieth and Balmossie which support just one train in each direction per weekday. For golfers, for sharpshooters (for the links are interspersed with rifle ranges in the dunes of Buddon Ness) or simply for those of a railway bent who take an impish delight in flummoxing travel centre clerks with requests for tickets to obscure stations? We must have had one on board, for the communication cord was pulled at Balmossie, and we shuddered to a stop at its short platform while the driver investigated. Whatever the source, it gave me time to take in the ravishing view across the Firth of Tay towards a huge conifer forest between Tayport and Tentsmuir Point. I felt like nipping off the train while the going was good and swimming for it.

Broughty Ferry was where the well-heeled 'Jute Princes', who had made their fortunes in Dundee, chose to erect grandiose residences and rest on their labours. I fancy there are no jute millionaires in Broughty Ferry now; besides an attractively refurbished station (which my train didn't condescend to call at) all I saw were some windswept sands, Malaga and Florida being perceived more popularly now than when, in 1955, British Railways Scottish Region *Holiday Guide* could wax lyrical about its 'bracing climate, excellent accommodation, wide range of recreations and surroundings of pleasant scenery'. A 15th century castle, built to guard the entrance to the Tay, is open to the public. Before the Tay Bridge was built, travellers for Dundee and beyond had to take a ferry boat from Tayport to Broughty Ferry, one with an unenviable reputation for rough passages. The Dundee & Arbroath Railway, completed between those two places in 1840, was for seven years laid to the gauge of 5ft 6ins, the so called 'Dundee Gauge'. The two Tay Bridges hoved into view, road and rail. On the Tayport shore a tall whitewashed lighthouse was a prominent landmark. I was surprised by the number of ships docked at Dundee. I counted three or four, though long grey corrugated warehouses may have hidden more. The preserved Frigate *Unicorn* ('Launched in 1824 - the oldest British built ship afloat') became briefly visible before the train began to descend below sea level into the 610 yards of Dock Street tunnel and what used to be known as Tay Bridge station. Though I was about to repeat my travels from *Rebus Country* as far as North Queensferry, the adrenalin was still pumping, and I was looking forward to reliving some of the highlights of that journey.

No one, for example, could easily get fed up of crossing the Tay Bridge. The Turbostar rumbled slowly over all two miles of it. This time I saw some of the old brick piers from Bouch's original cut down to water level just east of the new bridge, and in an unsettling sort of way they brought home the horror of the tragedy to me much more than any amount of reading I had done on the subject. The old station at Wormit, on the south side of the firth, seemed more significant as well, since I had come upon its station building, reincarnated at Bo'ness. Each time you make a journey new layers of knowledge are accrued. A Great North Eastern Railway HST was pulling away from

Leuchars as we slid to a halt. A good number of people boarded the train, and though in mufti, I sensed that a high proportion of them were in one way or another connected to the
Forces. Having spent seven years in a boarding school,
it is a look I know well, a disconcerting mixture of arrogance
and insecurity that evolves from belonging to any self-
contained community.

We thrummed up the Eden Valley under a brightening sky,
the river's banks were deep in butterbur. By the lineside, Dairsie
Castle was, according to my trusty, if outdated, *Shell Guide,* the
childhood home of King David II of Scotland, son of Robert
the Bruce: 'a lamentable king who fortunately died without
issue' - some epitaph! At Cupar I took in the highly embellished
road bridge that spans the line at the south end of the station
and which, with its battlements and elaborate decoration, has all
the appearance of a gateway to a castle. The statuesque figure on
the adjoining podium has every reason to look proudly down on
the bridge, for it represents none other than David Maitland-
Macgill Crichton who farsightedly campaigned to have a bridge
built across the railway as opposed to a level crossing. An
admirable Crichton indeed! The bridge at Cupar reminds me of
the well known entrance to Guthrie Castle where the Arbroath
& Forfar Railway (which was to become part of the sadly now
defunct Caledonian main line through Strathmore) had to provide an even more Gothically inspired structure to placate the
local laird. This was the second time I had spurned the opportunity of investigating Cupar further and I promised myself I
wouldn't let it happen again.

An American couple - father and daughter - had boarded the
train at Dundee and had begun to gain my attention on account
of their rich and meaningful conversation. They seemed somewhat at loggerheads with regard to how their time in Edinburgh
should be spent, shopping in Princes Street or hang-gliding
being the apparent options for the afternoon. Pop's interests
were obvious but he was playing the conciliatory father role and
backing himself into a dangerous corner. Knowing her place in
the scheme of things, the dutiful daughter finally exploded: "I

don't care *what* we do Daddy just as long as I don't have to carry your *cushions!*"

Their antics with the catering trolley assistant ("What's *corned* beef? Don't you have *any* candy? Is the beer *really* cold?") kept me amused as far as Kirkcaldy, beyond which the enchanting coastline of Fife became the cynosure again. Twenty miles due east I could make out Bass Rock, and knew I would be seeing it much more closely later in the afternoon. Not so far across the mirror-like expanse of the Firth of Forth, and slightly to the south, Leith and Edinburgh stood up against the Pentland Hills like a pop-up illustration in a children's story book. Before completion of the Forth Bridge railway travellers had to catch a ferry between Granton on the Lothian shore and Burntisland on the Fife one. Of the four ferry vessels, *Balbirnie*, *Kinloch*, *Midlothian* and *Leviathan*, the last named was capable of carrying up to forty goods wagons on its open deck, though not passenger carriages. A steam-powered paddle steamer built to the designs of Robert Napier, it plied the firth between 1849 and 1890, and by all accounts prospective passengers needed either a good pair of sea legs and an optimistic disposition, or an unavoidable motive to make the trip.

Burntisland was another place I would really have liked to have explored during this railway holiday of mine - still on the last journey yet already regretting all the places I had failed to step off the train at. Children were building extensive sandcastles on the shore and there were yellow patches on the grass where the fair had been when I last passed through. It looked like a Jeykll and Hyde sort of town, a schizophrenic mix of seaside and dockyard - right up my street in other words. At Aberdour I looked out to see if Trevor Francis was weeding the flower beds, but to no avail, he must have been up at Lonie's for a pie.

Subconsciously, I had been getting more and more excited about the train's impending passage over the Forth Bridge, and was glad that I had taken the trouble to view it from the North Queensferry shore, and gain a gist of its sheer size and magnificence. The railway approaches it through a sequence of big green rocky cuttings like scales on a dragon's back. You feel as if you are about to go for a ride on this fire-breathing monster's back as North Queensferry's little station falls away and the train launches itself onto the massive structure. You become a babe in arms again, cradled in the brawny bauxite arms of the bridge's cantilevers. An oil tanker called *Northgate*, registered in Gibraltar, passed under just as we went across. I saw erotically right down its funnel and could have leapt onto its stern deck. A ploy which seemingly did not occur to Hitchcock when he had Robert Donat escape from a train on the Forth Bridge in his hugely enjoyable, but hardly faithful to the original, 1935 film version of John Buchan's *The Thirty-Nine Steps*.

With Dalmeny came the anti-climax of dry land, and the fast approaching capital's green belt as we crossed the River Almond and passed Turnhouse Airport. Then the suburbs sucked us in: South Gyle and the Pentlands looming over pebble-dash; Jenner's Depository surrounded by allotments; bowling greens and golf courses; Murrayfield, where gods have walked and from where, once a decade or so, the arrogant English are sent with their tails between their legs, 'tae think again'. No Deltics or A4s on Haymarket depot, though, just Turbostars and Sprinters; the bland leading the bland. Haymarket station has the feel of an inner London suburban stop. Two thirds of the train's passengers alighted, and the rest of us rattled like peas through the tunnels to Waverley. Before continuing out of Scotland along the East Coast Main Line, I wanted to make a small pilgrimage to Musselburgh and the Newcraighall district where Bill Douglas, the film maker, had his roots. My companion in this excercise was Russell Cowe, an ideal choice, because he has a professional interest in film and a private one in railways.

The guy at ScotRail's Waverley ticket office wondered if I was off to the races. I knew my shirt was bright, but not *that* bright. The 305s were still hanging on in there and I enjoyed the gallop to Musselburgh just as much as if I'd been a bookie's runner salivating at the thought of some quick, tax-free profit. Quite a crowd got off the train, but they looked more like homegoing shoppers than punters. Russell and I hadn't met face to face and he sorted me out from the crowd by dint of simply shouting "Michael" very loudly from the down platform - I was the only one who *didn't* look round.

Russell and I had known each other about six months. Inevitably the shadowy choreography of Yellowlees lay behind our developing friendship. Russell runs the Scottish video company Panamint, who launched an archive video of the West Highland railway serendipitously around the time *Iron Road to the Isles* was published. When I was doing some initial research into the Bill Douglas connection with Newcraighall, I'd contacted Russell in his capacity as a film buff to see if he knew anything. He didn't, but he was intrigued, and we decided to meet up and explore Bill Douglas Country together.

So now you know why two middle-aged men - a writer/publisher and a video-maker - were wandering around an old mining community in the middle of the afternoon, tracing the roots of a highly respected, but far from widely known deceased film-maker, when they could have been respectably employed at the nearby race track. Bill Douglas made a trilogy of films about his Newcraighall childhood in the 1970s: *My Childhood*, *My Ain Folk* and *My Way Home*. They are bleak little films, blackly humoured, minimalist in use of dialogue, or perhaps folk in the Lothian coalfield just didn't have much to say to each other in the 1940s when Douglas was growing up. The miracle is that such an imaginative man could have emerged from such dismal origins: what was it D.H. Lawrence wrote of the tram car in *Ticket's Please*, 'a dainty sprig of parsely in a black colliery garden'? The tragedy is that Douglas died from cancer in 1991, in his fifties when he might have gone on to do even more wonderful things.

While he'd been waiting for my train to arrive, Russell had done a quick recce of the locality and reckoned our first port of call might profitably be the Miner's Welfare Club. Mid-afternoon on a weekday the only activity was a bingo session, but washing glasses in the bar we came upon Jim Russell, a retired miner who'd spent thirty-two years down the local pit. He 'kenned' Bill Douglas, but could only shake his head when we asked if any of the miner's houses featured in the films were still intact.

"The mine closed in 1968 - though it were retained for pumping for a weil a'ter that - and the houses would have been demolished o'er twenty year ago."

That was disappointing, because the houses featured in the film were distinctively styled with curved staircases to the upper floors. When I'd described them to him, Russell said they might be 'colony' houses with the front downstairs on the opposite side to the front upstairs. Jim told us the houses had been in numbered avenues: First Avenue, Second Avenue and so on, and that he had lived in one himself.

We went for a walk through the village and found a plaque commemorating Bill Douglas and, on the opposite side of the road, a sculpture which read: 'From the barren coal dust of centuries of poverty, suffering and sorrow flowered a spirit of community that sustained our miners and their families in the struggle to preserve mining heritage'. Just then a call came from behind us and Jim Russell was hurrying up the road with a videotape.

"I kenned you might like this, it's some old film of Newcraighall."

What a wonderful gesture. Two strangers walk into your club and ask about a long dead film maker and you rush home to get a video which you're quite prepared to lend them on trust. Talk about a 'spirit of community'. I may be wrong, but I don't feel you'd find a similar spirit of co-operation in well-heeled Morningside!

There was a bit of time to spare before my train back into Edinburgh, so Russell and I drove over to Fisherrow and its idyllic little harbour on the Firth of Forth. On the way we dropped in on Millerhill, the EWS freight yard and locomotive fuelling point. A solitary enthusiast was leaning over a bridge, watching a Class 66 pass underneath on a train of empty coal hoppers. In the distance we could see a Class 56 and a Class 37 stabled beyond number-taking reach. Russell's interest in film derived - not unlike Bill Douglas's - from boyhood visits to the cinema. "B movies at the 'Flea Pit' on Leith Walk, especially the cowboy films," he told me. Indeed the name of his video company, Panamint, comes from a place in Death Valley in California, which featured in the 1937 cowboy film *Panamint's Bad Man* starring Smith Ballew.

"I just liked the name, and thought it was ideal as I started the video business with B-westerns. Also it sounds a bit like Paramount, which makes it easier for getting past protective secretaries on the phone!"

The current Panamint catalogue lists three cowboy movies, nine documentaries about Scotland and seventeen 'shorts' in collaboration with Scottish Screen Archive. Russell's first production was *Squadron 992*, a 1940 film by the GPO Film unit concerning the RAF's barrage balloon defence of the Forth Bridge. One of his favourites is *Waverley Steps*, a 1948 impression of a Sunday afternoon and evening in Edinburgh.

It was interesting for two media moguls such as ourselves to 'talk shop'. Another common thread in our conversation was railways. Russell makes model kits of OO scale locomotives in what little free time he has from running a one man business. He and his six-year-old grandson are building a layout to run them on in an outhouse at his home near Queensferry. This interest is reflected in the Panamint video range which features two films about the West Highland and a number of other railway documentaries. *West Highland* had made a bit of a splash, and, like many things in life, had all come about by a chance meeting with the veteran film maker John Gray who'd made the film for BBC Scotland in 1960. Having five years advantage of me, Russell's railway memories go deeper back into the age of steam than mine. He'd travelled over the Waverley line as a wee boy, crammed into the luggage rack of a rugby special making a sixteen hour journey to Cardiff for an international. His father had been a sports journalist on a long defunct Edinburgh evening paper and such outings were commonplace.

"He also somehow contrived to write the programmes for both Hibs and Hearts," laughed Russell, "but don't ask me how he managed that!"

"Platform nineteen for the fourteen hundred hours Great North Eastern Railway service to London King's Cross," had come the announcement over Waverley's tannoy, and I was already comfortably ensconced in the first class surroundings of a dark blue, red banded Mark 4 carriage as Customer Operations Leader Alex Boyle told us that "the train doors are about to close, would anyone not intending to travel please leave the train as we are now ready to depart."

Even in our sardonic times, there is still something portentous about an express train's preparation for departure. If I hadn't marched up to the front to see what was pulling us, it was simply because southward bound GNER expresses from Edinburgh are *pushed* by a Class 91 electric locomotive positioned at the *rear* of the train. This is not something that men of my generation can ever be entirely comfortable with. It goes against the grain, like an unnatural practice. But however deviant the train operation to purists like me, the *frisson* remains. I could hardly have been enjoying myself more if *Ballymoss* or *Andrew K. McCosh* was going to haul me to Berwick upon Tweed. My enjoyment was multiplied by complimentary tea and biscuits, the latter wrapped alluringly in customised GNER packaging bearing an image of the Angel of the North. Waverley's stone walls seemed to smile back at me, and I relaxed happily as the train pulled out of the station and into Calton Tunnel, having furtively sniffed my package to reassure myself that its contents were not yet about to cause olfactory offence to the tweed-jacketed old gentleman opposite me, absorbed in his copy of the *Daily Telegraph*.

The shape of things to come stood in the sidings at Craigentinny in the shape of one of Virgin's new Voyager train sets, its sleek silvery aircraft like body an epoch away in design terms from the quadragenarian Class 305 slam door electric unit on the adjoining track. At Prestonpans an EWS Class 66 was waiting to take a train of coal hoppers into Cockenzie Power Station. From Longniddry there were views back across the Forth to the coast of Fife, so that it seemed to me that this last journey was a series of reflections of itself, a confusing hall of mirrors playing with the known parameters of time and space. From Drem the North Berwick branch struck northwards like a well placed conversion kick and I was back on fresh territory again, albeit for the last time.

Other than on The Queen of Scots (with Eager under the table) and with the dark haired beauty on the night train (with my mind doing somersaults like an overwrought acrobat) I had only been this way once before, behind an unremembered Deltic in 1963, and so I was prepared to relish my last, and increasingly sentimental run through the farmlands of East Lothian, and along the clifftops of the Borders Region, to my own personal buffer stops at Berwick. It had become a balmy afternoon, the cornfields ripening towards an imminent harvest. Bass Rock dominated the seaward view as the railway twisted inland to cross a lesser known River Tyne at East Linton. Three men of note lie in the graveyard here: Andrew Meickle who invented the threshing mill, John Sherriff, a pioneer in crop research, and John Brown, an agricultural journalist. My eye cocked seawards, I missed the NMS Museum of Flight at East Fortune, located on a military aerodrome dating from the First World War. I looked its web site up when I got home and learnt something of its fascinating history. How, when the vanquished German Fleet sailed into the Firth of Forth on its way to Scapa Flow in 1918, aircraft from East Fortune were up aloft filming the sad procession for posterity. How, in July 1919 the airship R34 took off from the base on the first direct flight between Britain and America with a consist of eight officers, twenty-two men, two carrier pigeons, a stowaway and a pet kitten. And how, East Fortune flourished again during the Second World War as a training base for night-fighters such as the Defiant and the Blenheim with, by all accounts, fatal accidents being more the rule than the exception. Board a train and there's history wherever you look, and not always in the 'age of the train'.

Approaching Dunbar (birthplace of John Muir who founded the Yellowstone National Park) I glimpsed the sandy width of Belhaven Bay, which made me think of the local brewery and its exceedingly palatable range of ales. The single platformed station (located on a bi-directional loop to the north of the main running lines) is unique for a 'local' station north of the border

in not belonging to ScotRail, being paradoxically GNER operated instead for, at present, ScotRail do not operate beyond
Drem on the East Coast Main Line. GNER, however, do a
good job on its upkeep, the booking hall is well-appointed and
there are copious horticultural displays on the platform. When
the line between Edinburgh and Berwick opened on June 18th,
1846 a party of distinguished guests were treated to iced cham-
pagne on the platform at Dunbar. A nice red sandstone church
overlooked the station whilst, inland, the horizon lay against a
backdrop of the rolling Lammermuir Hills, bringing to mind a
Jackie Leven song which ends with the sound of a steam train
passing by.

Everything has been so bucolic since leaving the outskirts of
Edinburgh, that a sudden flurry of industrial activity within
sight of the sea seems intrusive. One wonders sometimes at the
planning ethics of a country which will baulk at the erection of
a garden shed, yet cheerfully pass an application to erect a
nuclear power station on a picturesque headland within five
miles of a fishing town. A cement works seems small beer in the
face of such effrontery. Likewise a landfill site. The good news
is that all three eyesores bring valuable turnover for the rail
freight industry. From Blue Circle's Oxwellmains cement plant
EWS work flows to Uddingston, Aberdeen and Inverness; from
Powderhall on the south side of Edinburgh they carry waste to
fill the craters left behind by the manufacture of cement; and
from Torness high security flasks of nuclear waste are worked by
the dark blue liveried Class 20 diesels of Direct Rail Services to
Sellafield for reprocessing.

Thirty six miles out from Waverley the line crosses Dunglass
Viaduct, spanning an eponymous burn which forms the boundary between the regions of East Lothian and Scottish Borders;
East Lothian and Berwickshire to those of us of a certain age
who still think imperially, and cling to our Susan Maughan
forty-fives. Similarly we like to think of that irritating race track
beside us as the Great North Road, and like to picture it when
it was sparsely populated by Austins, Humbers and Wolsleys,
and Foden lorries of a passably human scale. Place names with

a Scots burr to them begin to peter out. Cockburnspath is plausible, Grantshouse more dubious. Between them the railway side-steps the former tunnel at Penmanshiel which collapsed (killing two workmen) in 1979 whilst alterations were going on inside to make the bore big enough to accept Freightliners. A reverse curve of rocky cuttings covered in safety netting illustrates that this was not necessarily a simple manoeuvre. If Beeching had still had his feet under the table the East Coast route would probably have been abandoned on the collapse of the tunnel. Risibly, he had always intended that it should become a secondary route. It seemed symmetrically appropriate that I should encounter again the Southern Upland Way at this point on my last journey, as on my first.

There were two DRS Class 20s with a nuclear flask in the loop at Grantshouse. I was counting down the minutes. Just fifteen miles to go, reminding myself not to forget the fish as once, on the West Coast Main Line, Jackie and I had inadvertently left a package of equally noisome potential, in the shape of a haggis, under the seat of a Plymouth bound train. I started tying knots in my handkerchief, to the mild consternation of the old gentleman opposite, who obviously thought I was headed for the beach. Sinuously, down the valley of the Eye Water, the train ran to Reston, junction once of a North British Railway branchline which wormed its way south-westwards to St Boswells, a sleepy by-way which had gleamed like a main line in the eyes of its chief promoter, Richard Hodgson, Chairman of the NBR. I saw its melancholy trackbed curve away into fields to my right, then looked left to see an auction mart and prodigious lines of cattle pens, wondering how the local economy had withstood the ravages of foot and mouth. We passed some gravel pits as the line continued to meander about the compass at one point, in the vicinity of the village of Ayton, bearing momentarily north-eastwards. Ayton Castle dates from the year of the Great Exhibition, and in the context of these soft Border pasturelands seems quite as eccentrically imposing as the Crystal Palace itself.

The three mile long branchline between the fishing ports of Burnmouth and Eyemouth bit the dust in 1962. Perhaps it considered itself lucky to have survived the great wash out of 1948. Russell Cowe had shown me a photograph of a J39 at the terminus with an extremely youthful version of himself, with his mother and sister beside him, circa 1951. If you are fortunate enough to own a copy of *The Splendour of Steam* by Hamilton Ellis you will know that Plate VI depicts a view of a North Eastern Railway train at Burnmouth, the white smoke from the green locomotive (a Worsdell bogie single) rising into a blue sea between precipitous headlands. It's a typical Hamilton Ellis painting, a tad naive for some tastes perhaps (though not mine) but marvellously evocative of a simpler age, and it cannot be faulted for authenticity for, as described in the accompanying text, the author/artist took the trouble to make preliminary sketches from the lineside 'as dawn broke bluely over the North Sea'.

Running along the clifftops, the railway reminded me of my morning departure from Aberdeen. A Rachmaninovian sense of sadness came over me; rapidly overtaken by an acute Mahlerian melancholy. Out at sea a yellow-hulled yawl was making towards the mouth of the Tweed. Fifty-four and a half miles from Edinburgh the train slipped unostentatiously into England. Down along the coast I could see the outline of Lindisfarne and what I took to be Bamburgh Castle beyond it. "Ladies and gentlemen we shall shortly be arriving in Berwick upon Tweed." I took down my fish, slung my haversack over my shoulder, and tiptoed to the door so as not to disturb my neighbour who was sound asleep; impervious to the change of country, and very probably the twenty-first century as well.

Berwick's long island platform stands like a launch pad at the north end of the Royal Border Bridge. The station buildings, which date from 1927, are built of Dumfriesshire sandstone, and very pretty they looked as I turned my back on them and trudged down into the town. The original station of 1843 occupied the site of Berwick Castle; corporate vandalism is not a new phenomenon. In many respects Berwick still felt like Scotland. 'Don't forget,' I told myself, 'that you and Eden went to Shielfield Park to see Berwick Rangers play East Fife in the Scottish Second Division.' And true enough there were Scots

pies in the butchers shops and Scots accents in the streets, mingling mellifluously with Geordie excursionists. I went down to
the riverside and watched the salmon netters at work. Six men,
two boats and a dog working from a bar of silt in midstream,
rowing out in a semi-circle with one net at a time. Hard graft,
judging by the way they had to heave on the oars. Then the nets
were drawn by hand in a diminishing circle of capture. The silver fish splashed frantically in their death throes, and the men
with 'priests' put them out of their writhing misery.

Who was going to put me out of my misery? Not even the
antiquarian delights of Bridge Street Bookshop could pep me
up. I wished life was like a Monopoly Board and that I could go
round to the beginning and start my railway holiday all over
again. Would I do it any differently? Not to any great degree.
My only regrets related to not having had more opportunities to
alight and explore. And those were good regrets to have,
because they could always be cured by doing it all again some-
time. Where next? I have a hankering for Ireland where, they
say, locomotives still haul trains over branchlines, and where
every other dark-eyed colleen is a dab hand at the accordion.
But the railway world's my oyster, and I will have to wait and
see. As an employee of the Inland Revenue once wryly
observed:

"Your whole life's one long holiday, Mr. Pearson, isn't it?"

Useful Contacts

Aberdeen Tourist Information - Tel: 01224 632727

Stonehaven Tourist Information - Tel: 01569 762806

The Grassic Gibbon Centre - Tel: 01561 361668

Montrose Tourist Information - Tel: 01674 672000

Montrose Basin Wildlife Centre - Tel: 01674 676336

Arbroath Tourist Information - Tel: 01241 872609.
www.angusanddundee.co.uk

Arbroath Abbey - Tel: 01241 878756

Arbroath Museum - Tel: 01241 875598

M & M Spink (Retail Fish Merchants) - Tel: 01242 875287

Kerr's Miniature Railway - Tel: 01241 879249

Caledonian Railway (Brechin) - Tel: 01561 377760

Carnoustie Tourist Information - Tel: 01241 852258

Broughty Castle Museum - Tel: 01382 436916

Edinburgh Tourist Information - Tel: 0131 473 3800

MacTours Vintage Bus Tours of Edinburgh -
Tel: 0131 220 0770. www.mactours.com

Rebus Walking Tours - Tel: 0131 557 6464

Panamint Video - Tel: 01506 834936

Museum of Flight - Tel: 01620 880308. www.nms.ac/flight

Dunbar Tourist Information - Tel: 01368 863353.
www.dunbar.org.uk

Berwick upon Tweed Tourist Information - Tel: 01289 330733

Index

INDEX